THE
ORGANIC
GARDENING
BIBLE

SUCCESSFUL GARDENING THE
NATURAL WAY

Bob Flowerdew

THE
ORGANIC
GARDENING
BIBLE

SUCCESSFUL GARDENING THE
NATURAL WAY

*Everything you need to know to create
your own paradise of flowers, fruits,
and vegetables, thronging with wildlife
and a joy to behold*

TAYLOR TRADE PUBLISHING
Lanham • New York • Dallas • Boulder • Toronto •Oxford

To all those gardeners who have gone before us; for creating and discovering the varieties and intelligence that now make our gardens beautiful and productive.

All the photographs in this book were taken in my garden by Christine Mackenzie Topping, an outstanding photographer best known for her plant portraits featured in Express Newspapers, *Radio Times* and *Gardeners' World* magazine. Here dedication and skillful expertise enable her to catch each specimen and scene at the point of most exquisite perfection.

Published by Taylor Trade Publishing
An imprint of The Rowman & Littlefield Publishing Group, Inc.
4501 Forbes Boulevard, Suite 200
Lanham, Maryland 20706

First published in Great Britain in 1998 by
Kyle Cathie Limited
122 Arlington Road London NW1 7HP

Distributed by National Book Network

Library of Congress Card Number: 2004115763
ISBN 1-58979-219-X (alk. paper)

The paper used in this publication meets the minimum requirements of American National Standard for Information Sciences—Permanence of Paper for Printed Library Materials, ANSI/NISO Z39.48–1992.

CONTENTS

Introduction   6

  Let nature do the work

1 The organic way   10

  How we can all become successful organic gardeners, benefiting both
  ourselves and our environment

2 The flowering of the garden   30

  The pleasure garden of flowers; combining aesthetics, color, and design into
  the productive garden

3 Making your garden naturally beautiful   48

  The art and skill of planning your garden both to look beautiful and
  to run efficiently throughout the year

4 Keeping your garden beautiful naturally   74

  Maintaining the garden's appearance and fertility—how to keep your garden
  beautiful, interesting, and fertile as well as neat and tidy

5 Seeds want to come up, plants want to grow   88

  Much of being a successful gardener is just tending our plants well

6 Fantastic fruits   100

  Fruits are fantastic, easy, tasty, productive, nutritious, little work, aesthetic,
  flexible, and ecological

7 Feast on fresh herbs, salads, and delicious vegetables   134

  Growing for flavor, health, freshness, and quality using the easiest and most
  effective means

8 Shelter from the weather   168

  Grow more crops and flowers for more months in the year, and be warm
  yourself

9 Harvesting, storing, cooking, and sharing our bounty   184

  Easy and effective ways to spread the enjoyment of our bountiful produce
  over even more months of the year

10 Successful organic pest and disease control and gaining freedom from weeds 202

  Simple strategies for avoiding problems; how to deal with them
  organically and effectively

The Yearly Calendar   218

  A month-by-month roundup of what tasks to do when

Useful Addresses Bibliography   223

Index   223

INTRODUCTION

Let nature do the work

Your own homegrown food is fresher and tastes better than anything you can ever buy.

It has long been recognized that it is easier to work with nature than to fight her. Much of the resurgence of organic and green gardening has come about because we have realized how precious the natural ecosystems all round us are, and how dependent we are on them. However, I want us to go further—not just cooperating with nature but enticing her. I have found it possible to make any plot into a paradise within a short time and without much hard work. But this is not achieved by letting nature have her way. No, we must guide and channel her so that we get what we want by adjusting the balance of nature's own interdependent systems. Nature always reaches a balance; we aim to move that point so that it is in our favor and not aligned against us.

Plants want to grow, wildlife wants to increase, so let them do the hard work By their very nature, seeds "want" to germinate, plants "want" to grow and flower and fruit, creatures of all sizes "want" to multiply. If we plan well and grow the right plants in the optimum combinations in the best places, and if we encourage various forms of life to accompany them in our gardens, we can let nature have almost complete control over pests and diseases, over maintaining and increasing fertility, and over producing bigger returns than we could ever wrest from her by coercion.

Using our wit and cunning to produce flowers, fruits, and vegetables fit for the pleasure and tables of kings Most of being a good gardener lies in giving the plants what they need *and* not giving them anything which hurts or harms them. Many pesticides have turned out to be as harmful to the plants as they are to us—one greenhouse market-gardening company found their yields went up by about a fifth when they stopped using insecticides and went over to biological control. We don't even *need* pesticides—almost every pest and disease can be outmaneuvered. The best way to do this is to utilize other bits of nature to do it for us. There are tens of thousands of different sorts of insects and only a few hundred in total do any direct harm to us, our property, or our garden flowers and crops. The rest are all engaged in their own world, but we can persuade them to do our bidding. For example, if we lure hoverflies to yellow flowers which are (to them) irresistibly full of honey and pollen, then they lay more eggs in our garden than elsewhere and their larvae control aphids for us.

Matching the needs of each plant to our soil and microclimate. . . It is as hard to change your basic soil type as it is your climate—both determine what you will find easiest to grow and it makes for more effortless success if you work with them rather than trying to modify them drastically. For example, trying to make a lime-rich soil suitable for heathers and rhododendrons by adding bags of peat bog is futile; far better to grow lime-lovers. Similarly, much as I enjoy the challenge, I know I'm making pain for myself by trying to grow watermelons in England. Far more sensible, less effort, and usually less expensive is matching the plants to the soil and the planting positions you can offer them. A useful guide is to observe which plants in your area are growing really well or of their own choosing. Looking at neglected gardens will soon show you the real survivors eminently suited to local conditions. If your neighborhood is full of heather gardens and camellias, then grow these, or plants with similar requirements such as azaleas and rhododendrons. Anything flourishing is worth growing—most good gardeners earn their reputation from growing the commonplace superbly, rather than by coaxing unsuitable plants in the wrong place.

. . .and not wasting our efforts: the lure of the show table and keeping our eye on the ball Saving unnecessary work makes for happier gardening. I have tried always to remember that I am growing crops to enjoy eating, not to show. The techniques required are just different; I'm looking for ease, taste, and texture, not size and appearance. A visitor once remarked that my tomato plants didn't look as good as his. I took up the offer and saw his tropical jungle of dark green plants cramming his greenhouse. True, his plants *looked* better, but where were the fruits? By overly boosting their vegetative growth he had so far prevented the plants ripening any of the heavy trusses; my harder-grown plants had already been providing me with ripe fruit for more than a month. So if you want to grow wonderful tomatoes, don't aim for wonderful tomato plants.

There is no work as bad as wasted work, so we must be careful not to make our beloved gardening into a chore. Obviously, as the old proverb puts it, "If we want strawberries we should not sow turnips." But how often do we grow vegetables that just go over unwanted or prune bushes that have long since passed their best? It is our garden and we should do and grow whatever we want, resisting pressure from "good old boys" who insist that a thirty-foot row of parsnips is essential if you are to have any gardening credibility. I've tried in this book to show the choices open to each of us and hopefully the best way of enjoying them as well.

Using natural processes to our advantage Nature rarely performs the equivalent of our annual digging. True, moles may turn over the topsoil and upended trees often tear up the ground. However, these are small and localized occurrences and the surrounding plants can soon repair the patch. Then their all-pervading, hungry roots will prevent nutrients

left
All of nature is profligate —plants are naturally productive, we just need to harvest some of their bounty for ourselves. These pumpkins are grown for their tasty seeds.

below
It costs nothing to leave surplus leeks to flower to feed the insects.

escaping. Of course, digging a plot initially is a good idea, if only to unearth and remove rubbish and roots, but as an annual chore it seems to me not only unnatural but unproductive. The effort would be better spent turning the compost heap or weeding, as for most crops any increase in yield from digging is less than that obtained from one good watering at the right time. Likewise, we can learn from nature to use mulches to keep the soil warm, moist, and alive and to encourage the worms underneath to dig far deeper and more thoroughly than we can ever manage.

Some years ago I wrote *The Organic Gardener* (long out of print) in which I demonstrated many of my methods. I have revised and updated the best of these for inclusion here and added much more that has been uncovered since. But more than that I have tried to make organic and natural gardening methods adaptable so that you can adjust them to your own situation. In particular I have tried to write this book to help you find the best methods, plants, and aids to make your plot into an attractive, productive, and satisfying garden that will naturally teem with wildlife and be a joy every day of the year. In the following chapters I explain these various components, with their advantages and drawbacks and the ways of modifying them that go to make up such an Eden. It is up to you to select and apply them in whatever combination you see fit.

Bear in mind an old gardening adage—you can have a proper job, a quick job or a cheap job, you can sometimes have two of these, but never all three together.

A note on measures Rather than give conceptually difficult and effectively meaningless precise measurements, I have chosen to go back to a more pragmatic method. As we already adjust so many garden measurements and spacings according to site, soil, variety, convenience, and expectation, it is ridiculous to give precise figures. Instead I suggest we use nature's natural rulers for the placing of plants. I have used the following indicators: a pace or stride equals approximately one yard; a foot means whatever yours is, about one third of your stride; an inch is about as long as the end joint of at least one of your fingers or thumbs; and your longest finger is probably near enough three inches. Obviously if you are very small or very large you should adjust these measurements accordingly, but even so for most of us putting our plants not twelve inches but a real foot apart or not quite three inches but a finger-length apart is downright convenient! And you always have the same measure to hand.

Also, to make the text more readable, I have wherever possible omitted Latin names, including only those that will genuinely help you select the right plant.

Bob Flowerdew Norfolk, England, January 1998

chapter one

THE ORGANIC WAY

*How we can all become successful organic gardeners,
benefiting both ourselves and our environment*

To garden naturally, you have to be organic. This is the
minimum foundation for any more ecological approach. But it
is not difficult. Indeed, tending an organic garden is an
enjoyable and practical way of caring for the environment,
naturally. In many ways it is one of the most satisfying and
worthwhile tasks we can find. Many of the world's greatest
thinkers, such as the French philosopher Montaigne, have
come to the conclusion that gardening is the only worthwhile
occupation: he wrote, "I desire death may find me planting my
cabbages." A century later the English essayist Joseph Addison
wrote, "I value my garden more for being full of blackbirds
than of cherries, and very frankly give them fruit for their
songs." Although some may disagree as to the degree, almost
everyone recognizes gardening as intrinsically good. However,
during the last century, much of the traditional gardener's and
farmer's harmony and closeness to nature was displaced by a
chemical approach where almost all creatures, great and small,
and all plants other than crops were regarded as parasitic if not
pestilential. We were misled into believing that pesticides and
weedkillers were essential to farm and garden practice, and this
resulted in a vast industry, with unsustainable reliance on
petrochemicals that polluted our water, destroyed wildlife and
wildflowers, and produced food and soil short of essential
nutrients and contaminated with residues.

Caring for the environment by
gardening naturally is one of the
most satisfying and worthwhile
occupations we can find.

Once the farming system had been coerced into such foolishness, gardeners were soon gulled into copying the same methods, to wreak havoc upon the ecosystems in their own gardens. Yet what resulted was an increased dependence on artificial means to obtain the same yield as before. Gardeners who came to depend on the chemical approach annually applied vast amounts of soluble fertilizers and mixes of chemical poisons to their land, yet rarely did much better than their forefathers. Increases in yields have usually come from better varieties of plants rather than from the methods used to cultivate them. These same gardeners may also have wondered why there were fewer and fewer songbirds, butterflies, and other wildlife to beautify and enliven the world, even as they were unwittingly poisoning them—and their own children and grandchildren. The steadily increasing list of once approved and supposedly safe pesticides now withdrawn makes salutary reading, as do the disclaimers on their packets.

Despite all the propaganda, we have come to realize that this chemical approach was an aberration. With increasing awareness of green issues, ecological and environmental concerns, and the search for a healthier way of life, many people are deciding to nurture their own small plot of earth in a more natural way. Although in isolation a small farm or garden may seem insignificant, it is not; if all the gardeners in the UK alone stopped spending their millions a year on chemicals they would produce an immense conservation area bigger than some countries and benefiting all of us. Indeed, in a world where we may often feel powerless, we do have the ability to improve at least that little bit of it in our care.

The benefits to each of us of cultivating our gardens organically range from the obvious ones of producing fresh, tasty produce and beautiful flowers free from contamination to enjoying a healthier lifestyle that makes better personal and ecological use of our time. As gardeners, we get a lot of pleasure, exercise, and fresh air, enjoy social exchanges with other gardeners (you try and avoid them!) and benefit from one of the few profitable hobbies.

Organic gardeners get the additional satisfaction of saving work and money by using their wit and cunning instead of chemical treatments. And it cannot be wise to keep poisonous substances in a home with children. Merely by recycling our household wastes for compost and reuse and minimizing our use of resources, we can significantly reduce the amounts of pesticides and fertilizers polluting our water.

Creating an organic garden enables us to rescue, aid and encourage a multitude of wildflowers and wildlife big and small at a local level, as well as saving from extinction old varieties of fruit, flowers, and vegetables, many of which are no longer grown commercially or sold legally. Most importantly of all, each of us can make our own small part of our Earth richer with plants and more teeming with life than it was when we found it.

We can each of us make our own small part of our Earth into a new paradise.

What organic is all about, and what it is not

There is no single "organic design" or method that you can copy by rote. Organic gardening is a different approach rather than a set of methods that can just be substituted for the artificial regime of sprays and fertilizers. It is sustainable, ecologically sound, more natural, and environmentally friendly, and has been carefully and scientifically developed in the U.S. over the last fifty years by organizations such as the Rodale Institute in Pennsylvania and the California Certified Organic Farmers (CCOF). Many state organizations, such as the CCOF and the Northeast Organic Farming Association have administered organic standards for crops grown by their members. Before a product can be labeled "organic," a Government-approved certifier inspects the farm where the food is grown to make sure the farmer is following all the rules necessary to meet USDA organic standards. The program is administered by the United States Department of Agriculture and based on certain principles designed to guide farmers and commercial producers. However, these principles can be applied just as well to the garden, and gardeners are free to choose which methods they employ within this framework.

There are other techniques that incorporate organic principles, but are called by different names. One system is called Biodynamics and is based on the work of Rudolph Steiner (who also founded the largest private school system in the world). The followers of Biodynamics pay special attention to companion planting, astrological timing, Steiner's special potions, and the more spiritual interactions between man, plants, and the universe.

Permaculture gardening is another approach that originated in sunnier lands and aims to use many layers of plant life to create a permanent but flexible ecology that is productive and requires little labour. Permaculture was modeled on the tropical jungle and works in areas of high rainfall and powerful sunlight. There is much similarity between all approaches worldwide, especially in their desire to marshal the forces of nature on our side rather than fight against them.

And it is not organic simply to stop using undesirable and unecological chemicals and replace them with "natural" products. Nor is it organic to give up doing anything other than grow and harvest! Some produce proffered as "organic" has merely been grown untended, such as surplus apples. These may indeed be pesticide free, natural or even ecologically sound, but they are not organic. Neither were the Victorian gardeners, nor anyone else prior to the First World War. They used extremely nasty chemicals such as lead arsenate and mercuric chloride, though some of their better ideas are still useful to us today.

We feed our soil, which feeds our plants, which then feed us.

The principles of organic gardening

Guarding and increasing the life in the soil is the first and most important principle on which the others depend. Without healthy soil teeming with life, civilization as we know it will disappear. We are dependent on our topsoil to feed us. If it is overworked and abused it will erode away. The only way to maintain, foster, and increase the fertile topsoil is by actively encouraging the multitude of organisms in the soil which convert inactive minerals and water into the building blocks of life. It is the dead bodies of all these forms of living material and the by-products they generate that build up the humus-rich, water-holding loamy soils that we all desire for the healthy plants they produce. Chemical fertilizers and overcultivating burn off this store and destroy the very organisms that could create more—in return for extremely short-term gains.

Organic gardening uses the policy of feeding the soil not the plants. We do this with organic material instead of soluble chemicals which destroy life and then uselessly run off to pollute our water. The burgeoning life in the soil utilizes the organic material, minerals, and moisture to produce more life. Our plants then feed on the by-products and breakdown materials to help them grow. The effect of adding organic material is cumulative—as more is introduced, it further encourages increased populations of soil flora and fauna. These larger populations then support yet more tiers and chains of life predating and living off them. This, in turn, increases and raises the fertility of the soil. The plants living off this balanced diet are healthier and more resistant to pests and diseases than those living in denatured soil pumped up with cocktails of chemical fertilizers and kept going with poisonous sprays.

In order to protect this life in the soil we use no poisonous substances that can harm them except certain, mostly "natural", ones as a last resort. The permitted substances are determined as safer because they are less wide-ranging in their toxicity than other chemicals and break down rapidly and naturally after use. However, it is not their "naturalness" but their effect on soil life that is important. Thus nicotine—a plant product—is no longer allowed as it is too harmful to many forms of life while Bordeaux mixture, a combination of copper sulphate and lime, is allowed. Although a chemical, it is relatively safe to soil life, so it is admitted but only if needed as a fungicide when other measures have failed. Similarly, basic slag—an "unnatural" phosphate by-product from blast furnaces—may be used because it aids soil life, but the very natural guano of petrified seagull droppings is not permitted because it is so soluble it can burn off humus and damage soil life.

The increasing life in an organic soil then goes on to support more and larger forms of life in the garden and surrounding environment. After all, if you want blackbirds you have to have worms. The effects on this bigger scale are also cumulative. As more larger forms of life come to the table of your soil, they concentrate and bring in minerals and nutrients, further enhancing the soil's fertility. For example, birds shed feathers, eggshells, nesting material, copious droppings and eventually their bodies, all of which contribute to the soil fertility as they are broken down and reabsorbed into the chain of life. At first glance this may not seem like much, but if you add up the daily amounts then the annual production of just one extra bird family encouraged to live in your garden is a whole bucket-full of very rich fertilizer, distributed for free. Other creatures, such as frogs and toads, all take part in the same processes, adding to the overall fertility of your soil and giving off precious carbon dioxide. This is a problem when it is pumped into the upper atmosphere, but released slowly in little breaths, it is rapidly reabsorbed by the plants in the garden. It is not often realized how important this gas is for their growth. It exists in the air in only minute amounts and growing plants can extract it all from still air in a very few minutes of bright sunlight. Animal life of any size in or on the soil gives off carbon dioxide continually and thus helps to promote plant growth. Indeed, commercial greenhouse management now supplements the natural levels of carbon dioxide with bottled gas in order to achieve the same purpose.

Good husbandry—growing plants well Good methods and conditions set the plants off to a flying start, and keep them growing without hindrance. Plants that have ever received a check in their growth never do as well as those growing consistently; their tissues harden and further growth is restrained. The aim of the organic gardener is to give plants the best conditions that can be maintained and to prevent them ever coming under stress. Freedom from extremes of heat and cold and, most importantly, from water stress is essential. The latter is most effectively achieved by increasing the organic matter and thus the humus content of the soil, which then acts like a sponge, retaining rain from times of plenty.

In many ways growing plants is a bit like caring for a baby—it is critical to get them through their earliest stages, but later on they are tough enough to endure less gentle treatment with little risk of permanent damage. Thus the good gardener ensures freedom from early stress and keeps down the competition from weeds and other plants. This then produces healthy, robust plants that grow well despite any later pest and disease attacks—in much the same way we shrug off colds and scratches.

Natural methods of controlling pests and diseases, using wit and cunning
This third principle is derived to some extent from the first two. We wish to guard and foster the life in the soil and also to give our plants the best conditions we can. We therefore need to control pests and diseases without resorting to harmful pesticides. Organic gardeners aim to prevent pests and diseases ever reaching the point where they need to use even an organically approved pesticide, by building up a wide variety of plants to create ecosystems that support the predators and parasites which then naturally control the pests. By growing a more varied selection of plants and mixing them together we also help prevent the spread of diseases, and encourage pollinators and recyclers such as butterflies and beetles, which further add to the fertility and health of the garden.

Perhaps our most important skill in this area is our ability to use our wit and cunning to outmaneuver pests and diseases. Simple traps, sticky bands, careful timing and mechanical barriers can defeat many pests, while techniques such as good hygiene and crop rotation prevent pests and diseases from building up. But these tactics come after our primary task, which is to grow healthy plants that resist attacks in the first place.

above
Healthy, robust plants shrug off pests and diseases and, when grown well, still produce a large and tasty crop.

right
Dragonflies are doubly useful: the adults eat gnats and mosquitoes in the air, and their larvae eat them under water.

Minimizing ecological damage and making best use of resources, time, and money The fourth principle is to minimize any bad effects we may have on the environment. After all, everything we do is using resources and creating waste. Even gardening is not exempt, as left to itself the soil would produce much more plant growth, though not of a form suited to our requirements. Given a season or two of neglect, bare soil disappears under a tangle of weeds and, in time, brambles, tree and shrub seedlings would turn it into dense woodland. All of this growth increases the soil fertility underneath. A healthy, natural soil can, however, be destroyed by bad practice in a few decades or less. Organic methods aim to increase plant cover as much as practicable, interplanting between crops and using green manure both before a crop is planted and after it is harvested. This approaches the natural soil cover as nearly as possible and ensures soil stability, preventing wind and water erosion while annually building up the soil. The increased mixture and variety of plants not only aids pest and disease control, but it also improves the local ecology by providing a conservation area from which beneficial wildlife can spread out to recolonize the surrounding environment.

The organic system further aids the world environment as it is far more sustainable than other methods. Homegrown fertility from green manures and compost is easily as effective as bought-in chemical fertilizers, and with subtler pest and disease control, there ceases to be a need for direct intervention with ecologically expensive agrochemical pesticides. This saves not only direct, but also indirect pollution—because the waste caused by these products' manufacture, packaging, and transport will not be created at source. Similarly, sensitive gardeners would not buy plants robbed from the wild or vast amounts of bedding plants that need replacing annually, since these consume excessive peat, heat, light, plastic, fertilizer, and sprays during their production.

BECOMING AN ORGANIC HOUSEHOLD

Converting your home and garden to an organic one may be easier than you think. Can you do these four things?

Most important of all, recycle all garden and household waste for compost and reuse A household and garden that puts valuable material into the dustbin is throwing away hard-won fertility. Anything that has ever lived can be converted back into fertility. Composting is at the heart of every organic household. It is the accelerated rotting down of once-living things, converting waste into a soil-like material that is pleasant to smell and use, is a perfect plant food and in a form readily available to their roots with no risk of overfeeding or imbalance compared with that caused by chemical fertilizers. Moreover, the vast numbers of microlife that have broken down the compost go on to inoculate and colonize the soil once the compost is added, further aiding fertility. Using compost to grow crops ensures their health, and that of the household.

Stop using all soluble fertilizers, all herbicides, most fungicides and most insecticides Although they are not allowed under most organic standards per se, the best way to dispose of existing stocks of chemical *fertilizers* is to use them. Once diluted down to a very weak solution, as for houseplants, they can be watered onto grass sward during spring when the nutrients can be rapidly taken up and converted to clippings for use elsewhere, with little danger of run-off. To dispose of unwanted chemical *herbicides, fungicides, and insecticides*, contact your local authority for advice. Please do not pour them down the drain.

Consume wisely and save nature Stop using peat from important wildlife sites, don't buy ecologically unacceptable plants, such as imported wild bulbs and mass bedding plants. Use materials from renewable sources, such as managed woodland, and avoid plastic if natural alternatives are available. (My secondhand galvanized watering can has outlasted four plastic ones and looks good for the same again given a coat of paint.)

Use wit, cunning, and companion plants to grow healthy plants and outmaneuver pests and disease problems Follow the advice given in Chapter 10 (page 203) to maximize the natural checks and balances in your garden by growing a wider variety of plants, especially more trees and shrubs. This helps create more habitats, especially if water is supplied in the form of ponds and pools. Add habitats such as piles of rubble or rotting logs hidden under evergreen shrubs or at the base of a hedge. These will soon be colonized by many forms of wildlife.

ENCOURAGING WILDLIFE FOR ALL THE OTHER BENEFITS IT BRINGS US

The most important part of good gardening method is to encourage all forms of life in the soil and the environment. The more wildlife there is in the garden, the more plant life it can support. More plant diversity encourages more wildlife, which then eats the pests for you. The greater the range of plants the more cycles of life we can squeeze in.

If there is little life in the soil there will be fewer forms of wildlife in the garden. Why stay where there is nothing to eat? The multitude of insect and scurrying life forms are increased by growing many diverse plants providing food, water, shelter, nesting, and wintering sites. Larger forms of life are thus enticed into your garden with yet more plants. However, a well-planned garden is not just filled with plants that benefit wildlife, but every nook and cranny is packed with nest boxes for birds of all sizes, bat roosts, hedgehog dens, frog and toad pits, piles of rotting logs in shady corners, beetle zones, and ladybug nests. Of course more pests are supported in the average garden than would be there in the wild because of the diversity of food sources. The balance point they reach is not necessarily one that suits us, so we try to move it in our favor by aiding the beneficial creatures. In an organic garden there are larger populations of predators and parasites to keep them all in check.

above
Guarantee seeing more small tortoiseshell butterflies in your garden by growing stinging nettles to feed their caterpillars.

right
The chirpy song of crickets and grasshoppers sounds throughout the summer in an organic garden planned around wildlife.

Although we may recognize a legal boundary at the end of our garden, nature does not; so unless we glass in our property we cannot absolutely control which forms of wildlife we have. But we can encourage the beneficial kinds by offering the habitats they prefer, and the more we gather into our garden the more it will throb with life. This contradicts the conventional view that almost every creature needs instant annihilation. The mix of inhabitants in a healthy garden is amazingly varied, from the larger creatures down to countless varieties of bacteria, fungi, and other forms of microlife, most of which are beneficial, especially the nitrogen-fixing bacteria such as *Rhizobium, Clostridium,* and *Azotobacter,* and fungi such as *Penicillium* and *Trichoderma.* All of these preying on each other, the plants and all the breakdown products in between, yet all powered in the end by photosynthesis fixing the sun.

We can categorize all these forms of life as pests, predators, pollinators, recyclers, and so on, but in reality they are all indivisible parts of nature's cycle of life. Each creature plays many parts interacting with other creatures and plants. For example, butterflies were once caterpillars eating leaves; blackbirds may be pests when they are scratching mulch onto the lawn or eating fruit, but are predators when eating wireworms or leather jackets. Such creatures are continually

recycling living and dead material. The value of all this fertility is easily the daily equivalent of several handfuls of organic fertilizer, distributed unseen and unnoticed in a healthy garden where the material is quickly incorporated by the soil life. Our aim, as organic gardeners, is to get as many chains of life going as possible, attracting wildlife of all forms to our garden for the hidden fertility they bring with them and the checks and balances that come from building up the natural populations.

Wildlife control and encouragement: aiding nature's ecosystems In order to maximize the number and variety of forms of life in the garden we must provide for their needs. All creatures exist in their natural habitat. If a niche exists, they will move into it. It is up to us to offer as varied and dense a planting as we can without choking the plants, and under and within this to provide shelter and refuges for the creatures to escape from our tidying, or to overwinter. Within each garden we can create damp corners, warm dry spots, and shady overgrown areas, avoiding over-cleanliness and uniform tidiness. Nests of dry twiggy material for small creatures can be hidden in every evergreen and bundles of hollow stems pushed under fences and sheds. Even a strip of long grass beside a hedge or along a fence is a surprisingly good habitat and will soon be found to be full of beetles, spiders, and other predators—add bulbs for spring interest and you introduce pollen and nectar into the bargain,

Lady's mantle (*Alchemilla mollis*) condenses dew on its leaves for thirsty insects and birds to drink. The leaves of lupins have similar water-trapping properties.

doubling the value of the scheme. Installing nest boxes for birds is a very effective method of increasing their numbers. We can supplement the food supply to this recycling system by adding organic material and natural fertilizer to the soil, and letting the leaves of fall and the fallen petals return to the earth to feed the wildlife.

All creatures need water, so make it as accessible and in as many places as possible. Indeed, water will lure and retain more different forms of life than any other attraction. Birdbaths, waterfalls, fountains, a deep pond, a shallow pool, a muddy stagnant ditch even just a buried sink will all appeal to different creatures. Even jam jars or plastic pots can play a useful role in providing water for small animals and birds—though they can equally be death traps if no egress is allowed for. Especially useful are plants such as teasel which have cupped stem/leaf joints that trap a little pool of water.

Sadly the natural breeding places for frogs, toads, newts, and other water-loving creatures are in rapid decline. Farm ponds have been filled in, ditches scraped clean or replaced with pipes, and marshlands drained. So it is up to us to provide alternatives. Fortunately, this is easy to do. Garden pools probably account for the majority of breeding sites, and an old bath, dug in and camouflaged, makes an excellent small pool at no cost. Do remember, however, to make an easy way out for small creatures by placing a piece of rough wood at an angle at the edge of the pool.

Much pleasure in the garden comes from seeing the beauty of Nature and observing her most intricate creations.

Pest subsystems Pests are an essential part of the ecology and a resource for others. Pests are only pests when they eat our crops or ornamentals, otherwise we would see them as wildlife, recyclers and pollinators. For instance, woodworm in a dead log is a recycler, but in the tree, post or table it becomes a pest. Some pests are also friends; thrips and capsid bugs damage some plants but eat tremendous numbers of spider mites.

Plants in nature come to a balance with their pests. It is only when we grow monocultures or eliminate the natural controls that they run rampant. However, pests seldom do much harm to healthy plants that are growing well—most things we grow are remarkably trouble free, after all. The pests we have to take note of are few and mostly concern a few susceptible vegetables and fruits. Pest outbreaks can be readily controlled by the methods described in Chapter 10. It is important to note, however, that it is *control*, not elimination, we are after. We need a few pests to survive or there will be nothing to keep the predators alive, and without them any new pest would soon escalate into a problem. After all, if there were no snails there would probably be no song birds, and even snails are useful since they consume diseased and wilted material.

Predator subsystems As with all natural food webs, some creatures are predators and some are prey. In the garden, the predators are largely beneficial as they eat pests, controlling their numbers and preventing their spread. The predators and parasites in a stable ecosystem need pests in order to live. Left to themselves they control pest numbers very effectively in a complicated web where they prey not only on the pests but also on each other. This is particularly true of the larger predators, such as skunks and birds, which will eat almost anything, regardless of whether it is a friend or foe to us. Ladybugs are well-known predators, but almost all beetles account for slugs and other small pests and their eggs. Spiders are predatory, every one, and can number many millions in a large, healthy garden. Hoverflies, lacewings, pirate bugs, and wasps all help control spider mites, aphids, caterpillars, and other pests. Similarly, there are numerous parasites such as chalcids, ichneumon flies, and other minute wasps that live on and even in their hosts.

The problem with these predators is that they breed more slowly than the pests. This is usually of no consequence, as other factors, such as lack of food, also restrict the pests. But if you use a pesticide and accidentally kill some of the predators along with the pests, then the latter resurge out of control. It can take many years to rebuild a complex, self-regulating system if it is badly disrupted. Thus all pesticides are better avoided, even the less toxic, organically approved ones. By growing a wide variety of plants—especially sacrificial plants that can have pests on them to little detriment such as honeysuckles, sweet cherries, nettles, and lupins—you can maintain a background level of predators that controls the pests on other plants throughout the rest of the garden. Ground-cover plants, even strips of rough grass, are important for the walking predators, such as beetles. You can provide flying insect predators with nectar and pollen to attract and keep them working in your garden, and further on I suggest plants for this purpose (see page 24).

Pollinator subsystems Bees are the best-known pollinator but hoverflies, flies, butterflies, beetles, and wasps all transfer pollen. Bumblebees are more important to early-flowering plants than honeybees (which fly only in warmer weather). They can be bought in cardboard huts to hang in greenhouses. The main requirement for encouraging more pollinators is more flowers, flowering through the longest season possible.

Recycler subsystems This is the largest of the subsystems; the vast majority of small creatures are recycling material discarded by larger forms. Of course, they may fancy a bit of meat with their diet and the apparently innocuous woodlice have been observed killing young caterpillars. The larger creatures often recycle without consuming, as they forage and disturb the litter or peck apart a rotten log in search of grubs. Pollinators are not only pollinating the flowers, but recycling pollen and nectar as more pollinators; these too live and die, adding their droppings and bodies to soil fertility. This is not insignficant. A colony of honeybees has from 30,000 to 100,000 bees in it at any one time and most of these live only six to eight weeks in summer. Thus a colony loses up to 10,000 bees a week to natural death and predators.

above
Flowering redcurrants bring us cheer early in the year and feed up the bumble bees so they can multiply to pollinate our crops.

above
Keeping bees gives you free honey, free beeswax, free pollination and even adds to the garden's fertility.

above

Honeysuckles perfume our air and carry aphid populations, which then support more predators, which multiply to protect the rest of our plants.

Insect bodies are rich in chitin, which makes up much of their tough skin, and is thought to be beneficial to soil and plant health.

In a sense we are all recyclers. Plants build up their materials from air, light, water, and the nutrients released from organic matter as it decomposes. All other life breaks down plants, other creatures and their by-products. The faster the turnover and the more forms of life we encourage the more our garden will support. Most of nature's recyclers live on or in the soil surface, where most things fall at the end of their life. Without them the world would long ago have filled up with smelly little corpses. Recyclers spend their lives converting dead and diseased material into plant food. These processes go on most rapidly in aerated, warm, moist conditions as found under groundcover plants, a layer of leaves or a mulch. By duplicating these conditions we aid recyclers and if we supply them with organic material they will convert it into fertility.

However, remember that the predators are just as keen to eat the recyclers as the pests, so we need to provide refuges as well. Small piles of rotting logs, rocks, bricks, or even bottles are ideal and can be hidden under hedges and evergreens. Some recyclers, such as snails, which are often regarded as pests, will also congregate in these refuges, so we can use them as collection points where they can be caught and dispatched.

Butterflies are often pests in disguise, but are more usually useful pollinators; their beauty alone is reason enough to encourage them. Many flowers can provide them with food, as butterflies have long tongues, and of course some rely on specific plants for their caterpillar stage. *Buddleja*, *Sedum spectabile*, golden rod (*Solidago*), valerian, and lavender all attract butterflies. So too do: *Dianthus*, *Hesperis*, honeysuckle, hyssop, lilac, *Lychnis*, *Lythrum*, *Myosotis*, *Origanum,* and *Viola*. Many other flowers are visited especially those with yellow, orange or red blooms. Night-scented flowers are appealing to moths which can detect their fragrance from further afield in the still, moist air of evening.

Bees Many species are under threat because of the widespread loss of native wildflowers. Each of us can help by putting a few bee plants in, and it is in our interest to do so. In the short term we benefit from the pollination of fruit; in the long term we may save ourselves. If bees die out whole families of plants may disappear. Bumblebees and leaf-cutter bees are even more valuable than honeybees (although they give no honey) as they fly in colder conditions and pollinate earlier in the year.

All bees need continuous supplies of pollen and nectar so many different flowers should be grown to spread the season. I have listed the best plants for honeybees under Livestock in Chapter 9 (see page 200). Bumblebees especially need early spring flowers such as *Aubrieta*, *Berberis*, bluebells, dandelions, flowering currants, wallflowers, and white dead nettle. From early summer they'll go for brambles and their hybrids, *Buddleja*, clover, comfrey, *Cotoneaster*, *Fuchsia*, globe artichoke and cardoon, golden rod (*Solidago*), jasmine, knapweed, lavender, mallow, Michaelmas daisy, raspberry, rhododendron, thistle, and vetch.

Hoverflies are the best aphid eaters we can encourage. Their larvae eat many more in a day than ladybug larvae—up to an aphid a minute! The adults are attracted to yellow flowers, such as broom (which provides their favourite aphid), yarrow, and knapweed. But the best plant to bring adult hoverflies into your garden is the low-growing, self-sowing annual *Limnanthes douglasii*. Commonly known as the poached egg flower, it should be grown anywhere you can fit it in, filling the garden with hoverflies and bees. Buckwheat and *Convolvulus tricolor* are excellent for supplying nectar later in the season. Most flowers will benefit hoverflies, including: *Alyssum*, *Arabis*, *Aubrieta*, cornflower, *Cosmos*, *Eschscholzia*, *Geranium* (but not *Pelargonium*), golden rod, grape hyacinth, heliotrope, honesty, *Iberis*, all marigolds, Michaelmas daisy, *Nemophila*, *Nicotiana*, *Petunia*, *Phlox*, all poppies, *Rudbeckia*, *Sedum spectabile*, Shasta daisy, stocks, sunflower, sweet rocket, sweet William and pinks, tansy, all the mints, and wallflowers. Letting celery and carrots go to seed will also encourage hoverflies and many other beneficial insects.

The Organic Gardening Bible

Ladybug and lacewing adults may take nectar or pollen from the same plants as hoverflies but they also like *Allium*, *Anthemis* (dill), fennel, and yarrow. In one experiment, lacewings fed only on aphids did not lay eggs. The best encouragement for any predator is plenty of tempting food. Grow plants that are regularly laden with aphids—patches of nettle, honeysuckle, lupins, sweet cherries—and you will soon be maintaining a healthy background level of predators and parasites. The overwintering adults of ladybugs and lacewings are fond of hibernating in conifers, evergreen hedges, and dense culinary herbs. Nest boxes made from hollow stems are particularly useful for them, and should be secreted in dry places.

Wasps are good friends for most of the year, eating pests in the spring and summer, but when fall comes they eat all the fruit! Dead rotting wood will provide wasps with the raw material for their paper-like nests. All the nectar-producers recommended for hoverflies will encourage wasps to some extent, but more importantly will benefit their relatives the predatory wasps which parasitize caterpillars, beetles, aphids, and spiders.

Spiders are all friends and are very sensitive to pesticides. The best way to encourage them is to provide the right type of habitat. Under cover, I supply strings to start their webs in the places that are convenient, as well as water and bundles of hollow stems for them to nest in.

Beetles are a very large group; most, such as ladybugs, are friends, but there are exceptions such as the wood-boring varieties. Beetles are good pollinators in cold, wet conditions when other creatures can't fly, though some, such as pollen beetles, can steal too much. Thick groundcover stops useful ground-dwelling beetles from being spotted by bigger predators: dense foliaged plants that collect dew are thus doubly useful. Plants with hiding places between their leaves, under rough bark, in congested twiggy areas and even in deadwood will help hide or hibernate beetles and other creatures.

Frogs, toads, and newts eat many pests, but they need water and wet places to live in. They will be keener to patrol the garden if there is good groundcover, preferably moist underneath. Provide a lush, moist overgrown corner in the greenhouse and you will have frogs and toads living and dining there. Newts are just as useful and more interesting to watch, especially their dance at mating time. I made the end of my polytunnel abut the pond and a low log wall provides access, so all these friends can come into the warm and eat pests while they are visiting. Generally, newts and frogs will not breed in the same small pond, so if you have the space consider having two small ponds instead of one larger one.

Birds Gardeners often wish to get rid of birds, but on the whole they are definitely beneficial. The main exceptions are the common sparrow and pigeons. Most other birds are hungry friends always looking for snacks—most of which are pests—and they control more pests than they spoil crops. Individual crops may need protecting, but in the end we all benefit from more birds. We can attract birds by providing the right habitat and a reliable food supply, but water is essential. Like us, they appreciate a bath—somewhere the cat can't get at them.

If you want to attract birds, grow fruit of any sort. As is all too soon apparent, birds prefer cultivated fruit to the wild fare nature provides. Redcurrants and cherries disappear fastest, but hardly any fruit makes it through winter. Berries of any sort are equally appreciated, though yellow ones apparently confuse the birds for a while before disappearing rapidly. Often they are just after the succulence, so you can reduce potential damage by providing water for them to drink. The more fruit you grow the less damage your resident population can do, so plant sacrificial crops of berrying trees and shrubs and enjoy all the wildlife that this brings. Seeding plants—especially sunflowers and wheat—will also attract and feed them, and some heads can be saved for the winter.

All dense-growing hedges, evergreens, and climbers favor birds by providing loads of useful nooks and crannies for nest building and shelter. Suitable nesting sites in the wild are increasingly rare, so provide nest boxes in your garden. Encourage the most useful birds, such as blue tits, great tits, tree sparrows, and other small insectivorous birds. The ideal nest site for most small insectivorous birds is an old woodpecker's hole—they always use them in preference, but few are available. The inside shape is more important than the outside appearance and a stark rectangular box is not a good substitute—a deep, rounded bowl is required and is best made with a papier maché insert. Robins, flycatchers, and wagtails prefer their box to have a bigger, wider, more open front. Boxes ought to resemble natural holes and should be fixed to trees, safe from cats and other predators. Put them where you can watch from a window, except for the robins, who like their boxes to be well hidden away in shrubs or hedges. Many of the other birds, such as blackbirds and thrushes, find ample nest sites amid dense evergreens or thick hedges. Bend suitable branches down out of sight and tie them together to form a nesting platform, or prune them back hard to form clusters of splayed shoots suitable for lodging a nest.

Swallows and house martins bind their nests together with mud—of which there is now a shortage, as garden ponds rarely have muddy edges. There are also fewer piles of strawy dung or livestock leaving hair on hedges, which deprives house martins of the other material they need. If they make them out of mud alone, the nests have nothing to strengthen them, so they fall off when the mud bakes and shrinks. So hang hair trimmings and put out bowls of mud by the pool edge for these useful insect eaters.

Choice plants to attract birds

TREES AND SHRUBS
Amelanchier gives a wonderful show of white flowers followed by edible berries and exquisite red tones in fall.
Beech hedges offer good cover for nests and perches—even during the winter as they keep their leaves, giving extra shelter.
Berberis has spiky leaves and thorns that help protect nest sites, with a bonus of berries.
Conifers provide good nest sites, roosts and weather protection.
Thorns, the *Crataegus* family, offer protective nesting sites and carry many berries.
Elaeagnus pungens is a dense evergreen offering good nesting places and hard weather protection.
Elder is one of the very best for perches, nests, and berries.
Holly is well known for dense, evergreen growth and winter berries—if you plant both sexes.
Laurel is useful for hard weather shelter, but not for nesting as it is so easily climbed by predators.
Mahonia is related to the *Berberis* family—it has holly-like leaves; the grape-like fruit is edible and loved by birds.
Pyracantha or firethorn has horrible spines and loads of berries—the yellow ones last longest.

Birds are valued guests—give them a good home.

Shrub roses are impenetrable to predators so are often used for nesting sites. The hips they produce are a welcome bonus.
The European mountain ash and whitebeam family, *Sorbus,* is renowned for its plentiful berries.
Yew is one of the best nesting trees, as the vertical trunks are full of nooks and crannies, hidden by the ubiquitous evergreen shoots. The berries are loved by birds—beware, the leaves are very poisonous to us.

CLIMBERS AND WALL SHRUBS

Ceanothus is a blue-flowered shrub that needs a warm wall for protection rather than support. Its dense growth (some varieties are evergreen) makes good nest sites.

Clematis romp everywhere and nests can be found all through them. The seeds of many varieties have fine floss that can be used for nesting material. (See page 47 for recommended varieties.)
Cotoneaster needs a wall to flop against. It offers good nesting places, but the wealth of berries is far more important.
Garrya elliptica is a large evergreen best grown against a sheltered wall and gives dense cover for nests.
Ivies are well known for turning a wall into a thicket full of birds; they also provide berries late in the year (see page 47).
Hydrangea petiolaris is a climber which starts slowly and can then become quite large and very dense, with good nest sites.
Honeysuckle Not all varieties are climbers—some, such as *Lonicera purpussii* and *L. fragrantissima* are shrubby and winter-flowering— but all produce dense growth that makes them good for nesting in, and they berry freely.
Virginia creeper (*Parthenocissus***)** can cover acres of wall with nest sites and also produces berries after hot summers.
Roses are unclimbable and easy to fix nests in; later they produce hips. Birds love them as much as people, so plant lots. I've seen the variety 'Kiftsgate' cover a house, and the gloriously scented 'Souvenir de Claudius Denoyel' hosting seven nests in an old rectory garden I visited.
Wisteria is slow to flower but worth growing as it offers good nest sites among its twisting stems, especially when old.

SACRIFICIAL FRUIT AND VEGETABLE COMPANIONS

The following are all loved by birds, so are well suited to the wild garden.

Apples are a staple food for birds, so plant as many of them as you can squeeze in and the fruit will be gone by the shortest day.
Cherries disappear with tremendous speed and the large trees make good perching and nesting places.
Mulberries are slow to fruit but it is far-sighted and worthwhile to plant one for the birds—and to rest under in your old age.
Peaches might go unrecognized on the tree for years, but as soon as one bird discovers them they all learn.
Pears are rarely given the chance to ripen on the trees or rot on the ground.
Plums hang on the ends of twigs and are less accessible to birds than most fruit, until they hit the ground. Wasps will get them either way.
Grapevines are good at producing berries and nesting sites, especially if allowed to ramble.
Blackberries are traditional nesting places and the cultivated berries feed far more birds than the wild.
Loganberries are rarely seen ripe, as birds will strip them from the stems. Tayberries are a new, even more bird-palatable variant.
Raspberries are a particular treat for the birds. The fall-fruiting ones spread the season, especially the yellow varieties— these may go unscathed for a while, but not for long.
Redcurrants are probably the birds' favorite, after cherries. Strangely, neither blackcurrants nor white currants appear to be anything like as palatable.
Strawberries are addictive to birds, so plant many varieties. Include fall croppers to spread the season.
Coastal black gooseberries have dense, thorny growth and resemble gooseberries but are larger plants with smaller berries. They are most suitable for wild corners.

When fruit fails to satisfy the birds' appetites, you can sow some of the following vegetables for tasty little seedling snacks:

Beet, including red and yellow beetroot, Swiss chard and leaf beet, are razored off as soon as they emerge. These are the number one favourite snack in my garden, unfortunately.
Brassicas are much liked by pigeons. Small leaves are attacked, but once established they become too tough for most garden birds.
Lettuce is a ready meal for birds until it bolts. Then it becomes bitter, although hungry chickens will still eat it.
Pea seedlings are another good snack for many birds. Those plants that survive produce peas for the birds to steal later.
Spinach seedlings rarely survive emergence very long.

Worms Remember, if you want to hear songbirds, you need worms! Worms are probably the most important creatures in the garden. They can excrete thirty or more tons of "casts" per acre per year—the very best soil texturizer and fertilizer. Worm casts are water stable (so soil containing plenty of them does not get too muddy) and have a granular texture that promotes plant root growth. Worm burrows also act as aeration and drainage channels, and when abandoned are followed down by plant roots for their nutrient-rich lining. The digestive process of worms reduces mineral particles in size, making them more accessible to microorganisms. Worms are encouraged by keeping the soil moist and covered with a mulch. I feed all bare soil and most mulched areas with a handful of grass clippings every month or so as they need "greens" as well as organic material, such as compost or well rotted manure. They will multiply if fed on ground seaweed, blood, fish and bone meal, and hoof and horn meal. It is better not to rotary-cultivate and to dig only by hand, and minimally, as both these processes kill worms. In acid soils, add lime every four years or so unless you grow lime-hating plants. Adding lime for the worms is most important for the vegetable bed and for most hard-wearing grass swards. Lime keeps the soil sweet and feeds the worms, which then ensure the efficient drainage, aeration, and recycling of all the material in the bed or under the sward.

Bats eat tremendous numbers of flying pests. They are best encouraged by providing both roosting and hibernating sites. The former are flat, wooden boxes, open underneath, which need to be attached high up on warm walls. The latter are harder to create. Some trees, such as limes, with large crops of aphids, will continually shower them off in the slightest breeze and these attract bats.

WORKING WITH THE YEARLY CYCLE

There's an old saying in gardening that there's a right time for everything and it was usually last week. It certainly can feel like it at times as most gardening jobs come in rushes and everything needs to be done at the same time. Less panic comes with practice and the familiarity of the annual cycle. Certain tasks are not only best done at the right time of the year, but they can also be much easier or more effective then. We do most heavy pruning during the dormant period of winter, when the plant is least shocked by it, but we prune in summer to control growth or promote flowers or fruit. The timing of sowing is, of course, often critical. Many cauliflowers need to be sown a year before they are wanted almost to the week, and biennial flowers, such as foxgloves, must be sown two years before they flower. Japanese onions must be sown as soon as the days shorten to less than fourteen hours. In my garden, in Norfolk, this means I have to sow during the third week in August—then and only then—if I am to get good crops.

I was surprised, when I investigated sowing according to astrological

left
Peaches thrive on the combination of grass-clipping mulches, lime, and the worm-worked fertility these produce.

below
Japanese onions (left) sown in late summer are at just the right stage of growth to come through the winter unscathed, while snowdrops (right) tell us it is time to start the gardener's yearly round again.

timings, to find how strong the results were. This is a complicated method whereby most gardening chores are done according to the phases of the moon. Although I found much contradictory evidence as to the best date to sow any given thing, what was plainly evident was how much difference sowing a few days apart could make. I conclude we ought to sow in at least three batches a few days apart, and then select the best—and there is rarely a doubt as to which batch that is.

Other tasks have their own schedule, for example cutting a grass lawn for neatness becomes progressively more difficult the later in the spring we wait to start. Clearing an overgrown area is much easier in late winter when all the growth is dormant. And, of course, we can only collect leaves when they fall in fall.

Becoming familiar with the seasonal change in activity soon enables every gardener to pace their workload so that it never overwhelms them. Indeed, one of the joys of gardening is that it can be done at so many levels depending on the amount of time and effort you are able and willing to put in. For instance, growing vegetables is a make-work scheme compared to a garden design based entirely on evergreens, or even a croquet lawn. But even so the same result can be achieved by a lot of hard work ill planned and too late, or by a little at the right time. It takes but a moment's thought not to plant fruit or flowers that will be at their best right in the middle of your annual summer vacation.

chapter two

THE FLOWERING OF THE GARDEN

The pleasure garden of flowers; combining aesthetics, color, and design into the productive garden

Gardens can be works of art. everyone's taste is different and in the end it doesn't really matter as long as you like what you have to live with. Some prefer order, symmetry, and regimentation, others like subtle shading and soft lines, or blazes of bright color. All styles are equally valid, but what tends to sit uneasily on the eye are contrasts of great diversity, unless they are skillfully blended with smooth transitions between them, or separated by an arch, opening or planting. What makes for a pleasing garden is a feeling of naturalness or oneness in the surroundings. As if the garden has always been as it is and could hardly be otherwise, changing every hour and day like a river or a shoreline, yet always remaining much the same.

This beauty of water and wild places has a wholeness— everything molded by everything else without intrusive elements. Creating such natural harmony of shapes, colors, scents, and sounds in our gardens helps us unwind and become more at ease, as well as giving us righteous satisfaction and pleasure on our conscious level. The gardener's art is in combining what few resources there are to hand to create this beauty, not only in the front garden or one particular bed, but in each and every part. Although some areas may well be completely given over to pure ornamentality a garden is only complete when every bed, view, and vista—even the most mundane functional and productive area—are a pleasure for the eye. Not only in itself, but also when seen as part of the whole garden.

Flowers are feasts for the eye and
food for the soul.

Furthermore, as we become more ecologically aware, even purely ornamental areas are seen to interact with and benefit the rest of the garden apart from giving us the pleasure of their beauty. They can be a source of fertility, providing grass clippings, leaves, and prunings to be composted for use elsewhere, and encouraging and sustaining many more forms of life which then go on to contribute their own by-products to the garden.

Visitors to my garden frequently remark, "I never expected to see so many flowers." As I am known for my organic fruits and vegetables they never expect anything other than stark utilitarianism, but of course I grow flowers, and as many as I can, though usually only scented ones—I just don't have space for the rest. Those flowers and noncrop plants that are a pleasure to see are also the tables to keep my tiny garden friends at home. Ornamental plants provide for the wide variety of species that create the balanced ecosystems which control pests and diseases in the other parts of the garden and neighborhood. The sheer diversity of plants, life big and small, and their many interactions mean that purely ornamental areas are exceptionally easy to manage organically with few pests or diseases ever causing problems. However, it becomes a little more complicated when you also want to grow crops in that same garden.

COTTAGE GARDENS IN MYTH AND REALITY

Often proffered as the epitome of design is the "cottage garden style," frequently simplified to masses of very mixed planting with flowers predominating and allegedly also producing useful crops. Though overworked, this vision offers some escape back to a supposedly simpler time and indeed the concept has much intrinsic merit which we can learn from. However, over the years the original has become perverted and now a twee and wholly mythical cottage garden is perpetuated by grotesquely expensive and transient follies at flower shows such as Philadelphia. Charming as these are, they have done much to mislead gardeners. Wonderful masses of flowers combined with luscious fruits and vegetables look terrific when staged for the cameras, but would be difficult and incredibly time-consuming to maintain. It is almost impossible in a real cottage garden to have all those flowers blooming at the same time—and, furthermore, in practice many of the plants would soon choke each other out and the birds would eat most of the produce.

Over centuries, the original cottage garden evolved from the primitive herb bed outside the rustic hut. As we now strive to understand and utilize more of the ecology involved, such utilitarian gardens as this—which arose through empirical trial and error—are enlightening. They were purely functional and developed with probably very little influence from the great gardens of the rich and powerful, whose garden styles reflected wealth and position. "Gardening" historically relied on scale, order, and geometry, and intrinsically depended on humans imposing

We grow peony-headed poppies for their show. Cottage gardeners would once have grown them for the medicinal opium they contained.

our designs on nature, fighting her all the way with unlimited cheap manpower. Little consideration was ever given to working *with* her! With the Victorian period came a desire for re-creations of a Rustic or Gardenesque style, but these are of no value to us as they were contrived from and not wrought with nature. Similarly, at the start of the twentieth century, Wild Gardening, as promoted by William Robinson, was concerned not with cultivating our native ecology but almost solely with growing pretty exotics in our native setting.

So only of real interest to us now is that pragmatic and very mixed planting employed by "ignorant" peasants who did what they found worked. Cottagers did not have their plants for staple food, but lived on beer, bread, and roots all grown elsewhere; their gardens were for herbs for flavoring and medicine, with few of our modern vegetables or fruits. Now we may again be searching for a similar harmony with mixtures of plants that superficially resemble this humble ancestral cottage garden, but the compositions are necessarily much changed. Some of the old herbs would be retained, but not the many medicinal plants, and our modern choice of vegetables, fruit, and flowers is likely to vary widely from their traditional few. Thus a modern cottage garden may well be completely different from the original in content, though not in its idyllic appearance. The only drawback is that serious quantities of food production are not easily obtainable when combined with an aesthetic cottage-garden appearance, particularly because of the intense plant competition. Nonetheless, there can still be valuable contributions to the household in terms of herbs and flowers. And as long as the plants are well chosen, there is great advantage in having such a wide variety of them—it provides that diversity which makes for a stable ecology, so that pests and diseases are no longer a problem. And a cottage garden immediately around the humble abode can act as a reservoir of guardians for the vegetable and fruit beds nearby.

ORNAMENTAL VEGETABLE GARDENS AND POTAGERS

For serious crop production we need to give more emphasis to the needs of the productive plants. A great mixing of plant types is fine for non-productive areas, but vegetables in particular require the best of conditions before they grow well, as will be explained in Chapter 7. Although they benefit in pest and disease control from a mixing and mingling with flowers and other plants they must never be in the least crowded or they fail catastrophically. Some vegetables such as squash will trail over other plants and produce some usable crops but their season of interest is short. Saladings can make quite attractive bedding in open spots but, unless you choose a cut-and-come-again variety such as frilly red lettuce, eating any inevitably leaves a gap. Many forms of fruit may be grown among flowers but they will be unlikely to do as well as in a specially prepared and protected area. Also, hidden among other plants ripe crops can be hard to find, unsightly if protected from the birds, and

difficult to harvest. However, mixing food crops and flowers is generally a good idea but the food crops must be given absolute priority in planning and position and flowering plants added in any niche left spare. Basically this means reworking the vegetable patch with an appealing design, adding companion plants and flowers and surrounding it with trained fruit. Trying to do it the other way round and growing our common food crops in among existing ornamental plants will nearly always give poor results from the established plants' usually fatal competition. There are alternatives; delightful gardens can be made almost entirely of ornamental edible plants, though I've tried most of these and find few of them very palatable. Indeed it makes more sense to go on to the next stage of small-scale farming, where the garden is made from plants to be fed to animals which you then eat. Of course you can forgo much of the productive side almost entirely and go for a naturalistic garden that runs itself ecologically and take what you can glean.

FOREST GLADES

These offer the nearest we can get to a totally natural garden, given the parameters of a modern plot. We can easily create the effect of the "open in the middle and shaded at the edge" hole left by the fall of a major tree in a woodland. This is soon colonized and can be a beautiful sunny spot until a successor fills the canopy over again. We can replicate such a glade with high fences and borders around a lawn and can play on this theme to make it beloved of all the wild creatures we wish to attract by planting predominantly native trees and shrubs for our perimeter and then filling the border with such typical woodland companions as foxgloves. The main drawback is that a small-scale forest glade soon becomes too shady for herb or vegetable production. However, as long as the sides are not allowed to get too high, then the central sunny glade area is suitable for most vegetables. Soft fruits, in a cage, can thrive as they are the natural accompaniment of the woodland's edge.

WILD GARDENS

These are often offered as a lame excuse by those who do not realize how truly they speak as they indicate their area of gross dereliction. Giving it all back to nature does have some merit: it is remarkable how rapidly a niche is colonized and, although a junk-strewn vista of scrub, weeds, and brambles is not what most of us wish to achieve, it offers a vast number of interesting habitats—but only if left completely undisturbed. The art becomes one of concealing all the junk where it can be of service to the various forms of wildlife, while also offering them the other things they need such as nest sites and water, and further planting up the garden to attract and hold them with food and cover. A well-planned wild garden that looks appealing and natural, and attracts wildlife, is a great achievement rarely wrought by mere neglect!

Roses are one of the most typical woodland's edge flowers. The pink ones shown here are 'Kazanlik,' the apricot are 'Buff Beauty.' The French lavender underneath helps deter aphids.

The golden compromise—selective companion planting for the health of the garden

Although plants compete with each other they are not all after exactly the same niches. This theoretically allows us to squeeze more plants into a given area without them choking their neighbors. Low-growing, shallow-rooting ground-covering plants can exist in the light shade of deeper rooting trees while climbers can grow up the latter, creating three tiers. Shrubs can be added but will do poorly unless the trees are well spaced. Then four tiers of plants can be built up, providing a rich habitat for wildlife and using soil and light so efficiently that few weeds get a chance to appear. Building up such a wide range of plants also gives the stable habitat that resists pest and disease problems from the very diversity of plants and the life they support. Unfortunately, such a garden produces very little that is tasty or nutritious, and it can even be unsuited to many ornamentals. In practice, some groups of plants just need to be isolated from the more vigorous woody and shade-forming ones. Most of our favorite herbaceous plants rarely do well in competition with other sorts of plant, so they are best grown on their own in a bed or border; likewise the silver-leafed and culinary herbs do best in a dry, sunny bed of their own. Similarly, vegetables are most successfully grown on their own open, sunny, airy plot—they do so very poorly anywhere else. But even they benefit from having the right permanent neighbors planted around the edges of their areas and from being grown with their preferred companions inside. But the companions have to be of the same transient nature as the main crop or the vegetables will be squeezed out. The best vegetable companionships are shown on page 145.

Even building up good teams of perennial plants can only be successful if the order of planting is patiently controlled to allow each form of plant time and room to establish. This applies to purely ornamental mixed beds and borders and to perennial productive combinations, but is definitely not recommended for most vegetables.

If you are starting a new bed from scratch, first prepare the area well, removing all weeds and rubbish and improving the soil as outlined in Chapter 10. Once the site is marked out and ready, plant trees, preferably fruiting ones as well as purely ornamental ones, and ensure that each has ample room to develop. After these have established for a year plant shrubs and fruit bushes between, again leaving each plenty of room. After another year, plant low herbaceous plants, groundcover and bulbs in any open spaces left available. Two or three years later, when the trees and shrubs have attained sufficient size, climbers can be grown to ramble over them. Careful weeding will be needed until the plants cover the soil, but thick mulches will minimize this and aid growth.

The temptation to plant up the apparently enormous gaps in the first two years should be resisted to give each form of plant room to establish successfully. More color and interest can be introduced in the first year or two by growing annual flowers in the gaps, but these must not be allowed to spread and choke the new plantings at all.

Choosing useful as well as beautiful flowering and scented plants

You can only have so many plants, so make them all multipurpose, and choose only the best. Don't have an annual when you can have a similar perennial. Don't choose a plant for its flowers if you can have another with flowers as good *and* scent, and better still with some part you can

False spikenard (*Smilacina racemosa*), also known as treacle-berry because the edible red berries taste of treacle. Not yet "improved" by commercial growers, this attractive plant has wonderful scented flowers and attractive herbaceous foliage.

eat or use in cooking, or just with attractive foliage. If you are interested solely in beauty, not production, you can still choose plants which benefit wildlife.

Plants are the most important part of our garden and deserve a little understanding. If we choose them carefully they will serve us well. Good gardeners try to go with nature rather than force her. Since plants respond directly to what we do for them, we can help them flourish if we understand their needs and responses. Plants can be better understood if we divide them up into groups so that we can give each the best treatment according to its nature.

Family ties All plants have a two-word Latin name, giving their genus and species. Often there is a third word, giving more description; this may be the cultivar name it is commonly known by. So we get names that seem complicated but which contain information to help us comprehend each plant. For example *Viburnum opulus* 'sterile' 'Snowball' is one of the *Viburnum* genus from the Caprifoliaceae family of plants. *Opulus* defines it as the particular species usually known as the guelder rose. This cultivar happens to be sterile, so is nonberrying, and 'Snowball' is a "commercial" clone name for this vegetatively propagated variety. Most species in a genus resemble each other with only minor differences, so once we know one we can often—but not always—guess at the needs and attributes of the others. For example, clematis and jasmine are both thought of as climbers and the needs for most varieties and species are similar, varying most in pruning, but there are herbaceous and shrubby clematis and even an evergreen shrubby jasmine, *J. revolutum*.

The important thing to remember about family ties is that closely related plants, those with the same first name, usually will suffer from the same pests and diseases. Furthermore, the more widely and commonly any of them and their relations are grown, the more pests and diseases there are to plague them. For example: members of the *Brassica* family—cabbages, cauliflowers, broccoli, etc.—are all both common and closely related, so they are attacked by the same large number of pests and diseases; the same applies to roses, whereas spinach and peonies are not grown as widely or frequently, so are less troubled. Any garden plants that are related to common native plants will similarly be subject to their pests and diseases, but these will usually be controlled by natural systems that have evolved with them, provided we have not inadvertently destroyed them.

Annuals and perennials Annuals live, flower, and die in a short period, usually from spring to fall. They are some of the prettiest flowers and their rapid growth is useful for filling gaps. Many vegetables whose fruits or seeds we eat, such as corn, peas, and broad beans, are also annuals. However, to complicate things, many perennials are grown as annuals

and either discarded or killed by the frosts to be replaced with fresh plants the following year. Annuals generally prefer to be sown where they are to flower and resent root disturbance; most are normally propagated by seed.

Biennials live longer, growing one year to flower the next. Many vegetables such as the roots and onions are biennials, but eaten before they complete their cycle. Some of our most attractive flowers are biennials, using the energy stored in their roots to throw up long spikes: foxgloves, Canterbury bells, hollyhocks, and sweet rocket are all examples. Some biennial plants, especially wallflowers, Brompton and East Lothian stocks, and sweet William, might live for another year or two before dying away, but they are usually replaced with fresh plants. Moving biennials while they are dormant will not harm them.

True perennials last for more than a year or two and although some live not much longer than that and some apparent perennials are monocarpic, dying once they have set seed, most are much longer lasting. Those that spread with creeping roots are continually forming new plants at the margins and are effectively immortal; some trees live more than a thousand years. Perennials tend to make up the bulk of the ornamental and fruiting plants in most gardens. They are semi-permanent, not in need of annual replacement, and their established root systems help them endure poor conditions. Most can be moved when young, but resent it increasingly as they grow older and larger; it is often easier to propagate and plant a new perennial rather than to move an old one.

above

A nearly hardy annual, the Cape phlox (*Zaluzianskya capensis*) has a rich vanilla scent when the flowers open in the cool of the evening.

You can also tell a lot about the requirements of a plant from its appearance.

Soft or shrubby? Perennials can be split into two groups: those with soft growth that dies back in winter and those with shrubby or woody growth that endures and regrows each year. The former, bulbs and herbaceous plants, spring again from the roots and are mostly propagated by division or root cuttings. Some also come true from seed and in a fairly short time. Bulbs and herbaceous plants form larger clumps, but do not grow taller each year and thus need no pruning, only a tidy up in fall.

Woody and shrubby plants grow larger each year and may need pruning if you want to control their size. They are mostly propagated from cuttings or layering, though some need to be grafted or budded on to suitable rootstocks. Shrubby perennials grown from seed may be variable and slow to flower or fruit.

Deciduous or evergreen? While herbaceous plants overwinter protected by the soil, most woody plants drop their leaves in fall and go partially dormant to protect them from the hard weather. This is generally a good time to prune or move a plant, as it will recover much better than if it is moved while in leaf. Although a plant may appear totally dormant, some processes continue and unless the soil is frozen they start rooting immediately.

Evergreens retain their foliage throughout the year, dropping their leaves only a few at a time. In hard weather they can suffer badly from drying winds and frozen soil. The moisture sucked out of their leaves cannot be replaced, leading to scorched foliage or even death. Evergreens have evolved waxy coatings to their leaves to prevent water loss and this is partly why the leaves are slow to break down and hard to compost. The dense cover they provide makes excellent winter shelter for ladybugs and other predators big and small, so include some in different parts of the garden as refuges. Most evergreens are never dormant, so should be pruned or moved only in early spring once the soil has warmed enough for them to recover quickly. See page 45 for a list of my favorites.

Tender or hardy? Plants that will stand in the open garden and survive several degrees of frost are considered hardy. Half-hardy is a term usually applied to those bedding plants which need sowing in warmth and hardening off before planting out after the last frosts in spring. Tender plants die at the least touch of frost and do badly if at all cold, while stovehouse plants require real heat. These last were popular with the Victorians, but most are now unsuitable except as houseplants or for those with well-heated conservatories. For exceptions to this rule, see Chapter 8 (page 169).

Hardy annuals are a large group of flowers grown from seed each year; they do not need protection and can be sown direct once the soil warms up in spring. Most can also be sown in the fall to overwinter for an earlier display. Some tender garden perennials survive many years in favorable sites, being killed only by extreme winters. Given a very good position against a wall some surprising plants such as *Opuntia*, passionflowers, and palms can be grown, especially if the roots are protected during the worst frosts. Other less hardy plants such as fuchsia and lemon verbena can be nursed through bad weather by mulching the roots thickly with straw or loose airy material. The tops may die back, but if the roots are kept warm and dry they shoot again in spring.

Plants that have been grown hard (outdoors), with strong but not too vigorous well-ripened growth (no extra feed from midsummer), tend to stand frost and temperature change better (survive) than plants grown soft (indoors or on a warm patio) or lushly (overfed and watered). Never feed plants heavily in late summer or fall as this promotes soft growth that does not ripen well and is then prone to disease as well as frost damage. Most plants are more frost resistant if they are not wet at the roots; well-draining soil and a warmth-retaining mulch protects roots against many degrees of frost. Often frost is not the killer—it is the warm, damp period afterwards that encourages rotting and finishes them off. This is one reason why dry spots, as at the base of a wall, shelter plants so well. For silver- and hairy-leafed plants rotting from damp is *the* problem and they survive almost any weather if the rain is kept off with a cloche or just a sheet of glass on two bricks.

Plants are shocked and checked by rapid changes of temperature, so keep these gradual. Plants being moved outside from a warmer place can be hardened off by putting them out during the day and bringing them in at night for a few days. Thus they deal with one shock before having to cope with the trauma of being transplanted. Similarly, do not move plants from outside to a hot room in one go—acclimatize them gently.

Plant pollination

One rarely needs to consider pollination except when saving seed or in the fruit garden, about which more is said in Chapter 6 (see page 101). A few plants, such as holly and *Skimmia*, are dioecious, needing both male and female plants if they are to berry, but requiring only one male to every half-dozen females. Otherwise ensure pollination by encouraging as many pollinators as possible in the garden. These useful friends can also be brought under cover if you grow companion flowers such as marigolds and sweet alyssum to attract them. If you want to be certain of seed setting, hand pollination using a rabbit's tail or cotton ball may be a good idea for plants growing under cover or early in the year when pollinators are few. However, most flowers last longer if they are not pollinated so cut flower growers may be better off without pollinators.

My favorite annuals, biennials, bulbs, herbaceous trees and shrubs, climbers, marginals and pond plants

I've chosen the following plants for all-round value. Remember, there are also lists in the previous chapter recommending plants for attracting different wildlife.

ANNUALS

These are invariably better sown in situ, but it is often more convenient to sow them in small pots and plant out in gaps as these become apparent in the main displays. Most will self-seed, and fall-sown seedlings overwinter and flower earlier than spring-sown plants, so extending the season.

Alyssum maritimum Sweet, honey-scented, loved by insects. The rose, purple, and dwarf forms are more attractive and compact but less well scented.

Convolvolus tricolor Like a petunia, but hardy, so does not require starting off with greenhouse space. Pretty white, blue, and yellow trumpets attract bees, hoverflies, and other beneficial insects.

Lathyrus odoratus Obligatory. What is summer without sweet peas? Grow the old-fashioned ones with strong scent. Sow in situ and in pots in fall and spring for succession of flowers.

Matthiola Ten-week stocks (*M. incana*) are opulently scented, but for color, ease, and the most divine evening scent sow mixed Virginian (*M. maritima*) and night-scented (*M. bicornis*) stocks.

Nicotiana Poisonous but beautiful, evening-scented sweet tobacco (*N. alata*) and more so flowering tobacco (*N. silvestris*) have sticky stems and leaves that trap small pests.

Phacelia tanacetifolia is a wonderful bee plant and a good space filler with absolutely masses of bluey-purple flowers.

Tagetes patula French marigolds offer

good color, are long flowering, and attract beneficial insects, so grow them everywhere possible. The other *Tagetes* marigolds are also useful plants.

Tropaeolum majus Sow nasturtiums direct in late spring and do not over-feed or they will be all leaves. Dwarf forms are often well scented, while trailers can cover large areas with flowers. All parts are edible, including the seeds.

Zaluzianskya capensis Cape phlox or the night phlox cultivar 'Midnight Candy' is little known but has the most heavenly evening scent of sweet rich vanilla.

BIENNIALS

Start these off in a seedbed during early summer and plant out in their final position in fall. Sow them two years running and most can be left to self-seed.

Cheiranthus Wallflowers are really perennial, but are better discarded once they become straggly. They have more scent value than most, particuarly as they flower so early in the year.

Dianthus Classic cottage garden plants, I equally like Pinks and Sweet William.

Digitalis Foxgloves that have self-seeded are always best. They have no scent, but they feed bees, thrive in woodland settings and can be fitted

Night-scented stock (*Matthiola bicornis*) is a hardy annual that looks poor during the day, but each evening the pale flowers open and their scent is glorious.

into most odd corners easily.

Hesperis matronalis Sweet rocket is an old-fashioned plant, with tall, stock-like flowers. It is easy, undemanding, produces lots of flowers, and self-

Foxgloves are said to be beneficial to other plants nearby—they certainly please the eye.

seeds everywhere. *H. steveniana* is similar but smaller, with one of the longest flowering seasons in the garden.

Oenothera Evening primroses are wonderful evening-scented flowers, full of pollen for the insects.

Matthiola Brompton and East Lothian stocks sown in midsummer give gorgeous heads of scented flowers the next spring. Many will be lost overwinter even if they are cloched. *M. incana* is the original and best, but is a short-lived semi-perennial.

BULBS AND CORMS

These can be grown like herbaceous plants as clumps in a border and most can be naturalized in grass. For the most natural effect, throw them, then plant them where they land. Bulbs are often best around trees and in front of hedges where the grass can be left to grow long. Wherever they grow, do not remove the leaves before they have started to wither as this reduces their vigor and flowering. When planting, tend to err on the deep side; on heavy or wet soils bed them on sharp sand.

Allium The onion family are tough, reliable flowerers loved by beneficial insects. Many are edible, such as garlic and chives, which are also believed to benefit other plants, especially roses. There are many ornamental alliums, such as *A. moly* which has lovely yellow flowers.

Crocus Often grown through grass, but they quickly die out if the leaves are removed too soon. The common Dutch types are useful to beneficial insects as they flower in early spring. Some other varieties flower in the fall and even through the winter. The Dutch types are inexpensive and best in groups. Black cotton thread tied onto sticks makes a barricade to stop birds damaging them.

Cyclamen Beautiful flowers, some with scent. Most have attractive foliage too, especially *C. europaeum*.

Galanthus Snowdrops are best moved

the flowering of the garden

41

Regal lilies (*Lilium regale*) are full of pollen for insects and full of scent for us.

or bought while in leaf, as dried bulbs die away. Divide them annually after flowering and they increase rapidly. Especially nice is the double *G. nivalis* 'Flore pleno.'

Hyacinthus Powerful scents and bright colors, but expensive. Hyacinths forced for indoor use can be hardened off and planted out but after a few years degenerate to resemble bluebells, though they belong to different genera. Bluebells prefer moist, light shade and are rarely offered for sale. Grape hyacinths (*Muscari*) are smaller, earlier, and seed freely.

Lilium There are many wonderful lilies. Most are not difficult to grow, though they need well-drained, rich soils. Some need acid conditions and most prefer full sun *or* partial shade. The easiest are the Turk's cap (*L. martagon*) and the regal lily (*L. regale*), which is outstanding—it can even be grown from seed to flower in two years.

Narcissus Daffodils come in many forms, from the early-flowering dwarf *N. bulbocodium* with rush-like foliage, through the sheets of 'King Alfred' all over England at Easter to the late, gloriously scented jonquils and *N. poeticus recurvus* or pheasant's eye.

Ranunculus verna Celandines can be more of a weed than most, spreading by tiny tubers carried from place to place in soil on shoes and tools. They bring early cheer with sheets of gold

for beneficial insects and look stunning with blue grape hyacinths.

Tulipa The strong colors make them overpowering in some settings, but give them tremendous impact on drab spring days. Some tulips can be naturalized in rough grass—try the wild form, *T. sylvestris*.

HERBACEOUS PERENNIALS

Herbaceous plants are more difficult to combine with other types of plant because they suffer from the competition. So they are usually best grown in their own bed or border. Some bulbs and smaller shrubs, such as lilies and fuchsias, can be treated as herbaceous to all intents and purposes. Herbaceous perennials are mostly best tidied in late fall, and divided or moved in the spring. When cutting back in fall, wait till the stems have withered so that all the nutrients have been re-absorbed. Then cut them off about a hand span high. This leaves the old stem bases to support and protect the young shoots as they emerge, and marks their position. Clean mulches, good spacing between, and planting in groups of threes, fives, and sevens give the best effect.

VERY LOW-GROWING HERBACEOUS

PERENNIALS

Ajuga reptans Carpet-like mats of blue bugle make excellent groundcover and attract bees, but are very invasive.

Alchemilla mollis Lady's mantle is good groundcover, with mounds of soft yellow-green flowers. Useful for wildlife, as it traps water droplets in its foliage.

Alyssum saxatile Trailing clumps of grey leaves good for rockery ground-cover with masses of golden flowers all summer long. It's rather vigorous and invasive, so cut back immediately after flowering.

Armeria maritima Thrift resembles evergreen cushions of grass till it flowers with pink balls on stems. It makes a good edging plant.

Aubrieta Similar to *Alyssum* with thick mats of evergreen leaves and masses of flower in red to blue.

Bergenia cordifolia Tough evergreen groundcover with large leaves that will survive almost anywhere. Pink flowers come in very early spring.

Gypsophila paniculata forms hummocks of tiny flowers that are loved by insects and flower arrangers alike.

Helianthemum nummularium Sun

Arabis blepharophylla is a sweet-scented, mat-forming beauty flowering in early spring.

The Organic Gardening Bible

roses are similar to *Cistus*, the rock rose, and are really shrubs. Ideal for dry walls or banks, they are evergreen but short-lived. Prune them hard after the reddish flowers fade.

Iberis sempervirens Really a dwarf shrub, this produces lax, evergreen foliage and masses of white flowers.

LOW- TO MEDIUM-GROWING HERBACEOUS PERENNIALS

These mostly stand up on their own or look best left to form their own shape. In windy areas on strong soil, support may be necessary, in which case tie them up early.

Aquilegia hybrids Columbines are one of *the* cottage garden plants with beautiful, low, fern-like foliage and tall, graceful spurred flowers in many colours and combinations.

Aster novi-belgii Michaelmas daisies reliably provide late flowers for insects in reds and blues.

Brunnera macrophyla Perennial forget-me-nots are tough groundcover plants for most situations. They produce heart-shaped leaves and blue flowers.

Campanula Bellflowers are good for bees and—unless you can grow gentians—provide the best blues in the garden.

Geranium Crane's bills are excellent groundcover and flourish almost anywhere.

Geum These tough plants form wiry clumps that make excellent groundcover.

Helleborus The Christmas and Lent roses provide winter and spring flowers for beneficial insects and their handsome evergreen foliage makes good groundcover. They are poisonous but rarely cause problems. I find they resent moving.

Iris Bearded iris are tough, beautiful and thrive even in dry spots. *I. unguicularis* is a scented winter gem, *I. foetidissima* a useful evergreen with magnificent orange berries.

Lychnis *L. chalcedonica* is commonly grown, but I love the double-flowered catchfly *L. viscaria* 'Splendens Plena.'

Granny's bonnet aquilegias are one of *the* cottage garden plants.

Nepeta Catnip or catmint (*N. cataria*) is loved to death by feline herbivores. The less loved *N. mussinii* is bigger with more pointed leaves. Both are loved by bees.

Sedum spectabile Although most of this family are invasive, this one is delightfully controllable, yet any bit roots or divides. It is loved by insects for its fall flowers and has good shape and foliage.

Tradescantia virginiana Attractive, odd, rush-like foliage and pale blue or pink flowers all summer.

MEDIUM- TO TALL-GROWING HERBACEOUS PERENNIALS

As these are taller, in windy areas some can be broken or fall without support. Keep them upright by tying them to canes or to long stubs left after pruning. Alternatively, grow them up through horizontal wire netting.

Achillea Yarrow with its feathery foliage and flat white flowers attracts beneficial insects for a long season. It is very tough and believed to be a beneficial companion to other plants generally.

Centranthus ruber False valerian—the true medicinal plant is *Valeriana*. *Centranthus* is unrelated and brighter colored. It is good for insects, but

self-seeds viciously, in any soil, anywhere, even dry spots.

Coreopsis grandiflora Good for cutting and liked by insects, tickseed must not be overfed or it will be all foliage and no flowers.

Eryngium Sea holly is loved by beneficial insects and has metallic-blue flower heads rising out of striking spiky bluey evergreen holly-like foliage. The roots were once eaten.

Kniphofia Red-hot pokers make attractive, almost evergreen grassy clumps which are surprisingly tough. They are excellent winter homes for insects while the flowers are very melliferous—I drink the nectar.

Lupinus polyphyllus This lupin bears wonderful flowers and its foliage traps dew. Divide clumps every third year or they lose vigor and fade away. They don't like overfeeding either.

Lysimachia punctata Yellow loosestrife will grow anywhere and everywhere and, as it flowers all summer long, benefits insects for many months.

Papaver orientale Brilliant orangey-scarlet flowers and copious pollen for the bees. Poppies will come back no matter how often you dig them out.

Rudbeckia purpurea Coneflowers are loved by insects and come usefully late in the year.

TALLER-GROWING HERBACEOUS PLANTS

Do not regiment a border short at the front to high at the back—have it coming and going in waves with some of these plants toward the front of a border for more height. These will probably need tying up to supports, but are worth it as the masses of flowers support many insects.

Althaea rosea Hollyhocks are one of *the* cottage garden plants. Sadly they suffer from rust, but nevertheless flower prolifically in red and yellow if given sufficiently rich soil. Hide them at the back of a border so that the worst affected foliage is masked by other plants.

Chrysanthemum These are members of the *Compositae* family, and many of them use exudations to combat pests and diseases. *C. coccineum* is effective at killing soil nematodes, while *C. cinerariifolium* and *C. roseum* flowers have been powdered for 2000 years for use as an insect killer. The commercial version, pyrethrum, is used in massive amounts because of its very low toxicity to mammals. Korean chrysanthemums flower late in the year, benefiting many insects. Though invasive, Shasta daisies are dependable and have good dark foliage that makes an ideal backdrop for other plantings.

Delphinium These wonderful spires of early summer are loved by bees and slugs! They need very rich soil.

Echinops Globe thistles are one of the best bee plants, statuesque and prickly with metallic-blue heads.

Eremurus Foxtail lilies have tall spikes of tightly packed flowers that rise from grass-like foliage and asparagus-like roots. They need sun and rich soil.

Helianthus These perennial sunflowers are as attractive to bees and butterflies as the annual kind.

Physalis franchetii Chinese lanterns are invaluable for winter color and decoration. They sprawl: grow them in front of a passion flower, *P. caerula*, which has similar, orange-colored fruits.

Verbascum hybridum Mulleins are beloved by insects and are another cottage garden must with their woolly foliage and tall spires of yellow flowers.

PARTICULARLY WELL-SCENTED HERBACEOUS PLANTS

These gems need siting where you can appreciate them—at the front of a border, concentrated around a seat or under an oft-open window.

Convallaria majalis Lily of the valley hates transplanting and needs a moist, rich soil, but once established, it romps and spreads, and the scent is divine.

Dianthus Almost all this family are delightfully clove- or sweet-scented, but the best of all are the pinks. These need regular repropagation from tiny pipings pulled off the plant, or they get straggly.

Hemerocallis Day lilies bloom for only a day, but keep on producing more for months regardless of the conditions. The flowers are usually edible.

Hosta Better known for their foliage's susceptibility to slugs than for their scent, so 'Royal Standard' may surprise you.

Melissa officinalis Lemon-scented balm is loved by us and by the bees. The golden-splashed foliage of *M. officinalis aurea* is beautiful.

Paeonia Peonies are exquisite, so soft and perfect, especially with the dew on them. The foliage is attractive after the short flowering season.

Phlox Strange spicy, musty scent, but these are long flowering on very upright stems.

Primula Wild primroses are sweet and easy to establish. Try the drumstick primula (*P. denticulata*).

Viola Not all violets are scented, but *V. odorata* is and works well under

Given enough water, phlox make a grand show, though their scent is not to everyone's taste.

roses as both like rich soil.

TREES AND SHRUBS

I consider a plant as a tree if it's shrubby with a single stem and can be used as a specimen. Most shrubs can be pruned and trained as small trees in the manner of standard roses and vice versa.

TREES FOR SPECIMEN FEATURES AND ADDING HEIGHT

Some fruiting trees are as beautiful as purely ornamental varieties, are not too large for most gardens and useful to us and wildlife. For individual varieties of fruit trees, their needs and treatment, see Chapter 6 (page 101).

Apple (*Malus pumila*) The fruiting varieties make excellent specimens, and most ornamental *Malus* varieties are good pollinators for the fruiters. Beautiful in flower and again with bright red or yellow crab fruits, try 'Adams' or 'Cinderella.'

Birch (*Betula pendula*) Silver birches look best in small, informal groups. Other birches have yellow foliage or attractive bark. Wine was once made from the sap of silver birch in spring and their presence in the garden is said to stimulate composting.

Cherry (*Prunus cerasus*) Fruiting cherry trees are very beautiful in flower and come on semidwarfing root stocks, so plant them to attract

bees and beneficial insects, as well as for the fruit. Avoid the larger-growing flowering cherries. Try 'Stella' on 'Colt' stock.

Hawthorn (*Crataegus laevigata*) The commoner *C. monogyna* has pink or white fishy-scented flowers, is thorny and berries freely. *C. laevigata* 'Paul's Scarlet' is double-flowered and dark red. It is of slightly less value to insects but very beautiful.

Quince (*Cydonia oblonga*) The best specimen tree, with a good framework. It bears big apple-like flowers, offers spring and fall leaf color and edible, aromatic, long-keeping fruit.

Rowan (*Sorbus aucuparia*) Mountain ashes are attractive in form and foliage and the prolific red berries are much loved by birds. I prefer the native species to ornamental forms, and there is a large-berried variety, *S. a. edulis*, whose fruit is sweeter and better for eating and jamming than the wild form.

EVERGREEN SHRUBS

Since evergreen shrubs are never dormant they are best planted in spring and kept well watered until established. They should rarely be pruned heavily, but if this is necessary do it in spring. Those with larger leaves should not have them cut or they brown.

Choisya ternata Mexican orange blossom needs shelter to protect its aromatic, evergreen foliage, especially the yellow form. Often a second flush of scented flowers appears in fall.

Daphne The whole family is poisonous, but all have exquisitely scented flowers from early spring, are very attractive and compact; most are evergreen. The most reliable is *D. odora* 'Aureomarginata.' Daphnes are often difficult to establish, needing well-drained, humus-rich soil.

Elaeagnus Tough, mostly evergreen shrubs that make good shelter for wildlife. All produce nondescript scented flowers and some bear edible berries. *E. pungens* 'Maculata' has a bright yellow spot on its dark green leaves and is a cheery specimen.

Leycesteria formosa This is an exotic, shrubby, bamboo-like plant with ferny foliage and jewel-like flowers with red bracts. It can be grown as a shrub or pruned, much like herbaceous plants, to the ground each spring.

Mahonia Attractive holly-like leaves, black berries, and yellow flowers are typical of this accommodating genus. *M. aquifolium* flowers in late winter but *M. japonica* is sweeter scented.

Osmanthus These look like holly or privet, but are more compact and have sweetly scented flowers.

Prunus laurocerasus Laurel is a tough evergreen and makes a big thick screen anywhere; the flowers are sweetly scented. The yellow spotted laurel (*Aucuba japonica*) is unrelated, but similar in appearance with flashy red berries on the females.

Rhododendron Magnificent displays of flowers and grand foliage, but rhododendrons must have lime-free soil. They can be confined in large containers. Most floriferous is *R. yunnanense*.

Sarcococca Winter box is a small, tough evergreen with lovely but nondescript, pale, sweetly scented flowers in midwinter.

Skimmia These make neat, well-scented and attractive specimens, with red berries on female plants if there is a male plant nearby to act as a pollinator.

PARTICULARLY WELL-SCENTED SHRUBS

Scent is the glory of the garden and I revel in it. The following are some of my favorites, but to each their own.

Buddleja *B. globosa* is semievergreen and makes a quick screen with orange ball-shaped flower clusters. *B. davidii*, the butterfly bush, draws all sorts of insects to long, strongly scented racemes in a wide choice of colors. Prune all buddlejas back hard in spring; the trimmings can be used as cuttings which root very readily,

The scent of mock orange (*Philadelphus coronarius*) is so strong it is reputed to give some people headaches.

but established plants resent being moved.

Cytisus The brooms like hot, dry positions, are generally short lived and small with yellowish, scented pea flowers. I love the tall-growing *C. battandieri* with its silky semi-evergreen laburnum leaves and pineapple-scented flowers.

Hamamelis The witch hazels are nondescript in leaf, but in winter the flowers smell divine.

Lonicera fragrantissima Shrubby honeysuckles are straggly messes, but the flowers come from midwinter till early spring and are gloriously sweet. Find space for one. For the best summer scent grow *L. syringantha*, which is named after and rivals lilac.

Magnolia These can get big like the wonderful evergreen *M. grandiflora* which has enormous scented flowers. They prefer loamy, lime-free soil.

Philadelphus Mock oranges all have glorious scents, but are a bit nondescript out of flower. Good for filling borders.

Rosa The finest of scented flowers. There is such a choice: old cabbage roses; the damask; I adore 'Etoile de

Hollande,' but for its spicy mossiness I must choose *R. centifolia* 'Muscosa' or 'William Lobb.'

Spartium junceum Spanish broom has rush-like growths and pollen-laden, sweetly scented, pea-like flowers over a long season.

Syringa There are many excellent lilacs from the common purple and whites (*S. vulgaris*) to the divine Persian (*S.* x *persia*), Canadian Preston hybrids (*S.* x *prestonia*) and several dwarf forms.

Viburnum There are so many attractive scented varieties yet the almost scentless *V. tinus* 'Eve Price' and *V opulus*, the guelder rose, are most commonly grown. Far better, in my opinion, are the compact *V.* x *juddi*, the *V.* x *carlcephalum* and the *V.* x *carlessii*.

DROUGHT-TOLERANT SHRUBS FOR DRY PLACES AND BY WALLS

Although the following will grow in such spots they need to be nurtured until well established. Prepare the planting hole well and water often until they are making strong growth.

Artemesia abrotanum Southernwood has feathery fern-like foliage and a delicious lemon pine scent. Plant lots.

Erica The winter-flowering heathers are more tolerant of limy soils, but none grows on chalk no matter how much peat you add. They suppress weeds once established, but will not smother existing infestations.

Escallonia Most species are not very hardy; many are evergreen or partly so. Some have aromatic foliage. Better grown by the sea or in very sheltered spots elsewhere.

Fuchsia These are hardier than most imagine if the roots are well protected. There are good foliage forms such as *F. magellanica* 'Versicolor' and all are easily propagated from cuttings.

Hyssopus officinalis See the entry under Herbs (page 150).

Lavatera maritima Not very hardy, but worth growing as it flowers long and late, benefiting many insects.

top

Fuchsias are especially valuable as they flower on late into fall, when color—and nectar and pollen—are scarce.

above

Forsythia has given a wonderful display every spring since it was discovered in the early years of Queen Victoria's reign.

Also easy to propagate from cuttings.
Lavandula See Herbs (page 148).
Rosmarinus See Herbs (page 148).
Santolina chamaecyparissus Cotton lavender is a tough, low-growing, evergreen, with lovely, aromatic, silver-gray foliage.

TOUGHEST, MOST RELIABLE SHRUBS FOR MOST SITES

Berberis There is an enormous number of varieties, many of them evergreen, some with colored foliage. Most are thorny with prolific yellow flowers and fruit freely. Many give brilliant fall color, too.

Chaenomeles japonica Fiery red flowers very early in spring, followed by iron-hard fruits on lax bushes. The stems are a bit thorny and best trained on walls, even shady ones.

Cotoneaster All are loved by bees for

their countless early-summer flowers and by birds for the prolific red berries. The branches arch gracefully or can be trained on walls. Good fall color, though some are evergreen.

Forsythia Much grown for their wonderful mass of early flowers in spring.

Potentilla These are very tough and very long flowering. Avoid red versions, as they are poor.

Pyracantha Firethorns have masses of flower and fruit for bees and birds, but mean thorns.

Ribes Flowering redcurrants come early, so are good for beneficial insects. Unfortunately, they smell like tom cats to us. They are easily propagated and flower in red, yellow, or white. *R. gordonianum* is particularly impressive.

Sambucus Wild elder feeds the birds with copious berries. Variegated, cut-leaved and golden varieties are more ornamental, especially the lovely gold *S. nigra* 'Aurea.'

Spiraea Slender, graceful, small-leaved bushes which flower profusely, especially *S. x arguta* 'Bridal Wreath.'

Weigela These have foxglove-like flowers in great profusion in reds through to yellow. *W. florida* 'Variegata' offers variegated foliage with slightly scented pink flowers.

CHOICEST CLIMBERS

Climbers, like any shrubby plant, need to be well established; apart from the self-clingers they must also have support. They eventually get big and catch the wind, so make the supports strong, durable, and renewable. Most climbers can be left to ramble rather than being pruned—they will then create good nest and shelter sites.

Buddleja alternifolia A lax shrub, easily trained up a pergola or wall for the long, hanging swathes of light blue, scented flowers.

Clematis These all need their roots in cool, rich, moist soil and their tops in sun. The large-flowered forms have good color, are rarely scented and can be hard to establish. They can be cut nearly to the ground each year except the early flowerers. There are many species with small flowers which are well scented and need no regular pruning. *C. armandii*, for instance, is a barely hardy evergreen. *C. montana* cultivars are good for covering large areas.

Hedera helix Ivy is much neglected, but a valuable self-clinger. It provides late flowers for insects, berries, and nest sites. Large-leaved variegated forms are not as hardy; cuttings rooted from fruiting bushes produce plants that flower soonest. *H. helix* 'Goldheart' has cheery yellow-splashed leaves and is very good in dull places.

Jasminum Winter jasmine (*J. nudiflorum*) is barely a climber, has pale yellow flowers in winter, and needs cutting to the ground afterwards. *J. officinale* is obligatory—no garden is complete without this sweet summer scent. It forms a twining plant best left unpruned.

Lonicera Honeysuckles are gorgeous, tough, easy and nearly all have wonderful scent, I have over a dozen different varieties. They attract fewer aphids when grown in semishade and not overfed. Leave them to ramble unpruned.

Rosa Rambler roses are much more vigorous than climbing ones, all need enriched soil and copious moisture. My favorites include 'New Dawn,' 'Rambling Rector,' 'Souvenir de Claudius Denoyel,' 'Mme Isaac Periere,' 'Maigold,' 'Handel,' and most of all the long-flowering, thornless Bourbon rose 'Zéphirine Drouhin.'

Vitis The vine *V. vinifera* gives wonderful fall color with bunches of grapes, if you can keep the birds off. White grape leaves normally yellow in fall and red ones redden. *V. coignetiae* has enormous leaves, but poor fruits.

MARGINAL PLANTS

Many waterside plants like moist soil, but cannot stand actual water-logging. Bog plants provide hidden wet habitats in and close to the water. This creates safe access, a nursery, and a feeding area for many creatures large and small. Bull rushes, flag irises and other vertical-shafted plants are necessary for dragonflies to emerge successfully from their larval stage.

Astilbe Goat's beard has attractive, palmate foliage and feathery plumes in tones of red throughout the summer.

Caltha palustris, kingcup or the marsh marigold, is the most beautiful blaze of gold in late spring and grows a foot or so high.

Hosta will thrive in any cool, moist, shady spots and are fodder for snails—keeping them away from the salads.

Lobelia cardinalis will grow in shallow water and provides a yard-high show of brilliant red from summer till fall, but take care that the slugs don't get it.

Mimulus luteus is a foot high and provides yellow flowers all summer, but can prove invasive.

. . . AND IN THE WATER

Oxygenating water plants are absolutely essential. Though not very ornamental, they oxygenate the water, feed and provide a habitat for many creatures, and prevent algae taking over the pond.

Elodia canadensis, Canadian pondweed, is invasive but a good oxygenator and then provides useful composting material when dragged out.

Ranunculus aquatilis, water crowfoot, has white flowers and is excellent in still or moving water.

Water lilies Proverbially beautiful, their leaves enable insects to gain access to the water. Preferring still pools, they thrive in plastic baskets of chopped turfs held down with a rock about a boot and a half deep. Choose any native variety.

chapter three

MAKING YOUR GARDEN NATURALLY BEAUTIFUL

The art and skill of planning your garden both to look beautiful and to run efficiently throughout the year

Before planning to alter your existing garden radically or beginning work on your new one, it is important to consider what it is you want from your plot. Is it to add value or interest, amaze your friends with your ecological or wild garden, or for the exercise? If you want to grow foods which ones do you want and when? After all, if you always go on holiday in August there is not much point in planting early apples. Similarly if you want flowers, are they for cutting or as outdoor beauty for you or your neighbors? All gardens need somewhere to sit, but are you going to be on a bench with the garden all around you, or have a more limited vista from a window? If you want privacy then effective screening may be more important than saving money or maximizing self sufficiency.

Once you know which are your most important parameters then it is much easier to plan around them. Consider and plan a garden in the same way you would when buying a newer car or refitting the kitchen, and similarly be prepared to spend realistic amounts of money initially. What you can have and what it costs in time, work, and money do not just depend on the size of your garden. All the factors are interchangeable, money being the most easily converted into the others, but size remains the most important arbiter, with choice increasing as the garden enlarges.

In very dry soil by an evergreen hedge, where even weeds are scarce, bearded iris flourish and the little-known and delicately scented *Hesperis steveniana* blooms on from early spring till fall.

PLANNING ON PAPER

To make an effective plan it will help to make a map showing the boundaries, walls, pipelines, immovable objects, future building extensions, solid paths, trees, major shrubs, and so on which are very difficult to alter. Given time and money anything is possible in garden design, but it is much easier to work around the permanent features rather than try to change everything. Use a pencil to mark the current areas of grass, vegetable plot, beds, and borders as these can be altered at will. Choose the best sites for production—vegetables, the fruitcage, and so on—then add other areas as your space allows. Work out your plan on paper first before translating it onto the ground as this saves much work and time. The plan helps you to see the garden as a whole and so organize it more rationally. Try to get the maximum use out of each item, for example, place a store shed to shelter a bed and so that the biggest blank wall faces the sun for a trained fruit bush while it can also be part of the fencing for a fruitcage or hen run, the overflow from the shed water butts can be fed to another store or a pool, nests put underneath the floor and bird boxes under the eaves.

Flowerdew's Five Fs

While it is quite possible to be completely organic and pay no attention to aesthetics or even simple neatness, you are more likely also to want to make your garden a beautiful place, with harmonious lines and a natural placing and composition of all the elements. A certain instinct comes in to play here, and I believe that if it looks right it is right. However, some aspects of appearance are harder to achieve than others. I have broken these down into five basic elements which combined form the garden portrait as a whole. To make them easy to remember I have called them Framework, Foliage, Flowers, Features, and Finish.

Framework Because of its permanence through all seasons the bare bones or framework of any garden is especially important to have right, particularly when it is visible from frequently used windows. The outlines, shapes, and views formed by the solid permanent features need to look good when there is little leaf or flower to help decorate or disguise them. The shapes and edges of beds and borders and paths are most important but pergolas, walls, hedges, trunks of trees, and evergreens also create the solidity and endurance of any design, so great care needs to be taken with their laying out and positioning.

Once you have drawn up your plan, mock it up in the garden using canes and string to try out different permutations before doing any work on the ground. A good idea is never to show all the garden from any one point so that there is a hint of more to discover. Create a hidden corner by extending the edge of a border or plant an island bed as an invitation

Herbaceous plants give foliage interest for far longer than their flowering period. They may form larger clumps as time goes by, but their eventual height remains the same each year, making planning their beds simpler.

to explore behind. Long, thin gardens can be made more interesting by breaking them up into a series of "rooms" with a meandering path just giving glimpses of spaces beyond.

Paths can be tapered and curved to change perspective and make gardens seem larger or smaller in different directions. They should always lead to something, be it nothing more than an urn of flowers. Bending a path so that it disappears round a corner invites more exploration and trompe l'oeil steps leading nowhere at a boundary can give an impression of size and of more garden to discover.

Arches, gateways, and pergolas add vertical interest and help heighten the feeling of rooms within rooms. They also allow smoother transition from one part of the garden to another with a different flavor, and block out unsightly objects and views. Remember that the closer the screen the lower it can be. The colors and materials making up the solid part of the framework tend to be more pleasing if they are compatible and consistent with their surroundings and each other. It helps to have all wood and timber work stained to the same hue; try also to use local materials, preferably recycled ones, within a single area or throughout the whole garden.

Foliage Although welcomed in the spring and appreciated in the fall, during summer deciduous foliage is noticed, if at all, as a backdrop for the flowers. Yet foliage is also important in its own right, the many different forms, textures, colors, and scents adding new levels of interest to any planting. Carefully selecting and combining these creates a more unified appearance than concentrating on flowers alone. One might even dispense with flowers entirely, as many plants have beautiful leaf color and not only in the fall. Some, such as the poplar *Populus candicans* 'Aurora' and *Jasmine stephanense*, have brilliantly colored new leaves in the spring and there are countless plants with variegated leaves in many patterns and shades adding more color.

Many evergreens such as *Elaeagnus, Euonymus,* and holly, have forms with white and yellow variegated and colored leaves and these are especially useful for brightening dull winter days and dark corners. Evergreens contribute much to the feeling of permanence in a garden and need to be considered along with the framework to give year-round interest, though too many can give a somber tone. The many shades and variety of evergreens plus the golds, reds, and blues of conifers and heathers create colorful gardens that remain almost unchanged throughout the year. Once established, these gardens require little maintenance but they are hard to blend in with many settings. Evergreens, especially ivy, are useful for providing shelter, nest, and hibernation sites for beneficial insects and animals; for this reason alone, as well as for aesthetic reasons, some should be included in each part of the garden.

The effect of foliage, particularly of the young growths of herbaceous plants, is enhanced if there is multiple planting. Single specimens can give a spotty appearance which is reinforced when the flowers come out. Most plants look best when grouped in threes, fives and sevens. Obviously this is not always practical, but generally in a bed with say three dozen plants, the effect will be better with two groups of seven, two of five and four of three than with 36 different ones. Deliberate and frequent repetition of a favorite plant in various areas can add much to the unity and ambience of the garden until it almost becomes a theme.

Flowers A garden is incomplete without flowers, not only because of their beauty but because they provide nectar and pollen for beneficial insects. The organic gardener wishing to increase the total life within the garden must ensure a constant succession of flowers using as many and as varied plants as possible to nurture and sustain the maximum number and variety of creatures. Of course, flowers are followed by seeds and berries, which then feed other beneficial insects and animals and so their value is increased. To us, these fruits may be as attractive as, or even better than, the flowers they follow, as is the case with holly berries and Gladwyn iris. Naturally few berries last for long, though those in unusual colors, such as yellow pyracanthas, last longest.

Growing flowers for their beauty it is a matter of personal taste. There are plenty of theories for composing color mixtures with emphasis on the harmony of colors, avoiding or promoting some combinations, as with single-shade borders or all white flowers. However some people seem to like violent discords and splattered paint box effects, others go for pastel shades and gentle gradations while many just want masses of color. There is only one way to find out what works for you and your situation, no matter how much planning and viewing of other's efforts you do beforehand: make notes of what works and what does not and, if you get it wrong, change the plants around as soon as they can be moved. No garden is ever finished, it can always be improved! As with foliage, constant repetition throughout the garden and multiple plantings of the same flowering plant, where space allows, generally creates a stronger impression than many assorted single specimens.

Features and themes These are the decoration on the cake and should not overwhelm or replace it. Features can be anything from classical statuary to a dead wheelbarrow full of gnomes. Water in any form, pergolas, timber work, rustic arbors, urns and containers, special beds, and specimen plants can all be features. It is setting and positioning that make them effective. As noted above, every path should lead to something and the path then makes it significant. Too many features, though, and the garden becomes a junkyard. One main feature in each view, area or "room" is usually sufficient. Particularly nice scenes are much improved with a seat for viewing them and this itself creates the centerpiece for another small picture, but should not be in competition.

A 'Zéphirine Drouhin' rose wound along a bent-down apple bough forms a natural arch, with roses now and apples later.

In fact no garden is complete without a seat, or many; though these are seldom used by the toiling gardener, they greatly benefit others and help give that atmosphere of relaxation we strive for so vigorously.

Themes are subtle features whereby individual areas or the garden as a whole have some common attribute. A water or a wild garden is a theme, as are scented gardens, historical gardens, Bible plants, silver borders, and herb beds. The danger with themes as with features is that they can become overpowering or constraining if followed too rigidly. Set the theme broadly and leave yourself room to maneuver. A wildlife garden that uses only native plants will have to leave out such charmingly useful ones as buddlejas and pyracanthas. A garden of all black flowers is going to be harder to achieve than a border of silver foliage and black flowers. A bed can have more variation and color if it is to attract bees *and* butterflies rather than one or the other. In the organic garden (which is in a way a theme itself), some features and themes are especially pertinent as they interact and benefit the life in the garden so much—ponds and other sources of water, wildflower gardens, native plants, beehives and bee gardens. Others may be worthy in their own right, such as wildlife sanctuaries and gardens of endangered plants be they wild flowers, rare fruits, or old varieties of vegetable.

Just using particular forms of plant about the garden can create a subtle theme without being too obvious. Spiky leaves like those of yucca and *Crocosmia* can give a drier, warm, Mediterranean appearance, while Chusan palms, bamboos, and large-leafed plants like figs give a lush tropical effect. I even had an *Opuntia* prickly pear cactus outside in a sunny spot for years and used a cloche over it only in the depth of winter till a damp spring and slugs got it. Conifers, heathers, and silver birches give a colder heath like effect, while rampant climbers rapidly create an enclosed feeling (and the reality).

Of all features and themes, scent is my favorite and I have consciously selected as many scented plants as possible so that my garden is a feast as much for the nose as for the eye.

Finish Finishing touches and immaculate tidiness make for the most perfect gardens (with much labor) and ignoring them spoils the overall effect disproportionately. Most importantly get rid of every bit of litter and junk; have a glory hole to hide away anything you cannot bring yourself to dispose of entirely. Junk includes anything that is not intended as a feature so garden tools, pots, canes, string, and buckets are best tidied into a shed rather than left exposed. The edging of turfed areas is critical; little improves the appearance of a garden more than neat, well-cut edges and the removal of tufts of grass growing up against trunks and fences. Uniformity helps, too. One plastic cloche made from an empty lemonade bottle looks unsightly, three dozen cut the same look neat. When adding to anything in the garden or repairing a fence, say, try to blend the new in with the old by painting them all the same. Most timber work can be stained to a similar hue and a coat of black bituminous paint will give an enduring, inexpensive and sympathetic finish to metal.

Crown imperial lilies (*Fritillaria imperialis*) flower in early spring. They have copious pollen for insects and an amazingly garlicky/foxy scent.

What you can change, and how and when, and what goes best where

Light Although all plants need light not all need full sunlight and many ornamentals, especially golden varieties, need partial shade or they get leaf burn. Generally, though, the problem is of insufficient light due to overhanging trees and shade from nearby buildings. Pruning may allow more light in and dark places can be brightened with white paint. Under-cover electric light can supplement weak winter sunlight, and all glass and plastic should be kept scrupulously clean to prevent light loss.

Some plants are very sensitive to day length. Spinach and Chinese cabbage bolt into flower if they are sown much before the longest day; strawberries and chrysanthemums need a short day length to initiate the formation of their flower buds, but will go on to flower in longer days. We can use this to persuade them to flower out of season simply by providing electric light or by covering them with a blanket on a frame.

Gooseberries thrive on good pruning and an open, sunny position, but will become disease-prone in stagnant air.

Warmth This interacts with light and shelter—the more light reaching the garden, the higher the temperature. The better the garden is sheltered, the less warmth is blown away by winds. In addition, a good hedge actually extracts heat from the wind. As the wind is filtered through hedge, twigs or trellis it is slowed and this slowing gives off the energy as heat. Thus a good hedge can raise the temperature of a garden by several degrees. So establish hedges and windbreaks rather than using fences and walls, though these can be improved by mounting trellis and/or climbers atop them. Warmth can also be increased by including brick walls, paths, and features which soak up and reradiate heat. Brick rubble, dark stones, and gravel all give off heat and have been used to help ripen fruit. Similarly, bare soil, especially if it is blackened with soot, will give off warmth to ripen fruit or protect flowers from frosts more efficiently than grass or a mulch.

Air Although we need to protect them from excessive winds, all plants need fresh air. Stagnant air encourages pests and diseases, especially mildews and botrytis. Good spacing and open pruning allows the plants to breathe. "Air" for leaves means the carbon dioxide content, which can be increased by encouraging animal life of all kinds into the garden and allowing filtered winds to change the air.

Moisture is crucial to success; probably more plants do badly through over- or underwatering than all other causes put together. In times of strong growth, it is almost impossible to overwater plants in the open ground. Indoors in pots in winter it is difficult to underwater. Between these two extremes is where the difficulty lies. In the open ground, try to conserve winter rains by mulching in spring, and except during droughts water only: before sowing, newly emergent seedlings, new transplants, and crops at a critical stage—usually when their flowers are setting. In times of drought water the most valued plants with one long soak rather than give everything a little and often as this will mostly just evaporate away. Never wet large areas of soil around each plant as this also mostly evaporates, but try to soak water down to the roots. Above all keep down weed competition and either hoe up a dust mulch by loosening the soil surface or mulch well. Where lots of watering is needed, consider installing irrigation or at least a hose (see Chapter 5, page 86).

Shelter In addition to what has been said under Warmth about hedges and walls, shelter can be provided on a smaller scale using dense, shrubby plants, sticks and twigs, netting, or cloches. These can all help nurse tender and establishing plants through hard weather, as well as

above

Elegant or maybe not, this tire wall ensures prodigious crops almost every year from the peach tree it shelters.

left

Akebia quinata is an excellent climber for adding shelter with attractive foliage. It flowers early and for a long time, filling the air with exquisite perfume.

providing privacy and security. Organic fruit, flowers, and vegetables may need protecting from two-legged pests as well as from nature's trials!

Fences have the advantage of speedy erection and take up little depth. They need some maintenance, but rarely last longer than a decade or two. Panel fences which stop the wind tend to fail before open fences and trellis, but they do allow borders in front, and fruit or climbers can readily be trained against them. Unfortunately, weeds come underneath very easily unless deep gravel boards are fitted. Open fences act only as boundary markers and are better in a garden if overgrown with climbers.

Walls are much more expensive but can last for centuries, and their deep foundations exclude weeds. They retain warmth and block wind but cause buffeting. Despite being harder to train on as the initial fixings take more work, they are excellent for ripening fruit but those that face the sun may be too hot and dry at the base for the comfort of some plants, especially roses. Red brick is best for retaining warmth and dry stone walls provide excellent niches for many forms of plant and animal life, especially snails!

Hedges are the best choice for most gardens other than the very tiny, as they can be the cheapest, though they take longer to be effective. They establish much more quickly when given a temporary fence of windbreak material. Their wind filtering provides warmth and they are a superb habitat for wildlife, as well as adding to the variety of plants in the garden. It is a good idea to have a path rather than a border right next to a hedge, as the latter will rob the former's soil and a path will make the trimming easier. See page 66 for my recommended varieties of hedge.

Extra shelter can be provided with cloches and coldframes, which can be as simple as a jam jar or large constructions of brick and glass. They keep off the worst weather, allow a longer season of growth and prevent pest attacks. Glass ones are most expensive but last longer and keep warmer than plastic, which degrades and becomes brittle. Larger models are expensive and more difficult to move than smaller ones; none is cheap, though a homemade version is described in Chapter 7. Clear plastic bottles with the bottoms cut off make excellent mini cloches for bedding plants, saladings, and transplants such as brassicas and corn; larger containers can be used to cover bigger plants such as pelargoniums, fuchsias, squash or tomatoes. When using rows of cloches, make sure they do not form a wind tunnel by blocking the ends off, and pay extra attention to watering. Secure them well in windy weather and always harden the plants off before removing the shelter completely (see page 93). Low, plastic film-covered hoops are least costly but because they use ecologically expensive plastic sheeting which does not last long, it is probably better to get a longer-lasting walk-in polytunnel instead (see Chapter 8, page 171). Sadly, shelter is often in conflict with aesthetics: we loathe winding a tender shrub with nets to ward off the frosts simply because it looks poor; and indeed plastic bottle cloches are never truly beautiful even when uniform, but they work!

Choosing the garden's "furniture"

As well as understanding and catering for the needs of the plants and the natural ecosystems, it makes sense to plan your garden to use recycled and environmentally friendly products to minimize your impact elsewhere. The garden has furniture literally and figuratively—you will want to have seats, birdbaths, and planting containers if not classical statuary. These need to be ecologically acceptable and aesthetically harmonious, which may cause conflict with the pocket, and the conscience as well. Well that's where your ingenuity is called for.

Oriental poppies (*Papaver orientale*) provide a vast amount of pollen for insects and a grand display of color for us.

BEDS AND BORDERS

In the design for a border it is obviously expedient to have shorter plants near the front, but do not regiment the heights too much—allow some tall plants to have forward positions. Taller, late-growing herbaceous plants can come in front of early flowerers that look drab and need hiding such as spring bulbs once they are past their best. Bulbs can also be grown under deciduous shrubs that come into leaf late, as they can use the winter light and enjoy the dark, dry shade of summer during their dormant period. As noted under Foliage and Flowers above, it is much more effective to group three, five or seven of the same plant together. Reworking a bed and splitting up herbaceous plants gives a good opportunity to do this.

Herbaceous borders are often considered a lot of work, but with careful planning and choice plants the only regular chores are tidying back the withered growths in fall and weed control. Spacing groups of plants well makes it easier to weed between them, and heavy mulches are an immense benefit.

Herbaceous plants combine well with bulbs which have a similar habit, but obviously climbers can only be added if a framework is provided for them. Many shrubs can be planted alongside herbaceous plants to make a mixed bed, but they soon predominate. This combination will only work if you choose dwarf varieties, prune them very hard or give them plenty of space.

Herbaceous beds, even those containing bulbs and annual flowers, tend to be rather empty much of the year, so are best positioned where they will be appreciated in summer, but not so conspicuous from windows in winter. Or you can give these beds year-round interest by adding a backdrop of winter- and early spring-flowering shrubs which will draw the eye before becoming obscured by the spring and summer growth.

Bedding plants, especially if bought in, are wasteful in ecological terms as they are started off with heat, peat, and plastic containers, and in order to get continuous color and interest their bed needs replanting for winter and spring interest. Some, such as sweet alyssum, zonal pelargoniums, *Impatiens,* and fuchsias are ideal for creating small, colorful features throughout the summer and will survive even if confined in pots and containers. One of the very best companion plants for any part of the garden is the French marigold (*Tagetes patula*); this is a bedding plant that everyone should grow. It attracts beneficial insects, discourages many pests and kills eelworms as well as having compact form and brightly colored flowers over several months. French marigolds should never be transplanted while in flower so nip out any flowers and buds beforehand to ensure more success later.

Many bedding plants are not annuals, but are merely grown for one season only, then discarded. True annuals may be used in their place.

Annuals offer some of the brightest blazes of color, often growing well in very poor soil and sites, particularly when direct sown. Some, such as sweet peas, night-scented stock, pot marigolds, and the poached-egg plant *Limnanthes douglasii* have outstanding value and should be included in almost every garden. One problem with annually replaced bedding plants is that most need starting off early in the year under cover, where they compete for space and time with the vegetables. There are several ways to avoid this, other than having permanent herbaceous or shrub beds. Sowing annuals in situ saves space, but they need very careful weeding and even the quickest do not flower till late spring. Hardy annuals sown in the fall and overwintered flower earlier than spring-sown plants, though they may also finish sooner and then need replacing.

Biennials are the best solution; sow them in a seedbed in late spring and summer, after the brassicas are planted out and no longer need the space, then plant them out in their flowering position in fall or early the following spring. Sweet rocket, sweet William, foxgloves, wallflowers, and stocks are all very useful in this way and give a lot of effect for little labor.

Flowers for cutting are better grown on the vegetable beds where their loss will be less noticeable than it is from the middle of your best border. Growing them on the vegetable plot also breaks the rotation (see pages 96 and 141) and benefits the crops as well as bringing in beneficial insects. Shrub borders need the least maintenance, especially if they contain many evergreens. The dense shade of large shrubs keeps most weeds under control and few ornamental shrubs need much pruning, as long as they are well spaced. As a general guide, leave most shrubs unpruned unless they get too big; prune those that flower early in the year immediately after flowering and those that flower later as soon as the leaves drop; prune evergreens, tenderer plants and those with hollow stems such as *Buddleja* in spring, and the *Prunus* family in midsummer. All shrubs benefit from soil enrichment and watering, but this is rarely absolutely necessary—they are mostly very tolerant of different soils.

ACCESS

It is no good having a lovely garden if you can't get round it in the wet or because of obstacles. Ease of access is important because human nature being what it is anywhere that is at all difficult to get to will be neglected. Good paths, stepping stones, easy gates, and no low branches or snatching brambles make the chores easier, so they get done.

Patios, from a few humble slabs by the garden door to a full terrace, are the viewing point as well as access for most gardens. Keep them tidy, as junk and litter not only spoil the appearance but make access difficult and dangerous. Loggias and overhead timber work combined with the patio help blend an unsympathetic building into a garden and cast a pleasing dappled shade, but drip in the wet. A patio makes its own

above
Clematis jackmanii, and other clematis, often flower too high for us to see them; train them up and over a wire pole so that they hang down into view.

right
Roses are happiest when the air can flow over them, rather than if they are confined up against a wall.

microclimate—hot and dry above with a cool, moist root run below, though it may be drier if sheltered from prevailing rains by the walls. This makes a bed let into a patio the ideal position for climbers such as *Clematis*, grapes, or roses, though the flowers do better climbing around posts than on hot walls which would be best used for grapes, pears, or other fruit.

Paths and drives These also create a microclimate as well as providing access. The hard standing again makes for a cool, moist root run with water run off; it gives off heat day and night, while its openness allows better airflow. Like walls, paths and drives can therefore be supportive to the less hardy shrubs.

Grass paths soon wear badly where traffic is heavy, but can be improved quite cheaply by setting in stepping stones. A slab path set on sand is probably the best as it can be moved yet is low maintenance and very durable. Gravel, done properly with board edging and hard core underneath, makes a very attractive path and if the gravel is deep enough can be kept tidy and weed free with raking. However, if you put a gravel path anywhere that muck, mud, and soil are frequently dropped or that weeds seed, it will become difficult to keep clean as plants germinate so readily in it. The same applies to loose brick paths, crazy paving, and badly done cobbles with many gaps. Point gaps well and fill all potential niches with creeping thymes or chamomile before they become a weed problem! Concrete paths are fine but can be expensive or arduous to make; they are rather permanent and somewhat utilitarian in appearance. Shredded bark or pine needle paths are good if they are laid over hard core where traffic is heavy, otherwise they can be churned to mud. These really look best in woodland or shrub settings but are also useful in vegetable areas as they repel slugs. This sort of path is best avoided near the house as it is carried in on feet.

LAWN AND HEDGE CARE

Lawns, paths, and hedges are all a major part of the framework of a garden—they are the backdrop and the foil. Their appearance and thus their maintenance is critical to the overall effect. If they are in poor condition they draw attention to themselves instead of enhancing the rest of the garden. Their shape and positioning also need careful planning. Giving them a good start will reduce maintenance work later.

Lawns and grass paths make up much of the typical "English" garden and the emerald green does show off other plants to perfection, but these areas take a tremendous amount of work, cash, and resources to maintain. In very small gardens, give serious consideration to dispensing with grass altogether, saving the need to buy and store a grass cutter as well as liberating ground space. Areas for sitting or sunbathing could be hard surfaced or graveled instead and surrounded or patch-planted with low-growing plants such as chamomile and thyme. In the largest gardens grass is a sensible groundcover because it is relatively easy to keep neat and tidy, though can be time-consuming if poorly planned. Grassed areas do compete with the plants in them, but grass clippings can be collected to use as a mulch (they are especially good for roses, shrubs, and soft fruit) and to suppress grass around and underneath trees.

Grassed areas can be established in three ways: seeding, turfing, and cutting the natural cover regularly. Seeding gives you a choice of grasses

Grass paths, neatly cut and with clean edges, are ideal for the larger garden where the wear is light.

and the option to include companion plants; it is not expensive but is quite hard work. The area needs to be dug, deweeded, leveled, and raked to a seedbed, removing all stones and rubbish. Then ground rock dusts, ground seaweed, and lime or calcified seaweed must be incorporated to enrich the soil. The first flush of weeds can be raked or flame-gunned, then the area sown in spring or fall with grass seed.

For most grassy areas, hard-wearing recreational rye grass mixtures are a better choice than the less competitive fine grasses intended for bowling greens. The former prefer limy conditions and produce a tough sward productive of grass clippings and resisting weeds and disease. The fine grasses can make a showy sward but do not take hard wear and prefer acid conditions, which in turn favor mosses and turf weeds. When sowing a lawn it is a good idea to include seeds of companions such as clovers, chamomile, creeping thyme, daisies, yarrow, and other scented and pretty turf plants. Of course if you are a recidivist and desire pure grass, then you can choose this, but mixtures are more interesting and ecologically sounder as well as staying greener in droughts. After sowing the seed rake it in, firm it down, and hang up bird scarers. Water religiously. Give the young grass a cut and a roll when it is more than toe high; thereafter mow regularly and walk on it as little as possible for a whole growing season.

Turfing is the most expensive way to get an area grassed, but is less work than seeding and gives more rapid results. The area still needs to be dug, enriched and leveled, but much less thoroughly, and weeds can often effectively be ignored—many will be killed by the disturbance, by burying, and by the grass cutting that follows.

Turfing theoretically gives a choice of turf, but this may be difficult in practice. It can only be done well in early spring or early fall with damp conditions and/or frequent watering. Concerned gardeners should be aware that much turf comes from unecological sources such as old meadow land, and that it is frequently pretreated with inorganic fertilizers and herbicides.

Cutting the natural groundcover regularly is the slowest method of getting a good sward, but produces the most ecologically balanced mixture of plants with the minimum work and expense. The procedure is the same as that for regularly maintaining or improving an existing sward and basically consists of making the conditions most suitable for grasses and unsuitable for everything else. If the area is too rough for a mower or contains hidden junk, use a nylon line trimmer or brush cutter for the initial attacks. Oversow with tough grass seed and keep strimming till the growth becomes a rough sward, then mow once a week from early spring to late fall, returning the clippings. If you like you can reduce the height of the cut gradually, but I prefer to keep it set as high as possible.

Regular mowing kills almost all the tall-growing weeds. Acid-loving weeds can be discouraged and the tougher grasses aided by liming heavily twice a year with calcified seaweed or dolomitic lime. Patches of clover which stand out green in times of drought are blended in by sowing clover seed in the remaining areas, as clovers are of immense benefit to the lushness of sward. Scarifying with a wire rake in the fall or spring is hard work but benefits the sward if done once every few years. Hiring a machine makes the job easier. (Scarifying produces a mass of thatch for use as a mulch or composting, but it needs moistening with dilute urine or liquid feed if it is to rot down quickly.) Follow scarifying by raking in a mixture of ground seaweed, rock dusts, and grass seed with sharp sand for heavy soils and lime or calcified seaweed on acid soil. This same feed can be used annually in spring, but I use diluted

This grass path was all weeds a few years ago. Regular cutting, oversowing grass seed, and liming have improved it beyond recognition.

urine instead and sprinkle this on the turf during light rain. It is absorbed rapidly and is converted by the sward into lush growth that can soon be removed as clippings for mulching elsewhere. Rosette weeds such as plantains and thistles may survive scarifying, cutting, and soil improvement treatments, but they can be hand pulled with a sharp knife severing deep underneath at the same time—they rarely regrow.

The regular cutting of grass is best done with a rotary mower that can collect the clippings. Cylinder mowers are not as good in damp conditions or with longer growths and mowers that do not gather the clippings build up too much thatch.

Although the design and shape of lawns and grass paths must be aesthetic and practical, they also need to be kept neat. With areas near the house the cutting needs to be weekly; further away and in orchards you can get away with fortnightly and in wild areas once or twice a year, but then these are no longer swards. This frequency of work means that a few minutes saved each time adds up to many hours in a year, so careful planning and possibly redesigning can be well worthwhile. If a low branch or object grazes your head or needs careful cutting around, remove it. Do the same with odd little corners where you have to push the mower in and out several times. Long paths should be made just to fit a given number of passes without leaving an odd strip which you have to go back over and finish up at the wrong end. Arranging your plantings so that there is a shrub or fruit bush deserving a mulch near to hand each time the grass box gets full can halve your working time. If you have to take the clippings far, a wheelbarrow will consolidate several loads in one trip.

As well as the main grass sward there are the edges to be kept neat. This can take more time than cutting all the rest, but is essential for a tidy appearance. It is really worthwhile reducing the amount of edging that needs clipping by amalgamating small beds and borders into bigger ones.

Using a nylon line trimmer first greatly increases neatness as it can be used not only to do the edges and to cut around trunks and bits the mower cannot reach, but also on the awkward and difficult spots, further simplifying the work for the mower. A nylon line trimmer is also good for trimming grass to different heights depending on the situation. For example, either side of a close mown path in a wild area or orchard the grass can be trimmed a foot or so high so that it does not fall over the path. With a nylon line trimmer the height of cut is so adjustable that chosen plants can be left standing alone after others around them have been cut hard back. Cutting grass and weedy areas with a nylon line trimmer can thus encourage bulbs, primroses, cowslips, and violets as the area can be kept neat without becoming overgrown and choking out these treasures. In heavy shade where ivy often predominates as groundcover, weeds such as nettles growing up through it can be eradicated and returned as shreddings at the same time.

Plants for hedges

Almost any shrub can be used to make a large informal hedge or screen, but few are suitable for a narrow informal or regularly clipped formal edging. Brambles, briars, and climbers trained over posts and wires make much more rapid and impenetrable barriers. The following are the most reliable choices, and I have ordered them with the lowest-growing first.

Box (*Buxus sempervirens* **'Suffruticosa')** Dwarf box is *the* edging for parterres and formal gardens. A very slow-growing evergreen, it's extremely neat and can be kept clipped to form a mini-hedge only a hand width high and wide. Beware the common box (*B. sempervirens*), which also makes a very dense evergreen hedge but ultimately reaches house height. It is excellent for topiary, however. Box thrives on chalky soils if they're not thin.

Lonicera nitida A tidy evergreen for low hedges, this one has tiny leaves. Planted a foot apart, it can be kept to one foot thick. Also good for topiary, it will grow in dry spots and on most soils if well established.

Worcesterberry (*Ribes divaricatum***)** is murder to do anything with as it has large, sharp, mean thorns. It produces edible red/black gooseberry-like fruit and forms layers and suckers that make it impenetrable except to small wildlife. Plant three feet apart near boundaries and leave well alone.

Rosa Vigorous, upright-growing roses make a loose but impenetrable hedge with glorious flowers in summer, with hips to follow. Plant them a foot or two apart, depending on vigor, in enriched soil. *R. rugosa* makes a poor, wide, lax hedge; far better are 'Queen Elisabeth' or 'Kazanlik.'

Privets (*Ligustrum ovalifolium***)** rob the soil nearby, but make neat hedges and most are semi-evergreen. The golden forms are less vigorous and less hardy, but make attractive yellow hedges. Common privet flowers sweetly and berries freely if left untrimmed. It can be kept to a foot thick and grows in most soils, even in shade.

Hollies are excellent as they are evergreen and prickly. Although slow to start, they eventually make large formal or informal hedges, and the berrying sorts can be trimmed just in time for the Christmas season.

Arborvitae (*Thuja plicata***)** A vigorous pyramidal grower with dense, rich green foliage with a graceful fern-like texture; easily maintained hedge or screen.

Purple Leaf plum (*Prunus cerasifera***)** is most use as an informal hedge, as left untrimmed it produces cherry plums which make great jam. The flowers are pure white in early spring. Trim once a year after these have finished, leaving

Hedges, too, need planning and consideration. They are much more ecological than fences as explained earlier as they warm the garden and provide a nesting habitat as well as decoration. Evergreen or beech hedges which hold their leaves have the most value. Informal hedges can have scented flowers, but clipping them into a formal hedge removes the flowering shoots and thus also any fruits. Informal mixed hedges are rarely pruned or cut once established; they are effectively just long, narrow shrub borders which take up a lot of space but produce a beautiful flowering screen. A formal hedge takes up much less space as it is cut regularly, preferably twice a year.

Because hedges need to grow densely, the ground must be well prepared and weeds controlled for the first two or three years until the hedge is well established. Planting through a strip of carpet or plastic is ideal for this. Most hedging plants are best spaced at about a foot to two foot apart—closer for small hedges and wider for tall ones. For the thickest hedges plant a double, staggered row. Sloping the plants over at a 45-degree angle gives a lower, thicker base and interweaving can increase this, giving a low, dense hedge from fewer plants.

some stems on top to fruit.

Beech (*Fagus sylvatica*) is not evergreen, but the leaves stay on through winter. Annoyingly, they drop in dribs and drabs which creates work if they are near patios and drives. Beech will grow in any soil other than very heavy clay or waterlogged ground. There is an attractive copper-colored form. Either can be kept to a couple of feet thick and only head high, but will soon grow bigger if allowed.

Leyland cypress (x *Cupressocyparis leylandii*) is a mixed blessing. It makes a quick, dense evergreen hedge or screen, *but keeps growing*, so takes a lot of cutting. It will easily overwhelm a small garden, but can be kept to a couple of feet thick with two cuts a year. Leylands rob the soil all round, but do shelter wildlife. The golden form is attractive and less vigorous. The Western red cedar (*Thuja plicata*) is similar, less vigorous and of neater habit; it makes a slower-growing hedge

Young hedges benefit from a temporary screen to reduce wind damage, but do not make this too close or dark or it may kill the foliage. Cut back the sides and top hard each and every winter until the hedge is nearly at its required size, then cut back again in late spring and once more in late summer for the neatest effect. Taper hedges in at the top slightly to allow more light and rain to reach the base. Like everything in the garden hedges benefit from monthly sprayings with seaweed solution during the growing season.

Planning for different sorts of garden

The advantages of small gardens and large Although, given the choice, most of us would prefer a larger garden, it is surprising just what can be done with a tiny one. In a small garden you can achieve a neatness, a richness of flowers, and grow incredible quantities of produce with the same labor that would be dissipated just cutting the grass in a large garden. Alternatively small gardens can be planned to be extremely undemanding once established. When only a small area is involved, any money spent is more effective. It can be used to buy more slow-growing evergreen shrubs or low-maintenance features such as paved areas, stonework, timber work, and thick mulches. In a larger garden far more needs to be spent on machinery and maintenance. The best features in a small garden must be concentrated near the house, where they can be seen from the comfort of the windows; in a larger garden they are spread thinner and further afield. Small gardens predominate in denser urban areas rather than in open country, so they benefit from the additional shelter and warmth that these provide. All the brickwork, tiles, and pavements act as heat stores, and the buildings reduce low-level wind. This protection is augmented by the heat from all the people, buildings, and cars, and enhanced by their carbon dioxide. These factors can give the urban gardener a great advantage, extending the season for several weeks over that of the country dweller. The last frost of spring always comes much later in pretty little valleys than it does in the city nearby.

Small gardens have close neighbors which can mean a loss of privacy, or equally, companionable conversation and friendly rivalry. With larger gardens the privacy increases—very rapidly once you can afford space for an informal hedge or windbreak. The choice of what you can squeeze in becomes much greater, but of course time, labor, and cash become spread more thinly.

One advantage for the organic gardener is the isolation that can come in a well-hedged garden. Spray drift, pests, and disease spores are less likely to arrive on your plants the further away their sources are kept. Similarly, with space for more plants and habitats, more forms of beneficial wildlife can be encouraged and retained and intricate ecological webs can be built up, aiding pest control. Large gardens also allow more robbing of Peter to pay Paul—you can, for instance, take prunings, grass clippings from lawns, paths and wild areas, and leaves from under trees to compost for use in the vegetable beds and elsewhere. With spare capacity the land can be less intensively cropped, which requires less labor to produce the same amount as from a small space and permits longer rotations with green manure leys to give better, cleaner crops more easily. In the larger garden, livestock can be converting wastes to eggs or meat and providing a source of high-value fertilizer, though there is no reason, bylaws allowing, why even the smallest garden should not have a chicken or two in an ark.

There are other benefits of scale for a larger garden. The bigger the task the more efficient machinery is, and the professional models work more effectively than small ones for home use. For example, it is much quicker (though noisier) to work with a hired petrol hedge trimmer than with a pair of shears or a small electric model.

Small town gardens Even the tiniest plot has room for herbs and many can be cajoled into pots and containers. With a patio area to sit on, scented plants around and water in some form, you can create a tranquil little retreat from the hurly burly of life. Fruit can be grown, in pots, trained on walls, and as screens; there may also be room for a small salad or herb bed or an ornamental area with mostly productive plants. There is always room for a compost bin and for bees! Beekeeping is ideal for town gardeners because bees add life and interest, are very productive, and thrive on the longer, milder seasons and myriad urban plants. They are more productive with increased attention, so are well suited to those with small gardens and more spare time. Nest boxes and food for birds can also be squeezed into the tiniest plots.

Small size does not so much prevent you from making any one sort of garden (except for those demanding forest trees!) as limit the number of internal subdivisions you can have. You cannot sensibly fit a fruitcage, a rose border, a vegetable plot, lawn, and a water feature into a tiny plot. However, you could make a very beautiful or productive garden from one or even a couple of these. It is probably better to make over the whole plot in one theme rather than trying to incorporate every possible feature to make a miniature of a larger garden.

The allotment is usually small scale but has other problems, theft being the worst and regulations the second; the distance from home does not help. Sadly too often the best things to grow are those that are least easy to steal in a hurry, so gooseberries beat corn!

Larger suburban Larger gardens need careful planning and good routines, otherwise too many chores eat up the time. Larger suburban is perhaps the optimum size for casual gardeners as it can be kept extremely attractive and productive without stealing all your time or forcing you to hire help.

A grapevine or two can be squeezed into even the smallest garden. If you have space why not try your own vineyard?

The typical garden for most people, the larger suburban plot has room for subdivision, though usually on a small scale. Often there's a formal front garden, and maybe enough space at the back to produce significant amounts of fruit and vegetables—if it's favorably situated and well planned. Concentrate on a few "bolt on" areas (see below) rather than trying to squeeze them all in, then each can have sufficient space and attention to become worthwhile. For example, have a wee vineyard or some cider apple trees, but not both. Site the less attractive greenhouse and vegetable plot behind the fruitcage and away from the house, and surround your home with flowers, a patio, and fresh herbs nearby for convenience.

Small country Once you get up to an acre of ground, what and how you grow is limited mainly by time and money. The choice widens, but the garden will need rigorous planning and/or ruthless maintenance or hired labor. I have squeezed more and more into my small acre, but it does take up the equivalent of every weekend throughout the year to stay on top of it. This is the optimum size for a very keen gardener—any larger and it needs to be simplified in many areas or help acquired. Intensive methods are better replaced with extensive, such as half-standard trees in grassed orchard rather than trained cordons, and vegetables on the flat instead of raised beds with fewer, bigger, more shrubby borders with sweeping curves and less edging.

Grass cutting is effective for maintaining large areas neatly but is one of the most time-consuming chores and it may prove a good idea to hire labor for this rather than for the more enjoyable work. Ensuring ease of access, installing good pathways, and putting the least visited areas furthest away are vitally important as much time can be wasted going back to fetch a tool half an acre away. The space available allows for a wide range of habitats and a garden this size can easily be made self-sufficient in fertility, becoming very rich in useful ecological systems with wildlife interest.

Lottery winner or large country With several acres then almost any garden imaginable could be created but time, money, and enthusiasm can become too stretched to maintain it. In order to keep the labor down, large areas need to be simplified, grassed and cut or trimmed regularly, but then can feed the rest of the garden with the clippings recycled as mulch and fertility. Machinery and hired labor become necessities for many more of the tasks, though four-legged lawnmowers can replace these to a great extent. Gardening as such becomes landscaping around the house. A very large garden then effectively becomes more like a larger suburban garden with a couple of acres of paddock or private woodland extending out from it. I think too much space may prove more of a curse than a blessing, but I'd love the chance to find out!

69

The options: "bolt on" garden areas

There are many different garden areas that can replace or be added onto existing ones. One can predominate and take over, like the ubiquitous lawn surrounded by borders, but it could equally well be made over as vegetable plot or orchard. You do not have to have conventional front and back gardens—it's your choice, you can have your garden any way you like with vegetables in the front and flowers at the back, an enormous fruitcage with parrots (muzzled, I guess) or the ecologically preferable and naturally green all summer pond could replace an expensively maintained sward of unused front lawn.

Herb bed Herbs are health-giving, useful, tough, and attractive and do not need very much space or work, so I have given them a space of their own in Chapter 7: please refer there for their uses, requirements, and how to situate them in your garden.

Patio area (scented!) The most essential area is somewhere to sit and relax outside—after all, this is one of the most important aspects of gardening. There are also plenty of chores, such as shelling peas, that need a seat and table for comfort. Hard standing, slabs or even gravel make this area available more days a year than grass and take far less upkeep.

A patio must be easily accessible from the house, ideally extending out from a conservatory or kitchen, or it will rarely be used. Patios in sunny positions act as storage heaters and help ripen crops of fruit planted around them—especially grapes, which can be wound round posts or over wires. Creeping thymes and chamomile will grow happily in holes or between slabs and give exquisite scent when walked on. The patio is best surrounded with more

Jasmines planted on a sunny wall or confined in a pot give the sweetest scents for a patio.

scented plants and aromatic herbs to add sweet smells and help discourage flies and mosquitoes. Bird boxes fixed to the wall and under the eaves can give extra interest and pest control; a table and bath will bring more bird life in for our pleasure.

Water features From birdbaths to pools and ponds, water is a pleasure to see and to listen to, it adds tremendously to the atmosphere—even a tiny pool and a wee fountain is a comfort to us. It is also a powerful attractant to birds, insects, and wild animals. These all need water and will come to your garden if you supply it; once there they help with pest control and fertility. Birds with ready access to water will eat fewer seedlings and fruit. A birdbath can be squeezed in every garden—position it where it can be seen from a window and is safe from cats. A fountain or cascade, however humble, is always a delight and can be combined with a pool (though waterlilies like still water). Pools do not have to be very large to attract wildlife provided they never dry up.

All water features need a sloping

edge to let creatures in and out and fencing if young children are around. With larger gardens several pools can be provided in different parts and a pond stocked with ducks will help immensely with pest control, as will the frogs, toads, and newts that are encouraged if you do not have too many ducks and fish. Large ponds create microclimates that can shelter tender plants nearby and reflect sunlight onto surrounding plants as well as providing an emergency source of water.

When making a lined pool protect it with newspaper and old carpet first to prevent the liner being punctured by stones. Similarly, hang old carpet upside down over the edges to protect the liner from light and wear. Butyl rubber is the best liner, as it outlasts all alternatives; however, as these are so much cheaper they will be used, so be sure to protect them and install them really well. Fill the pool and let it stand for a week to warm and to lose chlorine before stocking it. Take a bucket to a "natural" pond and scoop up some mud and water for an instant ecosystem.

Salad bed After fresh herbs, salad vegetables are the most valuable crop. Every garden should be able to find space for a small, intensive bed for salads, and with larger gardens this becomes part of the vegetable plot. See Chapter 7, page 150, for more details on salad crops.

Fruitcage and trained fruit As soon as any space is available, especially on walls, fill it with fruit trees, bushes and vines. Fruit can be trained alongside paths and drives and fitted into every garden, giving fresh food for years for little effort. In the smaller garden, have a fruitcage rather than growing vegetables—the rewards are much better. Well designed, it can be a much more pleasant vista than a vegetable plot for more of the year. Even in a larger garden a big fruitcage is better value than a vegetable plot as it takes less maintenance. See Chapter 6, page 106, for advice on fitting one or more fruitcages into your garden.

Greenhouse This is a great boon for raising plants and extending the season. Greenhouses come in all sizes to suit most pockets and gardens, but can take up a lot of time and money if you start to fill them with tender plants in pots. However, the smaller the garden the more valuable greenhouse space will be as it allows you to make much better use of the remaining space by starting off plants under cover, and planting out and intercropping only as ground becomes vacant.

A greenhouse needs to be near the house for access and services, but is difficult to site attractively as screening may block the light. In many ways a "working" conservatory may be a more practical solution and saves putting a greenhouse within view of the windows. Wooden greenhouses are slightly easier on the eye than metal-framed ones and tend to be warmer. Polytunnels are debatably even less visually appealing than greenhouses but can be screened more easily as their covers diffuse light effectively. They are ideal for the larger garden as they give a lot of space for the money and are easy to move. The cover needs replacing every four years or so, at which point the tunnel can be rotated to a different piece of ground. A polytunnel is a good addition to the vegetable bed as it can become part of the rotation. Siting a pool next to a greenhouse or tunnel acts as a source of predators, reflects light, and stores warmth and rainwater. See Chapter 8, page 171, for more details.

The tender perennial Marvel of Peru (*Mirabilis jalapa*) has varicolored scented flowers that open at teatime.

Orchard A small one can be part of almost any sized garden if you plant trees grown on dwarf rootstocks. In a larger garden the orchard is the most productive area in terms of both time and money, taking little maintenance for enormous returns. See Chapter 6, page 106 for the possibilities. Orchards can be easily combined with lawns, livestock, wild flower meadows, or play areas.

Vineyard Grapes are amazingly prolific and very attractive so some should be planted wherever possible. A vineyard is obviously more feasible in a larger garden but as well-tended grapevines do well in a town you may decide to make the whole garden into your own chateau! Vines can easily be trained up posts and over wires to combine them into almost any garden area; they can also be grown on most walls, but for serious production really need to be netted or in a cage. A vineyard is thus really a specialized fruitcage. See grapes in Chapter 6, page 123.

Livestock Bees, chickens, ducks, geese, rabbits, and goats can all add much to a garden and are such valuable adjuncts that they are dealt with in a separate section in Chapter 9 (page 197).

Vegetable plot When talking about organic gardening, most people probably think first of the vegetable plot, and it is certainly very important in gardens of all sizes. But those with little time may be better advised to grow fewer vegetables and more fruits, as I suggest strongly in Chapter 6. Chapter 7 deals with the siting and layout for vegetable plots and how they are most suited to different gardens.

The "front" garden Though most effort is often put into the front garden, this may be more for the benefit of passing pedestrians if you look out over your garden to the rear the most frequently. Do pay attention to make your entrance both safe and welcoming—or not, according to your taste.

Bog garden Although many attractive plants thrive in a natural boggy area and it is a wonderful source of predators, it is undesirable as it indicates low-lying, frost-prone and badly drained ground unsuitable for productive gardening. However, an artificial bog garden made over plastic next to a pond or pool will be very beneficial, encouraging many forms of life as well as adding to the beauty.

Rock garden These have been out of fashion for a while, but are a very good way of providing a better microclimate for certain plants. A well-made rockery with lots of big rocks with cracks and fissures and a stony, free-draining soil in pockets re-creates the conditions beloved by the compact and pretty little plants native to such conditions. However, as has often been noted, many rockeries are more a way of disposing of some spoil with lumps of rock dotted on top of them. Indeed, and they can easily be better done, but that is another book.

Wildflower lawn or meadow, with bulbs This can be any size and can even replace the front lawn, but be prepared for a lack of understanding from the neighbors! Most grassed areas are too fertile to make good wildflower areas and, if just sown and let go, the grasses overwhelm. Reduce the fertility by removing the turf (stack it to make loam for potting or use it elsewhere) and then plant out pot-grown wildflowers. Keep the grasses and weeds down by hoeing until the flowers have established and set seed for a year or two, then allow the grass back in. Cut the grass after midsummer once wildflowers have dropped their seed. For late-flowering wildflowers, have one piece that is cut in early winter instead. Bulbs are less demanding and can be planted under turf as they can usually out-compete grass. They look best if thrown into the area and planted where they fall, but are neater out of season if they are concentrated at the base of trees and hedges. The grass must not be cut until after the bulb leaves have started to wither. Areas treated like this can be under trees, in an orchard or coppice, and make great play areas for children as well as a habitat for wildlife.

Coppice If with great good fortune you can acquire a modest piece of land, a woodland is a beautiful extension of the garden, providing many habitats which can also be highly productive in fuel and free-range livestock. Something most of us can only dream about—*so recommend this book widely and buy it for all your friends!*

Paddock With more ground available, many people plan a paddock for a pet horse. This is exchanging a little grass cutting for a lot of horse care, but the by-product is great stuff for fertilizing the rest of the garden.

Play area Something I have noticed missing from most gardening books is any reference to children. I know many of us welcome them to our plots as we might a rabid dog—after all, they can do untold damage. But they are a cheap source of labor and rather necessary to the propagation of our species. The main problem is much as with other livestock—mostly one of confinement. As children are ingenious, unelectrified fencing is not enough; it is more effective to lure them to safer spots than to try to exclude them altogether. Swings and ropes, large trees, mud and water in any form will concentrate their attention on a suitable grassed or safe area.

Early spring crocus brighten up grassed areas—but do not cut the sward till six weeks after the flowers fade.

Building in the least effort ways of running your garden

A moment's thought can save a great deal of work, so try to plan ahead, not only on the large scale but also in the day-to-day tasks. Put compost heaps at the bottom of slopes, not on top of a rise, as more loads go towards it than come back. Put your tool shed near your crops, not half a garden away. Move heavy things only once, rather than putting them somewhere temporary and then lifting them again to move them on to their final spot.

A little maintenance goes a long way; if they are frequently used any doors and gates that are hard to open and close waste more time in a year than you might imagine! Make all your frequently used paths easy to walk in all seasons, and easy to maintain, and without corners to cut. If a path corner is often walked across, move the path. Pay attention to the tasks you find you're doing most often, especially grass cutting and watering, as time and effort saved with these adds up to so much in a whole year. And most important of all, as it's needed so often, make sure water is always available, quickly and easily.

chapter four

KEEPING YOUR GARDEN BEAUTIFUL NATURALLY

Maintaining the garden's appearance and fertility—how to keep your garden beautiful, interesting, and fertile as well as neat and tidy

A garden that is well planned and already running can take surprisingly little time to keep it that way once a regular routine is established. It may be hard to believe, but almost any average-sized garden can be kept neat, tidy and full of interest and production for only an hour or two a week if the tasks are approached methodically all year round. When I maintained gardens commercially I found that it was the frequency and focus of attention that made most difference. Of course, working professionally I had the benefit of a lawnmower that would start, shears that cut and a sharp hoe—tools which are beyond the scope of most garden sheds if I can believe what I've seen. It's not having a lot of expensive tools that gets a good job done, but the ones you use most often have to be good, or you will end up suffering more than your garden.

Most gardening activities are tied to the seasons and the advantage comes to the gardener carefully spreading the load to be in time with the rhythm of the year. Ideally we should all carry out tasks at their optimum moment, doing them efficiently, effectively and cleaning up afterwards. In the real world, it is harder to arrive at such perfection. Nonetheless, it is always true that persistently applying small but timely attentions will in the end give you the best results. The other thing to remember is that just maintaining a garden takes little time and effort compared to making any changes, especially major ones!

The buds of the old moss rose 'Nuits de Young' smell of incense if rubbed late on a warm summer evening.

The priority is nearly always watering whatever may need it, then
harvesting whatever is wanted, and ready, for the kitchen or store. Make
this the basis for a daily inspection tour, writing a list of anything that
needs urgent attention, as well as tasks coming up, such as seedlings that
need potting up or specimens that require pruning. At the same time,
collect and dispose of any litter, gather up any other superfluous items,
dead head and tidy or tie in the odd unsightly lax growth. If you have a
coldframe or greenhouse, open and close the ventilation and check the
min/max thermometer to ensure heating or cooling is adequate.

The weekly routine

The vital tasks are the daily ones; only once those are completed is it
sensible to commence the weekly. The most important weekly job is
sowing and transplanting whatever is due, as next week will be too late!
Afterwards, sharpen your hoe and weed the beds and borders. Only then
should you clip edges and mow grass. Collect the clippings, larger weeds,
and all other organic debris for composting. Finally, have a break, sit
down and think before proceeding to the next most urgent seasonal task.

The yearly cycle

One of the joys of gardening is that along with the regular jobs, such as
the weeding and grass cutting, there is a variety of activities that come
around with the seasons, such as the harvesting in fall and the
preparations for winter. To jog your memory for specific tasks, such as
when to prune currants, you will find a yearly calendar on page 218.

The biggest tasks

Some of these can become onerous chores if we don't plan to make them easier for ourselves.

Weeding By far the biggest stealer of time is the weeding, it is always best done sooner than later. The plants we want to grow are continually threatened by weeds which are far more efficient competitors for air, light, water, and nutrients. To get our plants to grow well we must keep weeds controlled, *especially* in the earliest stages of each plant's life. So please refer to Chapter 10 (page 211) for the easiest and most effective ways to achieve this.

Grass cutting For neatness and for the clippings, we need ideally to cut the grass on average once weekly throughout the growing season. In the U.K., this can last from March to November. In countries with milder winters, there may not be much of a dormant period. At the start and end of the season longer gaps can be left, especially if the soil is poor, but in the late spring, the period of maximum growth, mowing every four or five days makes a better sward and gives more clippings. Grass may be cut more often, but it should never be cut too short, though you can vary the height of cut during the season to control the growth. The shorter you cut it the less it grows, and the more the moss and weeds come in. The longer you leave it the more dew the lawn collects and the stronger and deeper the roots grow. The first cut each year must never be too close, though following spring cuts can decrease in height to slow down regrowth. In summer raise the height again to keep the grass greener and more drought resistant. If strong growth starts after heavy rain in summer, lower the height a little to check it. However, always start to raise the height of cut as the fall progresses, this makes the sward

hardier and banks up some clippings for spring, when they are often in short supply.

In the fall leaves can be collected with the grass clippings, since both break down better when mixed together in the compost bin than on their own. It is a good idea to return to the turf the clippings of the first and last cuts, as these then feed the worms which are most actively eating in spring and fall. Do lime the sward every other year to encourage the grass and discourage mosses and acid-loving weeds. For more on grass care turn back to page 62. Keep your mower blades sharp—they will work much better!

Digging and no-dig methods I have already mentioned these in the Introduction as there has been much controversy over them. Most of any garden is never dug anyway—it is really only the vegetable plot that the majority of people dig regularly, though I haven't dug mine for fifteen years. Digging annually breaks up the natural soil layers, the network of earthworm tunnels and decaying root systems. It exposes a few pests to birds et al, and aerates the soil, but this causes excessive humus breakdown, with a short-term increase in fertility which may leach out if the digging precedes the crop by too long. The need to produce a good seedbed does not justify digging unless the soil has been badly compacted. Instead, use a combination of mulching and surface cultivation to make a tilth every bit as good. However, most soils show benefit from a thorough digging once in five to ten years, which is often done anyway as crops come round in a rotation, with quite sufficient soil disturbance from harvesting the potatoes and root vegetables every other year or so. If nothing else, digging destroys mole runs, ant nests, and so on, but many successful gardens are never dug. No-dig vegetable plots mostly feature

permanent paths and fixed or raised beds so that the soil is not compacted by traffic. I discuss these in more detail in Chapter 7 (page 142), and I strongly suggest that you use fixed beds and dig but rarely.

If you still deem digging necessary, make sure you pace yourself. Never work too hard for too long, never dig sodden soil, never move too large a spit. Work slowly and methodically, breaking up each lump and mixing in sharp sand and well-rotted manure as you go. Heavy soils are least harmed by digging during the drier weather of fall; lighter ones can be left till late winter to avoid nutrients leaching out, but both need to recover and reconsolidate their capillary network before plants will do well. Digging may benefit heavy soils the more, as it can help break them down into a good crumb structure if well dug and frosted, but if badly dug can just make large clods and air gaps. Light soil which is easy to dig needs it least.

Pruning This is better left undone than done badly. For most woody plants the least pruning is the best although for some such as fruit, especially when trained, careful pruning is essential (see Chapter 6). Generally, we should need to prune only those shoots that are diseased, unhealthy, rubbing or where they are getting in the way or stealing light. Remember that growth removed is soon replaced and tends to grow back just where it was. Thus perfection in pruning is rubbing out buds that point in the wrong direction long before they become shoots.

When pruning, always either leave one healthy bud or shoot to draw the sap after the cut has been made, or cut off the growth flush with the point on the stem it springs from. Never leave a snag of wood with no bud, because this will die back allowing rots to get a hold. Painting wounds with pruning compound, paint or beeswax probably does little good at preventing disease but does stop water and pests getting in and makes the job look neat. I believe it is more important for larger wounds. *Trichoderma virides* paste contains a natural predatory fungus which efficiently prevents fungal attacks, but this is not currently available to amateurs in the U.K. In countries where it is legal—or in the U.K. if you are employing a professional—it should be applied before other pruning compounds. In the past much was claimed for Forsyth's Pruning Compound made of 1 part cow dung, ½ part lime, ½ part wood ashes and ¹⁄₁₆ part sand, finely mixed with urine and soapsuds. This was painted on and set with a powder of 1 part wood ashes and ⅙ part pounded burnt bone. I have recently tried Forsyth's compounds and am convinced their application has some virtue for stimulating healthy growth. If a wound calluses well the surrounding tissues will eventually grow over the painted dead wood. With large wounds this may take years, so check and patch annually. Similarly, clean out cankers and holes and fill with pruning compound to prevent water and rot getting in.

Prune most plants immediately if you spot something that requires attention. Pruning will do little harm as most plants can lose up to a quarter of their leaf area before they suffer greatly. So do not wait until the "right time" to prune—cut out problems before they get bigger. However, heavy pruning—where more than a quarter of the old growth is removed—is best done when the plant is dormant to reduce the shock. An exception is stone fruits and ornamentals related to plums, which are best pruned in summer to avoid silver leaf disease. Some soft fruits, such as redcurrants and gooseberries, are also very hard pruned after midsummer because this helps to promote fruiting. Younger plants and young growth recover far better from heavy pruning than old.

A necessary evil, but a jolly one!

Never cut into old growth which has no new buds because like snags, they rarely resprout. The exceptions to this include privet, yew, and quickthorn, which often come again from mere stumps. Before pruning a plant making poor growth, stimulate it for a year with water, compost, and a mulch to give it vigorous roots first.

Rose pruning is a special task all of its own. Forget the advice of the experts who grow flowers for show—they do not want the same as you. They are after a few enormous perfect blooms. Most gardeners, on the other hand, are after great numbers of blooms in several flushes, preferably with no feeding, spraying, or pruning. Once well established, rose bushes of most forms can be treated like hedges or like lavender plants and simply sheared back. This leaves lots of congested wood, but this is no problem as copious flowers are produced. Such treatment suits most varieties, but they will need more space as they now form fuller bushes. The climbing and most vigorous forms are better restrained than pruned and I prefer to weave them into themselves to form dense basketworks of growth. These make great hiding places for wildlife, as well as getting the whole surface covered in flowers.

Hedge trimming This can be one of the biggest tasks if your hedge is of any size. I have used both shears and an electric or petrol hedge trimmer, and although the power trimmer may seem quicker, I find shears much more enjoyable to use. They can do just as good a job much more quietly and safely.

If the hedge is high, make sure your steps or whatever are really solid. Trim or tidy the base first, then put down old sheets to catch the trimmings. Cut back the sides first, so that they taper in at the top, then do the top—this is the way to catch most trimmings. Look at your progress, from a distance, frequently.

Bonfires All prunings make good kindling once dried. Raspberry canes can be recycled as short pea sticks, while disease- and pest-free prunings, especially evergreens, can be used to make wildlife shelters. If you have a shredder they can be processed and then composted. But to prevent any buildup of pests and diseases, infected material should be burned as soon as possible. It is usually sensible to burn brutally thorny material, such as bramble stems, as well. Thus burning things is a necessary evil. It should preferably be burned piecemeal in a stove to warm the house. However, if you are about to have a bonfire, please drag it to bits and burn it a little at a time. This will save any creatures from a horrible death, and a small hot bonfire is far better ecologically than a great smouldering pile. Bonfires burn best when air can get underneath, so use some bricks and old metal posts to raise them off the ground. Try to wait until the wind is light, steady and blowing away from anything that might take harm. Light a small, fierce fire with dry kindling, and add material steadily as it burns away. When only glowing lumps remain, quench the fire with just enough water to put it out, but no more. Save any lumps of charcoal for barbecues and the ashes for the gooseberries, roses, and cooking apples.

Maintaining fertility without fertilizers

Rather than provide the plants with their nutrition as "junk food" in the form of soluble fertilizers, we want the plants, the wildlife, and the soil microlife to make it for us. Whereas in a pot we cannot expect to maintain fertility without adding it as a feed, in the open soil we can create it in situ. The rotation of crops on the vegetable plot leaves root and leaf residues and these are supplemented with green manures grown in between the crops or before a crop is planted. Green manures are dug in fresh, or composted first. Regular feeding of the plants, as such, does not take place. Instead, the soil is fed with these plant residues, plus compost or well-rotted farmyard manure mixed in whenever a heavy feeder or perennial is to be planted. Mulches of organic material break down and are incorporated, while rock dusts (especially potash) can be added to benefit plants at any time, but they take seasons to act. Ground rock dusts provide additional raw materials of the most needed elements in a finely distributed form, and benefit most soils, especially lighter ones. For poor soils in the first few years some supplementary feeding may be undertaken using organic fertilizers of a faster-acting nature. These should be considered as crutches to an ailing soil to be discarded as the soil becomes richer. Far more important for fertility is to ensure that the life in the soil is active—mulching and keeping the soil moist helps most of all.

COMPOSTING MADE EASIER
All manures and other organic materials for use in the garden are better composted before use. Fresh manures contain soluble nutrients which can be too strong to promote healthy growth, but if fresh manure is stacked and turned it will compost. The composting process converts most of the free nutrients into less soluble forms, so there is less danger of them being washed out, and into our water supply, by heavy rains. However they do leach out slowly, so composting heaps and rotting manures should always be covered. Garden compost is particularly valuable because it contains a greater spread of nutrients and more varied microlife than well-rotted manure, so it is more valuable and should be used in preference.

The composting process will break down almost all natural materials rapidly including old clothes made of natural fibers and wetted newspaper. Dry twiggy material will compost if chopped up and mixed with some nitrogenous material like fresh manure. Thorny material is better burnt. Seedy material is best put in the middle of a heap, and live weeds of a pernicious nature can be killed first by wilting them on a path or sheet of plastic before mixing them in. Diseased material may be composted, but only if you are confident that your heap will cook well. Large lumps of wood, bone, or fat compost too slowly and should be broken up or buried instead.

My compost-making and sieving area, with assistants on weed-seed and snack patrol.

There are many different ways of composting, but they all come back to one principle. In general composting proceeds best when there are many varied materials well divided, moistened, and thoroughly mixed together with plentiful air. It helps to have roughly equal amounts of dryish material and fresh green material as too much of either will slow down the process. Adding water when mixing is usually necessary as many materials are too dry on their own. Lime and wood ashes should be added in areas with acid soils where a sweeter more balanced compost is required, but this then must not be used for lime-hating plants such as rhododendrons.

An activator is not essential, but speeds things up if added during the mixing. Rather than chemical additives it is better to use personal liquid waste or poultry manure. Seaweed or blood, fish and bone meal will do instead. Sievings from previous compost heaps are the best activator of all. So if you are starting your first heap, scrounge some from an old hand to mix in. Add herbs such as stinging nettle, dandelion, oak bark, yarrow, chamomile, and valerian, as recommended by Rudolph Steiner, to encourage the microorganisms to thrive. A ready prepared version can be obtained

from Biodynamic suppliers. The May E. Bruce compost stimulator uses a similar recipe with addition of honey. These all work, but are no more effective than a few shovels of poultry manure in my experience!

Air and moisture are the most important elements of the composting process. You need sufficient but not too much of both, plus enough bulk to heat up, good insulation to keep the heat in and a thorough mixing. Perhaps the biggest problem with composting is how to accumulate sufficient material to make an effective heap, because the bigger the mass, the more heat it retains and the better it composts. Store material until enough is available. I spread mine on the ground for the hens to rummage through and their feet pack it down; later I can scrape it up and put it in the bins to break down. You could keep it in plastic bags until ready to be combined, but most people just put it on the heap in layers, then dig it out and mix it up and repack when enough has built up. In any case, it will always make better compost if any heap is remade after a week and the inside exchanged with the outside. Doing this again after another week will be of further benefit. Each turning mixes the ingredients and stirs in air which then speeds up the process. Do not pack a heap down as this has the opposite effect. There are commercial rotary composters and these speed up the process, but are more suited to warmer climates—they tend to be too small for colder climates.

Various compost containers are sold, most are a bit on the small side and so do not heat up enough to make really good compost unless given extra insulation. Simple constructions of wood, wire netting or brick about a yard each way are sufficient and considerably cheaper. I prefer to use four old pallets tied at the corners. Do not paint the wood with creosote as this will slow the composting process. A lid will keep out rain, but an old carpet and a plastic sheet will be better for retaining the heat—I stuff plastic bags with balls of crumpled newspaper. I plunge a crowbar down the centre of my heap—it has little effect, but I love to pull it out and watch it steam, showing me the heap is cooking well. If it fails, I merely remake the heap. Once it has been turned and cooked at least twice it is then left to mature for six months or so, when it is in the best condition for use. If it is left longer, the worms work it over too much, increasing its richness, but decreasing the quantity. Matured compost makes an excellent potting medium, though it is usually full of weed seeds. Do not believe anyone who claims clean compost, unless they are microwaving it!

Fresh compost, even when immature, can be incorporated into the soil when planting trees and shrubs, but if it is to be used as a top dressing or with small plants, such as when planting out cabbages, it is best matured, partly dried, and sieved. This takes extra effort, but produces a finer material which also makes a good potting compost. The sieving residues can then be used to inoculate the next heap. In almost every case, compost or well-rotted manure is best applied to growing crops in early spring so that the nutrients are taken up. If applied in fall, the nutrients simply leach out over winter. The commonest problems are too wet a heap, remedied by remaking with extra straw or dry material, and too dry a heap, remedied by adding water, fresh wet manure or grass clippings. The presence of a white coating on the material in the heap indicates that it is too dry with insufficient nitrogenous material—add water mixed with personal liquid waste.

If your garden is too small for there to be much compostable material available at any time, cooperating with several neighbors can allow each to make a heap in turn or to share in yours. As recycling your own material may not be enough, always be ready to acquire any wastes you can pick up from other gardeners, greengrocers, local stables, zoos, and so on. This is good for you and our environment.

WORM COMPOSTING AND OTHER ALTERNATIVES

Making worm compost is quite different and more akin to keeping pets. The wastes need dividing finely and are added a little at a time to a large container containing red brandling worms. You don't have to buy these, but unearth them from a compost heap or from under a plank or carpet laid on the ground. The worms need to be put in a layer of moist peat or leafmold in the bottom of the container and kept in the warm—say in the garage. The container should have drainage holes to allow air in and a drip tray to catch any liquids that ooze out. This liquid makes a good feed when diluted down. The worms convert the vegetable wastes into a very rich material that is best mixed in when planting hungry feeders or added to potting composts. The worms will die if put out into the soil with the material, so gently pick them out and return them to the bin. If you have an excess they can be sold as fishing bait. Worms cannot deal with large quantities of a material at a time, so they are really only suited to the smaller garden.

Another method is pit composting. Dig a hole and put the wastes in, covering each layer with a little soil. Once the hole is full and proud, start another and use the first for growing really hungry feeders on top such as squash, zucchini, runner beans or potatoes for a year or two. The pit can then be dug out and the rotted down material used as compost. A trench can be used instead, and can be fitted into the vegetable bed more easily.

GROWING AND USING GREEN MANURES

This is grow-your-own compost material. A green manure can be any plant grown as temporary groundcover predominantly for improving fertility, either incorporated directly into the soil or composted for use elsewhere. Usually grown on vacant soil over winter, they may also be grown in between crops and incorporated as seedlings. Green manures help prevent soil erosion, the leaching of nutrients and convert otherwise wasted winter sunlight into biomass. Any plants that grow over winter will do, but those which are easiest to incorporate or which create the most mass are best. Leguminous plants that fix nitrogen from the air are frequently used, as this nutrient is always in short supply. The manures are usually sown as soon as the ground is bare until the first frosts start. Those surviving the winter are then killed off by impenetrable mulches or digging them in before the crops need the space. Several weeks of breakdown are necessary for some of the more fibrous, such as rye-grass; those that produce succulent growth take far less time. Never let green manures flower and seed or the goodness is lost; it is better to grow two or three short crops of green manure in place of one long one.

Beans and peas Any variety may be used, but only hardy ones will overwinter. These are pulled up minus their roots before they form pods, thus leaving their nitrogen-rich nodules in the soil. Do not use them in the vegetable plot without considering rotational requirements. 'Banner' is a hardy variety of field bean often grown as a green manure.

Lupins A very useful leguminous green manure, but care is needed as most are poisonous. Lupins improve soil texture, are deep rooting, help improve sour acid land and are

Green manures such as this *Limnanthes* (top) are easily incorporated by the use of light-excluding mulches; here (above) plastic sheet is being pinned down.

generally beneficial—supporting vast populations of aphids and beneficial predators after flowering. Noted since Classical times for their ability to suppress weeds, especially fat hen. Ordinary lupins may be used, but agricultural ones are better and are sown in the spring to incorporate into the soil in the fall.

Clovers (*Trifolium*) Clovers are good for bees if allowed to flower, provide cover to ground-beetles, are hosts to predators of woolly aphids, and help deter cabbage rootfly if sown underneath a crop. One of the best short-term leguminous groundcover green manures. However, after a few years land may get clover sick from their own root exudates. Red clover inhibits its own germination when the exudate reaches one hundred parts per million. Before it reaches this level it inhibits vetches, alsike clover and white clover. Clovers in grass sward are helped by cutting the grass higher. Closer cropping encourages first daisies then moss instead. Clovers are poisoned by buttercups, but these can be discouraged by regular liming. A mixture of red clover and alsike is better than either alone at improving yields of hay. They are rich nitrogen sources, but need a year or two to give full benefit and the clovers are inclined to regrow. Alsike is the best for poor, wet or acid soils; white clover is better on lighter and more limy soils; and Essex red is considered the best for green manuring. Though not as hardy as the others, it does better on loamy soils.

Trefoil Another legume, similar to clover and related to alfalfa. It prefers a limy soil and is shade-tolerant, so can be used under taller crops. Short lived, it can be sown any time in spring and summer to overwinter.

Crown vetch Vetches are native legumes that will grow in adverse conditions and can be sown from spring till fall to overwinter. Excellent for producing bulk, fixing nitrogen, and suppressing weeds.

Fenugreek A quick-growing manure that is leguminous and can be sown after early crops, or on vacant land in between other crops. It is unrelated to vegetables, so causes no problem with rotation. It can be sown any time from spring till fall; then it is killed by the first frosts. It is probably the best green manure for summer use.

Buckwheat (*Fagopyrum esculentum*) One of the best hoverfly attractants, this is a calcium accumulator and useful green manure. It has pretty pink flowers and rather straggly growth, and should be grown more often in gardens. It is a quick-growing summer crop that can be left to flower to feed beneficial insects.

Phacelia (*P. tanacetifolia*) is beloved by bees and hoverflies, so should be grown for them anyway. Sow from spring till fall and it may overwinter. It is easy to remove or incorporate.

Poached egg plant (*Limnanthes douglasii*) I find this an excellent green manure as it is hardy over winter in California, very good at excluding other plants, and easy to incorporate afterwards. Some plants left for flower and seed are very beneficial for insects.

Mustard One of the fastest-growing green manures. If incorporated as seedlings, it can reduce infestations of pests and diseases in the soil, but will not stand hard winters. Grown in between crops or till the first frosts and allowed to incorporate in situ, mustard is very useful. However, being related to brassicas, it must be used with care in rotations and is best grown only to the seedling stage. It can, of course, be grown on for the condiment, but then needs more space per plant.

Fodder radish This is a not-very-hardy, deep-rooting radish that is killed by hard frosts leaving considerable bulk which can be incorporated easily in the spring. Unfortunately, it is related to the brassicas so be careful in rotations containing them.

Annual ryegrass Sown from late summer till midfall it provides quick groundcover for overwintering and resprouts in the spring. It must be thoroughly incorporated two months or so before the crop to give it time to rot.

MINERAL ACCUMULATORS

Some garden plants and many weeds are particularly good at accumulating very large amounts of minerals and trace elements. This is despite the soil being deficient in whichever mineral they accumulate. In fact, these plants often abound on deficient soils just because they are the most successful at grabbing a scarce resource. As they extract available nutrients from the soil water, the nutrients are replaced by more that are dissolved from otherwise insoluble mineral sources. In this way, they can go on accumulating from very dilute solutions. If you grow these plants as green manures they will remove the scarce resource while they are alive, but once composted, the concentrated material can be put back to boost the soil.

Nitrogen is best accumulated with leguminous plants, and by incorporating any succulent seedlings in their first flushes of growth.

Phosphorus is concentrated particularly by the weed fat hen, corn marigold, purslane, vetches, and the pernicious weed thorn apple (*Datura stramonium*).

Potassium, which encourages fruiting, is accumulated by chickweed, chicory, fat hen, goosegrass, plantain, purslane, thorn apple, sweet tobaccos, and vetches.

Calcium is concentrated by buckwheat, corn chamomile, corn marigold, dandelion, lambsquarters, goosegrass, melon leaves, purslane, and shepherd's purse.

Silica imparts disease resistance and is made active by plantains, couch grass, stinging nettles, and the most perfidious weed *Equisetum*.

Sulfur aids disease resistance and accumulates in the onion family, brassicas, fat hen, and purslane.

Rocambole is a gourmet form of garlic with unique twisted stems. It grows almost anywhere and accumulates sulfur.

Other minerals are accumulated by many plants, and especially by weeds, some of which are worth tolerating for this and other reasons.

BOUGHT-IN MANURES

Conventional fertilizers are ranked according to their Nitrogen, Phosphorus and K (potassium) ratio and content. These are regarded much as direct plant foods, replacing

these elements taken away with the crop. Nitrogen is considered to stimulate growth and leaves, phosphorus the roots and potassium fruiting and disease resistance. While it is true these same elements exist as salts in the soil solution naturally, it is not natural to have them in very high concentrations as occur when they are applied as conventional soluble fertilizers.

Organically, we guard the microorganisms in the soil by not using any substances that can damage them, so we apply fertilizers that are effectively insoluble and cannot become too concentrated. These need to be broken down and incorporated by microorganisms before they can increase the nutrient supply in the soil solution and be available to plants. Thus they do not leach as readily and are longer lasting. They may be considered more as soil stimulators than as plant fertilizers as they promote increases in soil life, and the byproducts from this increased population then feed the plants. Because they are stimulators or catalysts they do not need to be applied heavily, rather it is better to spread them thinly and more often than in massive doses. In established gardens every other year is sufficient.

ANIMAL MANURES

Be aware that providing a disposal method for their wastes is effectively supporting the factory farming they come from. Litter from very intensive units may also contain unacceptable residues. But one often takes what one can get—better that we use such wastes productively than let them go into landfill sites. All animal manures contribute directly and indirectly to soil fertility, but should always be well composted first. In order of preference I choose: horse, sheep, then goat which are all sweet to handle; cow muck is less pleasant; pig is vile and often contains unacceptable contaminants. Rabbit and pet droppings can be added to the compost heap, but cat and dog litter is best pit buried under trees. Poultry manures are very strong, highly nitrogenous, and a good source of potash. They certainly make a compost heap cook! *Never* put these raw droppings on plants, always compost them first. Commercial poultry composts are acceptable if organically qualified.

Human liquid waste is not a health hazard in temperate climates, and it is wasteful to use a couple of gallons of water to flush such a rich source of fertility down to the sea. Saved in a bucket it can get quite whiffy, but then makes a superb compost activator. Alternatively, apply each day's quota directly to the heap. Recycling personal solid wastes is not for most of us; though ecologically desirable, it is difficult in practice. Sewage sludge is also likely to be contaminated so is only recommended for ornamental plantings where it can be used as a slow release source of phosphate.

Traditional organically based fertilizer—blood, fish and bone meal—is first-rate in performance, but not so good on ecological and compassionate grounds. Many people find it unpleasant to handle, but it is very effective and fast acting. It should be used in moderation, raked in immediately before planting hungry feeders. Beware, cheap brands are frequently adulterated with chemical fertilizers and sand. Bone meal is unsavory to many, but is an excellent source of phosphates, which make up about a third of it. The finer ground the bone meal, the faster acting it is. It is expensive, but good for incorporating when planting, especially for woody plants and strawberries. Hoof and horn is just that, equally unpalatable and very expensive, but an effective slow-release source of nitrogen for hungry and woody plants. These last three fertilizers are all likely to be pinched

by animals or birds unless mixed in well with the soil, so keep the bags in a safe, dry place.

GROUND ROCK DUSTS

These are very slow-acting sources of fertility, but the most natural and long lasting and very good for revitalizing worked-out soil. Clay soils contain plenty of these ingredients in already finely divided form, so rock dusts are more use to those on poor sandy soils. Although rock dust is almost insoluble, if it is ground very finely water can act on an immense surface area to dissolve just a little. The plants can remove this from the soil solution, which then allows more to dissolve. The same huge area is also available for colonization by microscopic life which starts to eat the rock dust and convert the surface material into biological mass. So, by adding rock dusts rich in, say, potassium, we make more available to the plants, but only if our soils are moist and alive and teeming with the right microlife to be able to make use of it. Thus some rock dust can be added to the compost heap to make it bulk-up the right microbes. These will then inoculate the soil and make it more able to utilize the bulk of the dusts, applied more directly at a later date. Most dusts can be applied any time, but winter is convenient. Choose a still day so that it doesn't blow away and let light rain wash it in, or rake it in by hand. Never inhale rock dust. Some rock dusts are now supplied compounded to make them temporarily more granular and easier to handle.

Lime is commonly used on grass swards and on the vegetable patch. In a rotation, it is usually applied with peas and beans before or with brassicas, but never just before potatoes. It is the main source of calcium and in a form that can react chemically with acids and stronger alkalis in the soil; thus it is said to

sweeten and improve most soils. Garden lime is ground chalk, builders' and slaked lime is much stronger and not for garden use. Dolomitic lime is from rocks that also contain magnesium and so is doubly useful. Calcified seaweed is the best form of lime to apply because it contains all trace elements and so encourages healthy expansion of the microlife populations and is valuable added to compost heaps. It also has some use as a general-purpose fertilizer, except for lime-hating plants, and is especially beneficial for tough turf, brassicas, legumes, and stone fruits.

Ground rock potash is rich in potassium which promotes flowering, fruiting, and disease resistance. Especially needed on light soils and in wet areas. It is always appreciated by gooseberries and culinary apples. Apply it at any time.

Ground rock phosphate is rich in phosphorus which encourages healthy roots. It is useful for restoring healthy life to abused, over-acid soils and soils in wet areas. Mix it into the compost heap or the soil at any time. It is especially good for strawberries.

Ground rock basalt and granite may also be usefully added to any soil. These are rocks containing a range of minerals, so they encourage many microorganisms. Their use is claimed to revitalize exhausted soils almost single-handedly.

OTHER DUSTS AND MEALS

The following are also worth trying; I have had good results with them.

Wood ashes are a very rich source of potash, but this is soluble and leaches out. Apply wood ashes to the soil immediately around growing crops, especially fruit and onions where it will encourage ripening and disease protection. Wood ashes should be sprinkled on the surface and raked in or mixed with their compost or planting soil.

Soot from fires burning no plastic contains some value as a fertilizer once mellowed with age, but is especially useful for darkening the soil surface, thereby improving its warming. Sprinkle aged soot on the surface of the soil after rain around early crops, such as asparagus and do not disturb.

Cocoa husks I have been impressed by this nitrogenous waste. It is an expensive mulch, but a good binding agent with others and I've found the finely ground form useful in potting composts. It smells lovely to start with.

Seaweed meal contains a wide range of trace elements and significant nitrogen and potassium, but is a bit short of phosphate—add bonemeal or ground rock phosphate for balance. Organically, naturally and ecologically this is the best nitrogenous fertilizer and soil stimulator, and it is also a very good compost activator. Made from a very renewable resource seaweed meal is more pleasant to handle than blood, fish and bone meal for use as a general-purpose feed and is best raked in during spring.

FOLIAR SPRAYS
For abundant and healthy leaf growth, try one of these sprays.

Seaweed solution This is not so much a fertilizer as a catalyst or vitamin "injection." Although sprayed on as a foliar feed only in very dilute solution, the effect on plants is rapid and marked. They take on a darker, healthier color and are better at resisting both pests and diseases. Seaweed solution similarly stimulates the soil microlife, and is probably the most effective way of improving their variety and number. I spray the soil and every living thing in sight once a

Comfrey makes a useful liquid feed, but wait till the bees have finished with the flowers.

month from early spring. It can be diluted down and watered on as a liquid feed, but is better when combined with a cheaper source of nitrogen such as comfrey or borage liquid.

Equisetum tea This is made from the dried plant and boiling water, then sprayed as a foliar feed when cool and diluted. It is high in silica which is believed to give plants more resistance to pests and diseases.

LIQUID FEEDS
Plants confined in containers have a very restricted root run and cannot reach further afield for nutrients. Top dressing and repotting are possible solutions, but often we resort to feeding them nutrients each time they are watered. This seems at odds with the organic desire to avoid soluble fertilizers. But we are talking about plants in pots, not the soil, so we cannot apply the same rule. However, we should still follow the philosophy, only using feeds in a very dilute form, similar to normal soil-solution strength. The weaker the better, applied little and often—and never if the plants are growing slowly or under stress. Unfortunately, all organic liquid feeds smell a bit whiffy, but this disappears when they are absorbed into the compost. Although these feeds are for plants

with restricted root runs, they may be used with utmost moderation on hungry plants in the open, such as tomatoes or corn, and to bring on spring greens in cold years.

Comfrey liquid Comfrey leaves are collected, packed into a container, activated with a little personal liquid waste, weighed down and covered in water. They soon rot to form a black soup that smells horrible, but watered down to a pale straw color makes a well-balanced tomato (and other plant) feed which has considerable potassium as well as nitrogen. The concentrated soup can also be added to potting composts for added fertility.

Stinging nettle liquid This is made and used in the same way as comfrey liquid and is claimed also to make plants more resistant to disease and pests, especially if diluted and sprayed on.

Borage liquid Made as for comfrey. I have found this produces a highly nitrogenous concentrate that is worth trying for the hungriest feeders, such as melons and brassicas.

Dung bag tea Sacks of manure were once hung in waterbutts to produce a dilute feed. The resultant soup is obviously variable depending on the dung used; it can be effective, but is nastier than other options.

Fish emulsion This very rich source of nutrients is especially effective mixed with seaweed solution for use as a liquid feed.

Personal liquid waste Call it what you will, this is sterile at source, rich in nitrogen and with significant potassium and other nutrients. When it is fresh, it can be diluted down twenty or forty to one and makes an excellent feed, especially for citrus. Don't throw any away: save it all up and use it on the compost heap.

The importance of correct watering

Bigger yields and more vigor can be gained by one generous application of water, at the right stage, than by almost any other improvement you can make to reasonable growing conditions. Obviously, poor conditions like low light or compacted soil need improving beforehand, but once the general conditions are favorable then a single watering can be more effective than any fertilizer. Without sufficient water no life processes take place. Add some water and plants grow, but add plentiful water at the right time and they flourish. Add copious water to the crops in flower that produce seeds, such as peas and beans. Potatoes also respond best to water when they are in flower, which is when the little tubers are just beginning to swell. Give plentiful water to salads and leaf crops throughout their lives.

I cannot stress too often or too strongly that moisture is crucial to success. More plants do badly through over- or underwatering than almost any other causes. In times of strong growth it is almost impossible to over-water plants in the open ground. Conversely, during the winter pot plants indoors are difficult to underwater. Between these two extremes is where the difficulty lies.

In the open ground, try to conserve winter rains by applying mulches. During droughts restrict your watering to periods of critical importance such as before sowing, when seedlings emerge, after transplanting, and when crops are at a critical stage (see above). Water your most valued plants with one long soak rather than giving everything a little sprinkling often, as this will mostly just evaporate away. Do not wet large areas of soil around each plant as this also mostly evaporates, but try to soak water down to the roots. Above all, keep down weed competition and loosen the soil surface to form a dust mulch or cover the soil surface with an organic mulch. Making a hole or trench, or sinking a pot beside plants that need copious watering speeds up the task. A neat idea is to take clear plastic bottles with the bottom cut off, as used as mini-cloches. Invert and push one in beside each plant. A litre or two can then be poured rapidly into this funnel to soak in slowly.

A pair of watering cans with sawn-off spouts are easy to carry and pour faster than through roses or long, narrow spouts. And a butt by each greenhouse door, or in the middle of a plot, cuts carrying time down. This is almost essential if you have large numbers of pots or containers— around patios or in greenhouses, for example. Keeping the soil or potting compost in containers moist, but not waterlogged, is difficult, especially if you use a peat-substitute compost. A daily check, made by sinking your thumb into each pot, is essential. In winter, err on the side of caution, water rarely but thoroughly, and drain well. In summer, water frequently but still drain well. For large numbers of pots on benches, it is worth standing them on capillary matting fed from a simple reservoir.

Water control is really the key to a garden; indeed it is *the* basis of all life. Water is four fifths of every plant. It is the medium in which chemical and biological reactions take place, the dissolver of rock dusts and carrier of products from micro-organisms to roots, and vice versa. Evaporating water is the pump that lifts nutrients from the roots to the topmost leaf, and then transports sugars built by the leaves via photosynthesis back to the roots.

Many of the fungus problems, especially mildews, are aggravated if not actually caused by bushes getting too dry at the roots or by stagnant air around overcrowded tops. Sprinkling or spraying plants with a little water is worse than leaving them alone as it increases stress and makes them more vulnerable to disease.

Wet gardens are best enjoyed from the shelter of a summerhouse or potting shed, as a lot of damage is done by moving about in them. When it is wet, plants are more succulent and young growths more easily broken, the soil is compacted underfoot, breaking fine roots and excluding air. Later, during dry periods, the footprint marks evaporate water more rapidly than loose soil while their hard surface forms clods and cracks.

The worst problem in the wet is that touching plants spreads and lets in diseases. Many diseases wait for wet periods to release spores so that they can be carried in droplets of water. Bacteria can similarly travel protected from the danger of desiccation. Research on the ways viruses enter leaves has shown that they find it difficult to enter existing wounds as the defence system is repairing damage. The way they most easily attack healthy leaves is when the leaf is wetted with contaminated water and lightly rubbed—deep wounds were found to be less susceptible as they stimulated more of the plant's defense mechanisms. The moral is clear: walking among wet plants and particularly running their leaves through your fingers is probably doing them much harm.

Irrigation Sprinklers waste too much water, wet foliage, and cool the soil; a drip irrigation system is preferable. Even better are underground hoses that seep water to the roots—though these are harder to check! Where water is plentiful, trench irrigation is effective and cheap to install. When I could legally use as much water as I wanted, I periodically flooded trenches around particular beds and achieved fantastic yields. If you are permitted to use a hosepipe in your garden, arrange it so that all parts of the garden can be watered using a short length of hose, connected to one of several hidden points, as this saves dragging long lengths around the garden and decapitating plants. The permanent pipe layout can be made from ordinary hose buried in the ground or run along fences and hedges. If watering is easy it is more likely to be done.

Storage We seem to be experiencing more drought in recent years, so water must be guarded most carefully. To the gardener, rainwater is more valuable than tap water, and is free, so the more of the former that can be stored the better. Every effort should be made to save every drop. I've found old dead deep freezes make neat waterbutts. Waterbutts can be connected to one another with permanent siphons if they all stand on the same level. This can greatly increase your storage capacity and also help move water to where you want it. I have one big tank that saves the house's rainwater that is connected by siphon to a small butt in the polytunnel hundreds of feet away which thus is always full and ready for use. Siphons automatically move water for you, and if the butts are level you will need only a small one on view by the house or in the greenhouse as it can draw on many more hidden out of sight. Any excess is next best run into soakaways rather than down the drain, so it can benefit trees and other deep-rooting plants. Increasing the amount of humus in the soil increases the water-holding capacity enormously. Green manures, compost, mulches, and minimal cultivation improve the ability of the soil to store water that falls in winter until it is needed by plants the following summer.

"Gray water" Local laws permitting, gray water from sinks, showers, and baths can be diverted from the drains and run or siphoned down a hose to valued plants in times of drought. I use all my gray water for my espalier pears on a wall and for some grapes. Apart from it smelling if allowed to form stagnant patches, the only problem I've found is with the slower emptying, which causes more dirt to remain stuck on the bath! Water from washing machines and dish-washers may carry too many chemicals for safe use on plants.

Mulching A dust mulch used to be advocated as a water-conserving measure, but is mostly effective because of the simultaneous weed control. A proper mulch on top of the soil is much more effective at stopping water evaporating away. The mulch will itself hold about an inch of rain for every few inches depth, depending on the type of mulch. This can be a disadvantage if rain falls only a little at a time, because the mulch will absorb each shower and it will not reach the soil. Only heavy precipitation will penetrate through to the roots, which is why mulches are best put on after rainy spells not before. For types of mulch and their use as weed control, see page 214 in Chapter 10.

Using plants as their own mulch Well-mulched bare soil loses water at the least possible rate with no plants

Regarded as a pernicious weed, these celandines preserve the soil structure and provide food for early spring insects.

taking any moisture out. Grow only a few plants widely spaced out in hot dry conditions, and they will take out a lot more water to compensate, particularly on an exposed site. Thus a few weeds lose much water, and so will overspaced crop plants. To minimize water loss from crops, it is better to have them growing closer together intermixed with companion plants. The microclimate formed by the mixed layers of leaves traps moisture-laden air; the leaves thus keep themselves and the soil moister and cooler, then at night more dew condenses. The same occurs with deeper swards of grass and clover mixtures. These attract more dew than closely cropped grass. If the sward is allowed to grow up and tumble over, it then loses less water than when it is regularly cut, but there is less material being returned for fertility. Orchard management in the days before herbicides was to keep grass cut regularly until just after midsummer, then allow it to grow up. This would take up free nutrients, particularly nitrogen, causing the fruit to ripen better, and the long grasses falling over would use less moisture, leaving more to swell the crop. The grass would also cushion and hide windfalls. In the fruitcage, mulches are almost essential as soft fruits need plentiful moisture when they are swelling during the dry days of midsummer.

Drainage Waterlogging kills by driving out air, so is more of a problem on heavy soils because the finer particles hold much more water than the coarse grains of sand or silt. Obviously, drainage is needed in the very worst cases. However, more often reducing compaction, encouraging earthworms, adding organic material, or using raised beds will utilize that water rather than allowing it all to drain away. If drainage is needed, then ditches may work, or a herringbone pattern of drainage pipes leading to a soakaway may need to be laid.

chapter five

SEEDS WANT TO COME UP, PLANTS WANT TO GROW

Much of being a successful gardener is just tending our plants well

Our task is to learn enough about each and every plant's needs, so that we can look after them, not only lovingly, but knowingly. Seeds want to come up, so all we need to do is place them in a suitable environment at the right time and they will do their job. All of creation has arranged it so. Plants want to grow, flourish, flower, and fruit—it is their nature. All we must do is ensure they have the things they need, and prevent anything that will hinder them. If we get it right, so will they!

Sowing and growing methods vary with every plant, but certain basics must be adhered to. Seeds are better sown thinly than too thick, shallow rather than too deep, and late rather than too early in the season. However, it is important to remember that seeds are living things and need cool, dry conditions to stay alive. Store them in a sealable box, ideally with desiccant bags of silica gel. I use a dead refrigerator as I have many to store, but a wooden box is nearly as good.

Do not leave seeds in full sun, or in the greenhouse or kitchen. For the same reason, it is not a good idea to buy seed from racks standing in full sun or in heated rooms, far better and with a much wider choice is to buy from seed catalogs. These are usually packed with information, but take extravagant claims a bit sceptically—after all, they want you tobuy their own-brand special (price) seeds rather than the more economical standards.

Plants want to grow, flourish, flower, and fruit—it is their nature.

If you get good quality seeds and keep them well, then almost all will still be viable after three or four years. Never throw seeds away—if you are unsure what they are, you can always test a batch in a pot! The main exceptions are parsley and parsnip, which rarely keep for more than two years. On the other hand, larger seeds such as zucchini may still germinate after a decade.

Saving your own seed is remarkably easy for many vegetables—after all, they do it naturally. The large seeds, such as peas and beans, are expensive to buy and the easiest to save, especially as they tend to come true year after year. Let them ripen on the plants, and store them in paper bags until required. Carrots, parsnips, celery, onions, tomatoes, leeks, and lettuce are all fairly easy, but then their seed is not so expensive. The squash family are very promiscuous, so if you have different ones flowering together the seed will not come true. Most F1 hybrids do not come true and so we are told they cannot be saved. However, I have often had excellent results from seeds saved from some of them, so they are certainly worth a try. Potatoes, garlic, and shallots are all expensive to buy and very easy to save "seed" from. It is true that you can build up diseases and get poorer yields, but you can also save a lot of money. So save seed from only the best plants. If yields drop or you get a year with bad disease problems, buy new seed again the following year.

Young plants are like babies and have to be looked after as carefully: protect them from drought, draft, and extremes of temperature.

Sowing and growing

When seeds are sown in rows a drill is usually drawn out with a hoe. I find it is simpler and more accurate to press a thick straight cane or rod into the soil. When the plants are wanted at wide spacing, such as for parsnips, rather than sow evenly along the drill, sow a few seeds at set intervals (stations) and thin out to the best seedling as soon as they emerge. If seeds are sown as a block of several rows side by side, use a cane to mark out a hatch pattern in the soil to get equidistant spacing. For deeper holes, mark with a cane and use a blunt dibber to make a hole at each sowing station. Ensure there is sufficient moisture under the seed when it is sown by watering the drill or holes, preferably with rainwater plus a dash of seaweed solution. Let it soak in and only then sow the seed. Larger seeds, such as peas and beans, can be soaked for an hour or so before sowing rather than applying the liquid later. Never let young seedlings dry out. Do not forget that drying winds in early spring can parch the topmost layer of soil bone dry in hours—just when your seedlings have only made a few shallow roots.

Ideally, always cover the seed with dry soil or, preferably, any weed-seed-free material, such as a mixture of sharp sand and peat, leafmold, or old potting compost. This ensures few weeds come up next to the crop. Big seeds, such as peas, beans and corn, can have their planting holes filled in with the ordinary soil then covered with a thin layer of mulch which will suppress most weeds. Firm the lot down well then label with the date and variety. If the seed packet is empty you can use this as the label, weighted down with a stone inside. Keep weed competition down after sowing, especially during the earliest stages of growth.

When sowing in pots and multi-cell packs all the same rules apply as

Grass-clipping mulches keep the soil moist and suppress weeds around these broad bean seedlings.

A physical barrier is the most effective pest deterrent.

for soil. Use a sterile compost rather than weed-seed-filled soil from the garden. Some fine seeds may need to be surface sown and then kept in the dark to germinate, so read the packet! Generally, more seeds fail because they were sown too deep than too shallow. It is far better to soak the pots from underneath after sowing

and not to water them from the top. Sowing under cover in pots is usually more successful because of the warmth, but plants soon become drawn from low light and can quickly outgrow their pots if you do not pot them on or plant them out promptly.

Potting up Plants growing in pots need potting up as soon as they fill the pot, otherwise you get poor bonsai specimens. Better still, try and pot up just *before* it becomes necessary. Watch the rate of growth, if it slows for no other obvious reason, then the plant needs more root room. Knock the plant out of the pot and inspect the roots. If the roots run around the inside of the pot several times, then you have left potting on too late. When potting up, I often offset the rootball to touch the new pot at one side rather than set it centrally, because this seems to encourage faster rooting. More importantly, I try to keep the plant sun-aligned as it was when it germinated—having the label in the pot at the north point acts as a reference. Never grossly overpot as the compost will stagnate, and never use garden soil for potting, but choose a good quality potting compost. I use sieved garden compost from my compost heap, but can't recommend you do the same unless you make good stuff. If your garden compost is really good stuff, then dry it and sieve it for potting. Make it go further by mixing it with roughly the same amount each of sharp sand and peat (or an equivalent). After potting, I cover the surface of the compost with bought-in compost or just sand as these are weed-seed free and keep the surface clean.

Seed beds Although the best plants always come from seed sown in situ, often they do not make it this far because they get eaten by pests or damaged by the weather. To avoid these problems, it is safer to start them off under cover in pots or raise young plants in a seed bed where they can have special attention. A nursery bed is just a seed bed in use for a long time. It can be used for raising slower growing plants and for propagating from cuttings, which take a year or more before they are ready to be planted out in the garden. If you have a large garden, you may also find it convenient to have a small area dedicated to raising plants in bulk for use as hedging or groundcover, say.

Most often a seed bed is used to get crops through their most vulnerable early stages, ready to be transplanted out as young plants. This also keeps the main vegetable beds free to grow other crops and allows for easier weeding and intercropping. Seed beds do not need the high fertility of salad or vegetable beds, but do need copious watering. They also benefit from being sloped slightly to face the sun and sheltered from cold winds. Parsnips and other roots have to be sown in situ, where they are to finish, and legumes are usually treated similarly. Seed beds are most used for brassicas and leeks, bedding plants and biennial flowers, before these are moved to their final sites. Some plants, such as brassicas,

actually do best grown in a seed bed and transplanted once when they are very young to break the tap root—they then develop a good, fibrous root system. Transplant them a second time, to their final site, when they have four true leaves and they will romp away.

Choosing composts Although it is easy to do, it is unlikely that you will want to mix your own sowing and potting compost—it would just never be as good as the best quality commercial brands (though it could not be poorer than the worst). Most composts are based on peat, sand, and chemical fertilizers, while John Innes formula composts are based on sterilized soil, though they may still have some peat in them. Organic versions may duplicate these, or be based on composted or worm worked wastes. Sadly, in trials, many conventional and most peat-free and organic composts have proved inferior to the best peat-based or John Innes loam-based composts.

John Innes is a series of recipes for loam-based compost produced by different companies: John Innes No. 1 is for sowing; No. 2 for potting on; and No. 3 for permanent pot plants

or very hungry young plants such as tomatoes. If well made, John Innes is without doubt the best non-organic compost to use. Peat-based composts are as effective, if you don't mind using peat products. There are now many peat-free composts on the market, but you may prefer to consider peat as a renewable resource we should be encouraging the sustained use of. Any sort of compost will deteriorate with age: never buy old, wet or end-of-season cheapies! Your safest bet is to buy a popular quality brand from a reputable supplier—or try several brands and see which suits what you grow the most. It is most interesting to sow the same seed in three or four different brands in a mini-trial at home!

For sowing, use a freshly sieved seed or multipurpose compost, John Innes No. 1, or a homemade mixture—either peat and sharp sand, or sieved sterilized garden soil, peat, and sharp sand. For rooting cuttings, use a mixture by volume of any sterile sowing compost with sharp sand. For small, tender and valuable seedlings pot up into a reputable brand of potting compost, such as John Innes No. 2—stronger and bigger plants may prefer the richer No. 3.

For robustly growing plants, pot them up into either a fresh organic compost or sieved garden compost. I use the latter for almost all my potting, making it extra strong for hungry feeders such as zucchini, melons, and cucumbers by thoroughly mixing in grass clippings.

Light, temperature and water control for sowing, seedlings, and young plants Although the very best plants are usually grown where they are sown, many accidents can happen on the way. A dedicated seed bed improves their chances and the hardier seedlings grow away well. But often even with cloches a sowing may be unsure in cold soil or the germination may inconveniently be

Homemade compost mix

Making a homemade mix of potting compost is easy provided you use good quality ingredients. Mix three buckets of peat, coir, leafmold or composted bark (leafmold is best) with one bucket of sharp sand. This mix will aerate and drain freely, but contains little plant food. So add one bucket of worm compost or casts, or three buckets of sieved garden compost, or a measure of a balanced organic fertilizer. The latter is better if you need a

weed-seed-free mix. I used such a balanced mixture successfully for years. For every four 2-gallon buckets of the "peat" and sand mix I added 3 ounces of calcified seaweed, 4 ounces of blood, fish and bone meal, 4 ounces of hoof and horn meal and 3 ounces of wood ash. I used it immediately and although not perfect it was better than many cheap brands. If you wish to avoid animal byproducts you can replace those ingredients with the same amount of seaweed meal, but it is not quite as good, so pot up generously.

expected to take years. Seed is usually easier to germinate in warmth under cover, and success is more certain with plants started in little pots or multicelled trays and planted out when they and the site are ready. Indeed, some long-season and tender plants, such as tomatoes *must* be started this way, otherwise they would never have time to crop in our short growing season. However, although ensuring survival, transplanting almost always checks the plant's growth and it rarely does as well as it might have done sown in situ. We must minimize such checks, and with pots we must take more care as we affect their conditions more than in the soil. Almost all crops that are best started off in pots benefit from being started in multi-celled trays, because these give each plant its own little space with minimal root interference. The insulated trays are easy to fit in a propagator and move around.

In pots or cells, never risk letting seedlings crowd each other. The commonest mistake is sowing thickly in one pot, intending to prick out later, and leaving this operation a day or two too long, which causes severe losses of yield. A few annual and bedding flowers, beetroot, and onions can be allowed to have two or three seedlings growing together to produce clumps of smaller plants. For other plants, sow two or three seeds in each cell or pot and thin *as soon as possible after they emerge.*

When sowing in pots or cells, extra care needs to be taken with watering, so as not to waterlog the seeds, nor allow them to dry out. It is best to fill pots with damp compost, then stand them in a tray of water till the top looks wet. Remove and drain well. Do not rewater until the seedlings appear unless the compost starts to dry out badly. Never use stale rainwater for seeds or seedlings as this can spread damping off disease. For valuable seeds even bottled water is not too great an expense, but tap

Multicelled tray seedlings each grow separately, so when they are planted out their rootballs are undamaged.

water will usually do. Once the plants are growing strongly then rainwater is preferable, because it contains no added chlorine, fluoride, etc.

A greenhouse is not needed for starting off hardy plants in cells or pots, because they will be more than happy in a coldframe or a sheltered spot until they are ready to go out. However, a greenhouse allows you to control conditions more easily and can later be used for growing tender crops to fruition. Cloches are nearly as good, but do not have as much space and are difficult to use. A polytunnel gives the best value for money, though they are not very nice to look at. Whatever you choose, be careful to keep the glass or plastic clean as light is more important than heat for most plants, especially hardy vegetables. Ventilation is also important, since it is easy to cook small seedlings if full sun hits them while they are tightly sealed up, so either be extra vigilant or invest in an automatic vent opener.

Once hardy plants have started growing well in pots they can be planted out into the main plot. However, they *must* be hardened off. This simply means getting them used to the tougher conditions by standing them outside during the

day and bringing them back under cover at night for three or four days. Do not skimp on this—it is most important. If you have to plant out partially hardened off plants, protect them after planting with cloches or clear plastic bottles. If the weather is poor or the plot is not ready for planting out when the plants are big enough, they *must* be potted on into larger containers or they will stop growing. When planting out hardened off or seedbed-grown seedlings, water them well the day before and, if possible, prepare the planting holes and water them too. Certainly water the holes long enough before planting to allow the water, with a dash of seaweed solution, to percolate away. Do not plant in mud! Make the holes bigger than the rootball of the plant, but not too deep. For the hungry feeders—including brassicas, corn, tomatoes, and cucumbers—mix a handful of sieved garden compost in with the soil before you replace it firmly around the rootball. As most seedling transplants are succulent, protect them from bird damage.

Growing tender plants from seed is more difficult, because most of them require starting off in warmth early in the year when light levels are low and they easily get leggy. They also need repotting several times as they cannot be planted out even under cover before summer unless you give them extra heat. In fact, the biggest problem is not germinating them, as any little propagator on a sunny windowsill will do that but where to keep them in the warm while they get bigger and bigger in larger and larger pots. Heating the greenhouse is an excellent if expensive option, but I suggest constructing a heated coldframe in an unheated greenhouse—it's cheaper, and the same place is useful later in the year for luxury crops such as melons (see Chapter 8, page 180).

Planting out bought-in and larger plants Only vegetables and bedding plants are usually transplanted while growing strongly; most other plants are better moved while dormant. In either case, the bigger the rootball and the more associated soil that can be transferred undisturbed the better. Some gardeners recommend cutting back woody plants very hard when planting to encourage strong regrowth, but I find it is better to let most plants establish for a year before pruning them back. If a plant has been too long in a small container, it may be root-bound—the roots encircle the base of the pot and do not grow outwards when planted in the soil. In these cases, tease out the roots before planting. If plants have been out of the soil for a long time or have dried out, the roots need a good soak before planting. If they have been under cover or in a protected environment they need to be hardened off (see above).

It is not a good idea to prepare planting holes a long time before your plants arrive, as this may allow the soil to dry out, *but* it is better to dig the holes early and do a good job than to rush it at the last minute. Water a planting hole well, but let it drain away before planting. If drainage is slow, break up the subsoil in the bottom of the planting hole. Always try to dig a generous hole to give the roots a free run—this breaks up existing root systems and aerates the soil, stimulating the microlife.

This, in turn, encourages the plant to reroot quickly, but the microlife needs raw materials to convert, so mix compost and rock dusts well in with the planting soil.

The hole for a tree or bush needs to be as big and as deep as you can make it, not just large enough to squeeze the roots in. Deeper is no better than wider; do not mix different soil layers, although breaking up the bottom of the hole with a fork is useful. Mix enriching materials into the topmost layer. Everything added to the planting hole needs to be mixed in well. I have seen many promising trees killed by too much peat packed around them by gardeners enthused by adverts. A layer of peat isolates the roots and dries out the rootball, so that the tree fails in its first summer because capillary moisture doesn't reach it. Equally important is the firming in of each root so it is in direct capillary contact with an unbroken soil network. For a new plant to establish quickly the soil needs to be firmed around each root and just moist enough to pack well. Too wet is as bad as too dry or frosted—the soil must be friable and moist.

Watering is the next most important part of establishing transplanted plants, especially the slower growing ones. Fast-growing annuals sown in situ with enough soil moisture initially fend for themselves. However, a large newly transplanted woody subject may need watering right through the first season of growth while it builds up a root system in the soil. Herbaceous plants fall between these two extremes—if moved when dormant they can usually look after themselves, but will benefit from watering during dry periods. Mulches will help by retaining moisture, suppressing weeds, and aid quick establishment.

Buying in wisely Market stalls and

"cheap" garden centers may not be the best places to buy from. Sadly, most of these stock only fast-moving lines, and offer a poor choice of variety with little, if any, choice of rootstock. Never buy "special offer" large or old plants, as these are slow to establish and would be soon outgrown by vigorous youngsters. Often plants are grown in containers for convenient sale, but this can make for a cramped root system. This is little problem for herbaceous plants, small shrubs, or most soft fruit, but planting a tree that could live a century or more with its root wound into a circle hardly makes a good anchor. Buy from a reputable nursery, where possible bare rooted, because you can see the roots and ensure that there are no hidden pests. Choose certified, virus-free plants and always order early. Get several catalogs to compare and plan your planting on paper. This is well worthwhile because the plants are of a higher quality, you get more choice and you will often pay *much* less by mail order.

Catalogs give glowing descriptions of plants, but it is still hard to visualize them—sometimes even when a photo is provided. Going to visit garden centers and gardens, especially those where the plants are well-labeled, provides a much better idea of what plants look like. Visiting regularly—say, once a month— enables you to observe the continuity of color and foliage though individual plants are out of bloom. Gardens are better for this, because garden centers tend to stock "fast movers"—predominantly plants in flower as these sell most easily.

When ordering by mail, be prepared to send back anything that is poor quality. However, most nurseries send plants that are as good if not better than those offered by garden centers and at a lower price. At a garden center, though, you can choose which plants you want. Do not always go for the biggest, as these may not grow away so easily. Look for health in plants with plenty of young, strong shoots and avoid anything that looks thin, spindly, or sick—no matter how cheap it is. Plants that have been on the shelf too long will have roots coming out the bottom of the pot and weeds growing in the compost. Buying weeds with your plants is like getting litter with your shopping, so if you are assertive enough, remove them and leave them at the point of sale.

Replenishing your own . . . Sowing always gives the best, most vigorous plants especially when sowing in situ because they are never disturbed. This is often inconvenient, especially if the plants are slow growing. For this reason most plants are started off elsewhere in pots or a nursery bed and planted out when they are big enough to survive in their final position. Growing plants from seed has one major drawback, namely that most of the best varieties of perennial plants cannot be propagated from seed, but have to be vegetatively propagated from cuttings, layers, grafts, buds, or root division if they are to come true. For many woody plants the simplest way to propagate them is by fall cuttings (also known as hardwood or ripe cuttings). These have the summer's energy stored away, and cleanly cut young shoots a foot or less long root easily. Firm them in a slit trench lined with sharp sand. Keep them moist and sheltered from the worst of the weather over winter, and they will be ready for planting out next fall.

As a rule, cuttings are best able to root from the leaf joints (nodes) in the stem, so are cut close below one at the bottom. For a few plants, such as clematis, they are best cut halfway between nodes. Lower buds are removed unless many shoots are wanted close to the ground to form a stool, as for blackcurrants. Fall cuttings root well, but have to endure the winter. In hard areas, store the cuttings in moist sand in a frost-free place, then plant them in spring.

Cuttings of some less hardy plants, such as rosemary and lavender, will not stand hard winter or storage, but they can be rooted successfully from cuttings taken in early spring. "Lazy cuttings" (semiripe cuttings) are best for this; small shoots are pulled off with a tiny heel of old wood. Summer cuttings (also known as unripe or soft cuttings) are of the fresh young growth, and would wither before rooting unless given special conditions, which a propagator can provide. They need warmth underneath, high humidity, and shading with a sheet of paper to prevent them scorching in strong sunlight. Summer cuttings are shoots of current growth long enough to have several pairs of leaves. Usually one pair of leaves is left and two or three pairs at the base removed to give a short, bare stem to firm into a sterile medium. Sharp sand in pots is excellent, because it is well aerated and the grittiness helps rooting. Once rooted, the cuttings must be potted on into richer potting compost. They form smaller plants than those produced from fall cuttings, but they root more readily and after

Most roses, such as this 'Buff Beauty,' can be propagated by rooting foot-long cuttings in the fall.

overwintering can be planted out into a nursery bed or potted up.

Layering is used for plants that do not take easily from cuttings, and is simply rooting the cutting while it is still attached to the parent. If a branch cannot be pegged down into the soil then a pot of soil can be held up to the branch. In either case, the bark is damaged and held in moist, sharp-sand-enriched soil till it roots and can then be detached and planted. Hormone rooting powder may encourage rooting of difficult subjects, but although naturally occurring, it is not generally accepted by organic gardeners.

For woody plants that do not layer easily, such as many of our fruit trees, grafting and budding are used. This is a more difficult technique to master, but basically consists of joining a bit of the desired plant to the rootstock of another, compatible plant that is more easily propagated. The cut surface of one is attached so closely and firmly at the cambium (growth layer) of their bark, that they join.

Root division is used to propagate most herbaceous plants. As plants grow they form large clumps that get old and woody in the center. They can be dug up, the vigorous perimeter divided into chunks for replanting and the worn-out middle discarded. If many plants are wanted, every segment which has roots and a bud can be replanted in fresh ground to make a new plant. Often the clumps just need splitting into two rather than being chopped up small, while others can be teased apart by hand, or have tightly entwined roots pulled apart with two forks placed back to back.

Most plants can be grown from seed in the same way as vegetables, though some need to spend time in a nursery bed before being big enough to plant out. This can be a long time for some trees, so you may be better off buying these in, but is quite short for many shrubs, though most of these are quicker to flower when

New apple trees never prosper where an old one grew, or still is, so replant as far away as possible.

grown from cuttings in the fall, or layering if cuttings are difficult. If you want named varieties you will have to propagate from cuttings, as few will come true from seeds. However, if you want to take the risk, you might just grow something completely different!

With patience, a garden can be replenished or even stocked with little expense. Most gardeners are only too willing to donate cutting material and seed, and few begrudge bits off the side of herbaceous plants especially when they are replenishing a bed anyway. Beware the over-generous gardener who comes with a barrowload of any plant. It is more likely to be an invasive peril than a rare and choice item, so accept it graciously and compost discreetly.

. . . and profiting from your surplus
There are strict laws preventing the sale of seeds of most vegetables in many countries, and plant-breeders' rights govern the sale of protected varieties. Generally, though, you are free to sell your surplus plants and produce. However, I counsel against selling produce because the returns are so low compared to the efforts, and one always ends up selling the best and retaining the poorest for oneself.

Give your surplus crops and plants to friends or charity stalls instead—and never give away too much, or the best, which is yours by right.

Replanting and rotation In any garden there comes a time when, for some reason or another, a major tree or shrub dies or is evicted. Never ever try to replace it with the same or similar, because the new one will seldom prosper. The proximity of any established similar plants will also severely handicap the newcomer. In the worst cases, if you want to replant part of a hedge or rose bed, you will have to remove and replace all the immediate soil and give the new plants a heavy feeding and regular watering if there is to be any hope of success. See Chapter 7, page 141, for advice on vegetable rotations.

Recognizing your soil type and improving it organically

We rarely have the opportunity to choose our site or the soil for our garden, and have to make do the best we can. Most gardens are on old sites and may be exhausted and pest ridden. Those in towns are likely to be polluted and out of balance, especially if many chemicals have been used. New sites and country gardens may have been treated better, or worse if they were recently formed. Sites run derelict and full of rampant weeds will probably have better soil.

Generally, most soils will produce flowers, shrubs, or tree fruit without much improvement, but need to be better for vegetables and soft fruit. Problem soils tend to be local problems and it is always a good idea to see how neighbors cope. Almost all soils can be improved, but it may even be an easier option to put on extra topsoil if the existing soil is very poor. Most types of soil need basically the same treatment to improve them: the addition of

copious quantities of organic material. Anything else is of little consequence by comparison. Soils can be divided into types in many ways, but what concerns the gardener most is their effects on plant growth and ease of labor. There is no need to know their exact composition, but how they behave.

Loamy soils are produced when old meadow or grass sward is dug up, or where other soils have been heavily enriched with organic material. This is the best type of soil for most plants. The best loams have a rich, brown, sugary texture, made mostly of earthworm droppings, which encourages plants grown in them to produce masses of fine root hairs that pull up granular soil particles with every root. You can make your own loam-like soil for your most favored plants by stacking and rotting down turfs of grass.

Heavy clay soils are hard to dig, stick to every tool and boot, drain poorly, and pool with water in heavy rain. However, they are the richest soils, rarely suffer mineral deficiency and resist drought well, though eventually set like concrete. Clay soils must never be compacted while wet, so *do not stand on them*. They need copious amounts of coarse organic material, sharp sand or grit, and they benefit from liming and fixed bed gardening. Heavy soils encourage slugs, but also produce the best cauliflowers and roses.

Sandy soils are a joy to dig, wash easily off tools and shoes, and never pool with water even in downpours. They need much more organic material, rock dust (especially ground rock potash) and organic fertilizers than other soils because their wonderful aeration burns off humus quickly. They warm up quickly in spring for early crops, but dry out badly. If not too stony, they will produce super carrots.

Silty soils are more like sandy soils than clays, because they do not retain water and are fairly easy to work. Often built up on old river beds, they benefit from ground rock dusts. They are good for most crops if well fed, but tend to splash and cap badly in the wet.

Lime-rich or worse, thin, chalky soils cause chlorosis (yellowing leaves with green veins) in lime-hating plants by locking up iron and other nutrients. Slightly lime-rich soils suit most plants though, especially brassicas, if they are also rich and moist. Good for many trees, figs, and grapes, these soils need feeding and mulching. Thin ones over chalk or limestone are then hot and hungry, so raised beds will significantly improve them.

Light, silty soils like mine need generous composting and liming to produce good cauliflowers.

Stony soils tend to be freer draining, though not always. The stones are of little consequence to most plants, but frustrate cultivation, especially hoeing. These soils are better with permanent plantings and mulches rather than for growing annuals and vegetables, though these can thrive on cleaned beds. "Hoeing mulches" of sharp sand make hoeing and sowing much easier.

Peaty soils are not always advantageous. Though very high in organic material they can be short of nutrients, dry out easily and are not stable enough for large trees. They

will grow good salads and soft fruits, though, and will be naturally suited to lime-haters such as rhododendrons. With the addition of lime, many other plants can be grown, and weeds thrive.

Wet soils tend to be sour or acid, they may need to be limed and drained, especially if low lying, but be cautious not to overdo it. Water gives life and it is only water-logging that is a problem. Adding copious amounts of organic material improves the drainage and water dispersion.

Having your garden soil analyzed for nutrient content is unnecessary. It is supposedly accurate, but you'd be better off simply applying a bag of

97

seaweed meal. It is difficult to get accurate readings from the patchy soils in gardens, containing all sorts of detritus from dead cats to car batteries, so it is best not to worry about this sort of fine tuning. Aim to incorporate some broad-spectrum organic fertilizers and as much organic material as possible, and most soils will be productive.

The only thing worth checking if you're doubtful is the pH—the acidity or alkalinity (lime content) of the soil. Don't bother with cheap meters—they are invariably inaccurate. Instead, use a simple chemical test kit with an accurate color chart. These are inexpensive and available in most garden stores. The basic pH may vary between ground level and deeper if the soil layers have built up a rich surface mold, so take several samples from a typical worked soil. The pH may change as the soil is enriched particularly as more organic material is added, so most soils tend to become more acid. For this reason, liming the soil every few years will be of benefit especially for vegetables and grassed areas. Lime can be plain chalk, or better still Dolomitic lime which contains more magnesium and other nutrients. Best of all, though, is calcified seaweed which contains all the trace elements too. Never apply lime at the same time as manures or compost. Apply it before rain on top of the soil or grass and rake, brush or allow to leach in during late fall or winter.

Although most soils can be improved and thereby made acceptable to a wider range of plants, there is a difference between improvement and change. Various materials are sold as soil improvers and some flocculating agents based on lime or gypsum, do help lighten textures when applied to clay soils. But for most soils, applying generous amounts of well-rotted organic matter will give the greatest benefit. All soil types contain the same materials; stones, silts, sands, clays, and organic material—it is their proportions that change. What affects plants most is not the nutrient levels of a soil, but the physical texture, the aeration and moisture retention.

All these are improved by adding more organic material, especially when combined with a mulch. Introducing organic material adds to the nutrient level directly and increases another component of healthy soil, its microlife. This then attacks not only the fresh resource but also the soil's mineral content. This almost limitless resource is then made available to the plants. There is sufficient in the soil of almost every element to last for millennia of heavy cropping if the microlife has other materials to enable it to break the particles down. Most of all, they need water.

Air is the next most important component of garden soil. Almost all microlife and plant roots need oxygen and give off carbon dioxide. Much of the latter is reabsorbed by the soil, but fresh air has to replace the former. The size and shape of organic particles in various stages of decomposition keep soils open and allows aeration. This is greatly augmented by earthworm burrows which descend for several yards. So it is the earthworms that are most effective at bringing the greatest depth of soil into use—gardeners cannot dig this deep. The soil composition also varies with depth and only the top few inches throb with life. A foot deep is subsoil containing almost nothing but worms and plant roots. Initially, digging may be necessary but it does disrupt the soil layers. You should never mix the sterile subsoil with the fertile topsoil. The most active and productive part is those top few inches, and these are optimized with several more inches of an organic mulch keeping them warm, well fed and moist.

Growing in containers

Even in the smallest gardens, with only a patio, it is possible to grow many different plants by confining them in containers. This cramps the root system and prevents them getting too big, and tends to bring the plants into flower earlier. However, plants in containers are prone to drop their leaves or even die unless extremely good care is taken to stop them drying out. This may mean watering three or four times a day in summer. Similarly, attention is needed to prevent the roots freezing in winter. One advantage of growing in containers is that the whole pot can be taken under cover to prevent frost or bird damage, or to bring on earlier growth.

If you must grow in containers, use the biggest you can manage—plastic garbage cans can be converted with holes in the base and are much cheaper than pots. Plants in containers cannot get enough nutrients from ordinary garden soil and need an enriched medium. For most plants, choose a John Innes No. 3 potting compost which is based on soil. It is heavy, so helps keep top-heavy plants upright in plastic pots. Peat and peat-alternative composts are as good from most points of view, but potted plants are unstable and hard to re-wet if they do get dry. These composts are usually based on chemical fertilizers, but organically formulated versions are available.

To be more organic and for economy, I use sieved garden compost for the bulk of my potting. I adjust it for strength and openness with sharp sand or mole-hill soil, but otherwise it is used as it comes to fill the bottom three quarters of each pot. Each container is topped off with a sterile mixture of sharp sand and peat, or similar, so I do not suffer a plague of weeds. This works excellently for me, but I recommend it only if you can make good compost!

If you can, choose a dwarfing rootstock and arrange some form of automatic watering system. Wherever possible, try not to use very small pots, baskets or organic growing bags. These may be attractive or temporarily convenient, but they are not kind to plants. Plants have amazingly extensive root systems stretching for yards all round them, and to confine them in small amounts of soil or compost makes their life very difficult. Narrow borders in greenhouses or against walls are much the same, though they usually give a cooler root run than a pot. Any very restricted root run provides too little fertility and risks the soil or compost drying out or waterlogging. Thus any plant may be checked, and it will never do as well as it would in open ground.

Be sensible about watering plants in pots. Keep most of them on the dry side all winter—and much moister all summer.

Watering really is the biggest problem with plants in containers. Either constant attention or an automatic system is needed. Sprinklers activated by a timer or sensor, drip feeds and capillary matting can be used in a greenhouse, but become more difficult when the containers are spread about a patio, for instance.

Automatic watering is almost essential where large numbers of pots or containers are maintained, such as around patios and in greenhouses. In pots and containers keeping the soil or potting compost moist but not waterlogged is difficult, particularly with the new peat-substitute composts. It is essential to check all pots regularly to see if they need watering. Do this by pushing your thumb into the compost to check how moist it is.

In winter, err on the side of caution. Water rarely but thoroughly and let the pots drain well. Overwatering is a serious risk at this time of year, so good drainage is essential. In summer, water frequently but still drain well. Standing the pots on gravel trays improves drainage and creates a beneficial humid atmosphere around the plants. The gravel soon gets dirty, though, and may harbour disease, so I just use and empty drip trays instead.

All plants growing in containers or small borders soon use up the goodness in the rootball and require supplementary feeding. Liquid feeds can be added to the water at regular intervals, but it must be a very dilute solution so as not to burn delicate roots. Never feed when growth is slow or when the plant is under stress. Foliar feeding with seaweed sprays at monthly intervals will greatly aid all plants in containers.

You can save a lot of effort by choosing plants that will stand water stress well. Pelargoniums, aspidistras, spider plants, succulents, and cacti are all good examples. For outdoor containers all year round grow the tougher herbs such as thymes, mints, and marjorams—and best of all house leeks, which require less maintenance than plastic flowers. Unless you wish to check their growth, always pot up plants regularly as they fill their container. For permanent pot plants, this means repotting every spring.

Where several plants are in the same pot, use fewer and they will all do better. This applies to growing bags, too. For example, three tomato plants in an organic growing bag do no better than two, and one would produce as much fruit as all three.

chapter six

FANTASTIC FRUITS

Fruits are fantastic, easy, tasty, productive, nutritious, little work, aesthetic, flexible, and ecological

FRUITS ARE FANTASTIC . . .

I find there are few other foods that have the range of color, texture, and flavor, and there are few other plants that can give me the satisfaction offered by a fruit tree or bush laden down with a ripe crop. Yet it is easy to be successful with fruits, they're tasty, productive, nutritious, and little work; fruit trees are aesthetic and flexible, fitting into almost any design; and most of all a garden of fruit makes complete ecological sense.

. . . EASY . . .

As a form of gardening fruit culture is not only rewarding, but also rather easy, especially when compared with vegetables. It is the nature of fruiting plants to fruit—we must simply provide suitable conditions. Some fruits will even grown on shady sites vegetables would completely fail in. Fruits are easy because they are so much less demanding than highly bred vegetable crops, such as carrots or cauliflowers. These vegetables are being asked to give a terrific performance in ways that they wouldn't left to themselves.

'White Grape' whitecurrants (left) are prolific, while an apple tree like 'Discovery' (overleaf, top) will fruit year after year whether you do any more or not. Strawberry flowers (center left) are soon followed by sweet fruits. Gooseberries (center right) grown fully ripe at home are better than dessert grapes. Blackcurrants like 'Ben More' (below) are tasty juiced and jellied, and *so* good for you.

Fruit is easy to grow organically because the plants tolerate poorer soils and conditions and, being perennial, their pests and diseases are more simply controlled by the natural ecology. Because the majority of fruiting plants are perennials, there is no annual digging or seed-bed preparation, no sowing and planting out, while harvesting and storage is easier for fruits than vegetables, with less bending and no mud. Pruning is easy compared to digging. Thus growing fruit is ideal for the lazy or hard-pressed gardener, as even total neglect is less detrimental. Most fruit trees will crop for years with no care or attention as nearly all the work is done when planting and then we only need to harvest—and even that can be left to the birds.

. . . TASTY . . .

The delicious taste of a really good fruit is a subtle blend of flavors and aromas, with the acidity balanced by sweetness. Store-bought fruit can rarely be as really fresh or well ripened as your own grown at home. The varieties in the stores are invariably of commercial varieties chosen predominantly for their high yields. Growing your own at home you can choose old-fashioned varieties with exceptional flavor. Furthermore, as you can grow your fruit organically and pick it when perfectly ripe, you can eat it without peeling thus savoring all the textures and flavors. It's the fruit's good clean taste that tells you it has even more value than fruit grown conventionally.

. . . PRODUCTIVE . . .

Of course most people with a large enough garden plan to grow some fruit, but it makes sense to fit fruit into even the smallest plot. Economically fruit can give much better returns in weight or cash value than most vegetables using the same area. For instance, one gooseberry bush can yield a baby's weight of fruit yet occupies little more space than a cabbage or cauliflower. Although the initial cost may be higher for trees and bushes, it is an investment that you will recover in the first years of fruiting. The costs of growing vegetables, on the other hand, both occur and increase annually. Vegetables will be cropping the first season, but many fruits are not lagging far behind. Strawberries and fall-fruiting raspberries can be cropped a year after planting, all the currants and berries give good crops the second year after planting, and even tree fruit, such as apples, peaches, and pears, will start to crop in their second or third year. Yields increase every year for most fruits, reaching peak production after five to ten years. Some maintain this level for many decades with little expense or work required in return.

. . . NUTRITIOUS . . .

Although some fruits may contain fewer vitamins and minerals by weight than some vegetables, it is far more pleasant and easier to consume much more fruit. There is almost exactly the same value in

drinking a glass of mixed fruit juice as munching your way through a whole plateful of salad—and which would you rather have more often? It is certainly much easier to get children to eat more fruit and fruit juices than more vegetables! Fruits are most valuable nutritionally when picked really fresh, ripened naturally, and kept uncontaminated. So homegrown can be much more health-giving than commercial fruit which is sprayed with chemicals and picked underripe so that it can withstand being transported great distances.

. . . LITTLE WORK . . .

Growing fruit makes much more sense than growing vegetables, yet gardeners who go to the effort of cultivating a vegetable patch often don't consider making their garden over to this labor-saving form of cultivation instead. Care is needed to establish the plants well, but thereafter little work is needed for top fruits and not much more for the soft. Fruit-bearing plants benefit from soil enrichment, but it is not essential. Pruning is required most by the soft fruits, but it is not arduous and far less effort than digging. Trees or bushes of top fruits can be left unpruned for years and still give excellent crops, and some, such as stone fruits, are best left well alone anyway. As I said, it is easy to be organic when growing fruit, and even if pests and diseases do strike, a fruit crop is often still usable for preserves. Although fruit will benefit from careful watering when fruits are swelling, it tends to withstand droughts better and still produce good crops in seasons when the vegetables fail.

. . . AESTHETIC . . .

It is easier to make an attractive and productive garden using fruit trees, vines, and bushes than it is with vegetables, and the length of their season of interest is longer. Fruit trees can have a pleasing appearance even out of leaf when the bare branches are silhouetted against a winter sky. The changing months bring the green shoots of spring, the billowy masses of blossom, the ripening fruits and the leaf colors of fall. Trained fruit forms can enhance a wall or be used as screens to divide up the garden or block unsightly views. Climbing vines can be encouraged over trellis, pergolas or used to cover sheds and eyesores.

. . . FLEXIBLE . . .

Many fruiting trees, such as pears and cherries, are very floriferous and can be planted instead of ornamental trees. Quinces and medlars have interesting shapes and leaves and are much more attractive than many alternatives featured on small front lawns. In Europe at least they are cheaper too, because fruit trees currently carry no VAT. Fruit trees and bushes are also good competitors, and may still produce crops when grown among vigorous plants in overcrowded borders or in wild gardens, where vegetables would be overwhelmed.

Fruit trees planted as standards with a clean trunk will shade the pram the first summer, can be grassed underneath to make a play area, will be fruiting before the kids reach school, be robust enough for a goal post and soon enough be of a size for a swing for the grandchildren.

. . . ECOLOGICAL . . .

The ecology around us is, of course, of vital importance to all of us, and the permanent nature of most common fruiting plants means their cultivation makes fewer demands on peat, heat, and consumables than other types of gardening, such as ornamental bedding schemes or the vegetable patch. Once established, most tree fruits can be grassed or mulched around leaving no bare soil to erode or leach. Their long season in leaf fixes much carbon dioxide and their root systems go deep enough to utilize more of the soil's nutrients than do other plants. Fruiting plants necessarily have flowers in quantity which are especially valuable to the pollinating, parasitizing and beneficial predatory insects. The permanence of fruit makes it easier to build up a beneficial ecosystem around them and they support wildlife with nest sites, shelter, and of course food—especially if we are not very careful to protect it. Indeed, if we do not utilize, and protect, our crops then the wildlife can, and will, take advantage of it. Whereas rows of surplus vegetables are mostly only good for composting.

We can, therefore, choose to make a fruit garden partly for wildlife, adding the shelter, water, and other conditions needed to encourage them. If we are cunning, we can have sufficient fruit for ourselves and yet have enough spare to share with all the other garden inhabitants. Indeed, the birds are not only nature's guardians, controlling insect pests, but also the heirs to the crop. Much of the fruit gardener's work goes in to preventing them and other pests from making off with the results of our efforts. However, with cunning and nets, we can prevent them stealing more than a modicum. Nature intends them to eat and spread her fruits, so we should not take their depredations too personally. After all, a fruit encourages us, and other creatures, to eat some of the sweet flesh, if in exchange we distribute the plant's seeds. Thus it is with a clear conscience that we consume fruits, the plants give them freely, providing food so we can travel on and spread their seeds as we go. How different this is from growing cut flowers, which we take to a sterile death indoors, and vegetables, which we so thoughtlessly hack to pieces, possibly even while we feel righteous about giving up meat!

Cultivating the very finest fruits, nuts, and berries

Currants vary little in flavor, apples, gooseberries, and grapes vary tremendously. Without trying each and every sort it is difficult to know which are going to be the best from the vast numbers on offer. Over

Homegrown walnuts like this 'Franquette' are different from anything you can buy—really fresh, the bitter skin of the kernel peels off easily and the flesh is soft and buttery.

If you want aromatic, sweet, juicy peaches, fully ripened and warmed by the sun, grow them yourself. There is no comparison— a real peach requires a bib for safe eating and a finger-bowl afterwards.

6000 names for perhaps 2000 or 3000 varieties of apples are recorded, and it is still possible to buy several hundred. You can have a different one for every day of the year! And if you are growing for yourself and "commercial viability" is not in question, then your choice of fruit can be a gourmet's delight. My 'Bredase' apricot bush only gives me fruits one year in six, but in that one they are magnificent with a flavor and texture that puts all others to shame.

When buying fruit trees use the year of introduction as a guide because an old variety must have some good attributes if it is still around. Naturally some new varieties are higher yielding than the old and many offer some resistance to disease. But where flavor is concerned it is a matter of taste, and many of the old varieties were grown solely for that quality. Indeed, that is why they were developed in the first place, whereas modern breeders are after the commercial market which wants high yields and a long shelf life.

The best way to choose varieties is to go somewhere with a wide selection of fruit on trial, such as a pick-your-own farm. Carefully gleaning around local stores and supermarkets may also produce several varieties to taste and, of course, "expert" local recommendation is always worth listening to. Otherwise, read the catalogs carefully; with a sceptical mind to nurserymen's claims. When choosing for yourself and family, try to spread the season of harvest by choosing early-, mid-, and late-fruiting varieties. This is especially important for apples: with careful storage you can have them most months of the year. It also spreads the workload as picking and preserving do not come all at once. Growing different varieties means there is much less likelihood of all the crops being lost if catastrophe strikes. Even if space is limited, you can still grow many trained forms in a small garden. For real favorites it may be worthwhile also extending the season by planting two trees—one in a warm, sheltered spot and one in a cool, shady place to spread the cropping period by a week or two. It is also worth remembering that the fruits on the sunny side of the tree ripen ahead of those in the shade, so do not pick them all at the same time.

Successful harvesting and storage will affect both the quality of your fruit and its shelf life. Always handle fruit as gently as possible, because the slightest bruise will start decay. Please also note that fruit picked wet rapidly rots, and that fruit kept with other strong-smelling items may become tainted. But if a little care is taken, your homegrown fruit, harvested at the right moment and lovingly ripened, will be beyond compare. See Chapter 9, page 185, for more on harvesting and storing.

The fruitcage, the backyard orchard, and the nut patch

Fruitcages Cage fruits are predominantly the soft fruits, the currants and berries, or bush and cane fruits which like the dappled shade. Birds, which live on the woodland's edge where most of these fruits are native, are the most likely cause of lost crops, so it is sensible to keep the most vulnerable in a netted cage. Netting draped over bushes can help protect fruit as this keeps some birds out, but is not really effective. Ready-made cages are expensive, but you can easily build your own. Once built, the roof-net is taken off for the winter to prevent snow build-up breaking the cage. Removing the top also allows birds in to eat overwintering pests, and storage of the net reduces weathering, so it lasts longer. However, I rarely bother—I simply shake off the odd layer of snow when it comes. Cherries are sometimes included in a fruit cage, but tend to make too much growth to be contained, though the newer dwarfing stocks ought now make this possible. Grapes demand the sunniest spots.

Orchard Although several fruit trees on dwarfing stocks could be fitted into almost any small garden, if you have the space tree fruits are always best grown in an orchard. If planted on half standard or standard with strong roots then an orchard can still be a play area, paddock, or wildlife meadow as well. If fruit quality is to be the highest, a fruitcage for each tree or the whole orchard becomes desirable, but this is rarely practical. When planning an orchard, put the tallest trees on the shady and windy sides, and the tenderer peaches and pears on the sunny and sheltered. Although planting in neat straight lines may seem excessively formal, it does allow for easier grass cutting. However, for modern small orchards

The blossoming of fruit trees is as beautiful as that of purely ornamental plants.

with dwarf trees or cordons the area will be more productive and easier to manage if it is heavily mulched instead. Those with very little space can still grow an orchard of trees by keeping them in containers. Indeed, orchard houses were greenhouses used in prior times just to bring on earlier and better crops of many common tree fruits, especially cherries.

Nut patch Nuts are different to fruits, because we eat the seed, not the covering. Nuts are big seeds which are very exhausting for the plant to make because they are rich in oils and nutrients. So they have a high dietary value to us, but of course that does not help the plant. The trade-off is that the plant "hopes" that if it produces a lot of tasty, edible nuts, some will escape the slaughter to be trampled underfoot or carried elsewhere and stashed, but never recovered—thus starting new colonies. Squirrels, rodents, and birds all hide nuts and there are plausible stories of attics filled with nuts popped singly through a knot hole for years. Most nut trees are wind pollinated and bear catkins so generally they do not have scented flowers and give little nectar to insects, but of course they are a rich source of pollen. Unfortunately, though nut trees are little work, most of them grow rather too large, which makes them difficult to protect or grow under nets or cover. Indeed, except as bonsai, nuts are almost impossible to keep constrained. Nuts are more reliable in warmer countries than the U.K. because they are rather susceptible to frost damage and prefer a hot summer and fall two years running—the first to ripen the wood and the second the nuts.

CULTURAL REQUIREMENTS AND CALENDRIAL INSTRUCTIONS

Soil and site As with almost any plant, better results in fruit growing come from a deep, rich moist soil full of organic material. So every effort should be made to improve it before planting as it is more difficult later! Equally important, the ground *must* be cleared of weeds! Consult Chapter 10, page 211, for methods. Top fruits need soils that are neither extremely acid nor alkaline. Apples prefer a slightly acid soil, and stone fruits, such as cherries and plums, like it more alkaline. Soft fruits generally do best in acid conditions, especially blueberries and cranberries, which thrive in peat bogs. Thus, dry soils especially over chalk will be unfavorable, particularly to pears, though apples may just succeed. Once established, grapes, hazels, and figs will grow in gravelly or chalky conditions, where other fruits would not be happy. Few plants other than relations of blueberries and cranberries will thrive in soil prone to water logging, so drainage may be necessary—or consider planting in raised beds or mounds of soil as a cunning alternative.

No fruits will do superbly in heavy shade, especially from large trees, and the root competition will make establishment and cropping poor. Light shade will not severely handicap most soft fruits, but they make sweeter fruits with more sun. Fruit grown on windy and exposed sites often suffers poor pollination, slow growth, early and excessive loss of blossom and leaves, and premature fruit drop. You can prevent these problems by erecting a windbreak. But don't go to the other extreme; stagnant air pockets—especially in hollows—encourage molds and mildews. If you have the space, productive windbreaks can be made from hazels, damsons, and cherry plums. Apart from birds, frost damage probably causes more loss of fruit than every other problem.

We cannot change our garden's climate, but we can improve the microclimate for each plant by putting them in the best place. Frost pockets are places that collect the coldest air which is dense and flows like water down to low-lying places. So they are unsuitable for growing strawberries, early-flowering fruits, and low bushes. Instead, grow taller forms, such as half-standards, to keep the flowers up out of the coldest air. Early-flowering fruits can be grown against walls where they are less likely to be damaged. If given further protection, in the form of a cloth or fine net, they will probably escape unharmed. Similarly, tree and bush crops can be saved by throwing some form of protective layer over them to stop the heat escaping to the night sky. Warm, sunny spots on walls, patios and in places with extra heat, such as near a boiler flue, should be saved for the most susceptible fruits like pears, peaches, and apricots. Soft fruit in a cage is often protected by the roof net and this can be augmented with an old sheet or even wet newspaper spread on top. Frost will also damage young fruitlets for a fortnight or so after pollination, so protect these whenever a frost is predicted.

Pollination In order to set and form fruit most plants need to be pollinated. Some figs do without pollen entirely and others produce malformed fruits, as do Conference pears. Where there are different varieties of the same fruit nearby, say within fifty paces, you may get away without ever considering pollination. But if you want to be sure of certain choice varieties you should also plant a suitable partner to act as a pollinator. Most widely grown varieties of bush and cane fruit are self-fertile, so problems rarely arise, but heavier crops usually result where several varieties are grown together.

With top fruit, more care is needed. Some popular tree fruits, such as Victoria plums, are self-fertile but again give better quality and heavier crops if cross-pollinated. In most cases you can choose two varieties that will pollinate each other, but there are exceptions. For example, planting just a Cox, or a Cox and a Bramley, which are not compatible, means no crop, but add a James Grieve and all become pollinated and fruit. Family trees partly solve this pollination problem by having compatible varieties grafted on the same roots, but these tend to grow lop-sidedly. Pollinating partners have to be compatible and be in flower together, so the biggest problems arise with very early- or late-flowering varieties. Some varieties are biennial bearers, that is, they produce crops every other year, so they are a bit tricky—if they don't flower, you lose not only their crop but

right

Grapevines are often best grown in large containers; they can be persuaded to fruit without taking over the entire garden.

below

Of all fruits, cherries most need a suitable pollinator.

that of the supposedly pollinated partner as well. Don't panic, a good garden center or nursery will indicate suitable pollinators for any proffered variety. Where a pollinator is required and no space is available you could try grafting a branch of a pollinator onto an existing tree. Alternatively, the wild forms of a fruit, such as crabapples, are usually excellent pollinators for the cultivated forms and can be grown in the hedgerow to save space where they are also sacrificial crops for the birds.

Rootstocks The type of root system a plant grows can affect your success with the way it grows more than the care you give it. The majority of cane and berry fruits are grown on their own roots. Fruit trees are generally grafted onto special rootstocks. Normally these are dwarfing rootstocks that prevent the tree growing as large as it would if grown on its own roots. Such trees need staking throughout their life and inevitably produce less yield per tree. For larger crops or more vigorous trees to cope with difficult soils, different stronger rootstocks may be preferable. Most trees sold for specific purposes, such as full standards for growing in orchards, are normally supplied with a suitable rootstock by the nursery. At the other end of the size scale, rootstocks for cordon training or growing in containers are very dwarfing. These include the rootstock M27 for apples, Quince C for pears, and Pixy or Colt for stone fruits. The exact type of rootstock ought to be shown on the label by reputable suppliers, so don't buy where you can't find out what type of rootstock has been used, and what effect you can expect.

Container growing Modern housing comes with small gardens yet with only a patio it is still possible to grow fruit. Many types of trees, soft fruit, and even vines are suitable for growing in containers. This cramps the root system and prevents them getting too big, and usually tends to bring them into fruit much earlier. Obviously, the total crop must be small and the plants need special attention. They will need watering regularly, possibly three or four times a day in summer. One advantage of container-grown fruit is that the whole pot can be taken under cover to prevent frost or bird damage, or to bring on earlier growth. Always use large containers—plastic garbage cans are ideal—fill them with a good organic potting compost. Choose a dwarfing rootstock and arrange some form of automatic watering system. Don't forget the need to pot up every couple of years, so rather than increase the size of container I start by only half-filling it, then I lift the lot up and add a layer underneath and repack around. Eventually, the container gets full and too heavy to move. At this stage, propagate and start again, planting the old one out if you have space.

Spacing and staking Spacing is most critical with fruit culture as it affects the quality by allowing more nutrients, light, and sun to each plant. Do not skimp. Give each plant more space than you think it needs and you

Good establishment and weed-free conditions are ensured for these soft fruit bushes by using old carpet as a mulch. In spring this is augmented with loose straw, which also makes it prettier.

will be surprisingly successful. With limited space you can squeeze them in, but you need to pay them more attention. Don't forget when spacing trees that the soil and site will affect their growth rate and space requirements. As a rough guide, I have given the planting distances in paces for the average-sized person—adjust for yourself accordingly.

With fruit trees you need to give each tree the spacing it requires according to the rootstock. This applies particularly to trained fruits and principally to apples which vary the most. Standard trees on the vigorous apple stocks M2, M25, and M111 will need to be at least seven to ten paces apart and need staking only the first year. Cordons, or those on the very dwarfing M27 and M9, will need to be just a pace or so apart and need permanent staking or wire supports. For medium-sized gardens, M26 and MM106 are probably best rootstocks to choose—plant at least four or five paces apart. They do not need staking once established, and grow vigorously enough so you can still use the space underneath. Stakes should support trees as low down as possible to ensure the development of a strong trunk. The tie should be wide, padded, firm, but with some give, adjustable and removable. Plastic string and wire are not acceptable alternatives to tree ties, but old tights and bicycle inner tubes are.

Grapevines do not need special rootstocks in the U.K., so they can be propagated from root cuttings—which strike very easily.

Propagation: replacement and replenishment Growing replacement plants is quite simple for most of the soft fruits, provided you can get cuttings from healthy bushes. Unfortunately, your own plants will probably need replacing because they have picked up disease and are not a source of suitable material. This is particularly so for blackcurrants, raspberries, and strawberries, which tend to suffer from virus diseases. As a general rule, eradicate any of these plants you inherit with a garden, and periodically replace old with new. Strawberries need to be replaced every third or fourth year, but you can root runners from healthy plants to get up to a dozen years from a batch before buying in new stock. Blackcurrants and raspberries need replacing after ten to fifteen years. The other currants and gooseberries last a couple of decades, and most of the tree fruits we plant will still be producing crops long after we are pushing up daisies.

If you want multiple plants of one variety of soft fruit, buy one good certified virus-free plant and take twice as many cuttings from it as you need. Hardwood cuttings of about a foot long, taken in the fall from healthy new growth, should produce excellent fruiting plants in under two years. Rub off the buds from the lower half of each cutting. Push the cuttings a hand's breadth deep and a foot apart into clean, gritty soil in the open ground on a seed, vegetable, or nursery bed. On heavy soils, force sharp sand into the bottom of a slit trench and plant the cuttings in this. Firm them really well. Keep them sheltered from the worst winds—cloche them during hard winters. Keep the soil weeded and moist and new plants will be ready to be moved out the following fall.

Blackcurrants are the easiest to raise from cuttings. Each plant is grown as a stool with many shoots from ground level, so do not rub off the buds on blackcurrant cuttings. Other currants and grapes are very easy too. Gooseberries fairly so. All the blackberry family and hybrids can be grown from the tips of the canes allowed to root into pots in late summer. Raspberries produce suckers all over the place, choose strong ones with fat underground buds and a mass of fibrous roots, transplant these in fall and cut them back to knee high.

Strawberry runners coming from clean, deflowered, vigorous plants are easily rooted into pots in early summer and can then be planted out in late summer to fruit well the following year. Don't bother trying to root cuttings from tree fruits—they do not take easily, and even if they do the resulting plants are not controlled by a dwarfing rootstock. It's also hardly worthwhile growing most common fruits from seed, because they take a long time and are not very good. Seedling raspberry, Japanese wineberry, and currant plants are less disappointing than most.

Above all, it is absolutely essential you use healthy plants for propagating, so avoid obviously dubious specimens and especially avoid old blackcurrants, raspberries, and strawberries as these are prone to more disease problems than most others. Remember not to plant your new fruit crop on exactly the same site as the old, because they are likely to suffer from replant disease (see page 205).

Companion plants It is essential to keep a clear circle of at least a pace or two around a tree or bush for the first few years, so it can establish without any competition. The bigger the mulched or weeded area the quicker the tree establishes. Having other plants nearby initially inevitably leads to poorer growth and lower, later yields. So don't plant companion plants until after the fruit has established. Companion plants can be of immense benefit, bringing in and maintaining larger populations of predators and pollinators. Rosemary, thyme and sage, lavender, chives, garlic, *Limnanthes douglasii*, *Convolvulus tricolor,* and nasturtiums are all of particular benefit to fruit trees and bushes. Red dead nettles and stinging nettles, docks, and thistles also help, but these are not so pretty. Traditionally, orchards were furnished with grass, alfalfa, and clover as companion crops, though pears were only grassed if overvigorous. Grassing down must never be done until the trees are well established anyway, then it is worthwhile for the appearance and reduced labor. The grass competes with the trees, but if the clippings are returned their fertility returns, and the sward prevents soil erosion. Orchards need cutting at least once a year to prevent shrubby weeds taking over. Grassing down increases the danger from spring frosts because bare soil keeps the air above warmer at night.

Planting See page 91 for general advice. Sprays of seaweed solution will be of immense benefit during the first year and should be done routinely at monthly intervals. Never let trees or bushes fruit in their first year, because this diverts energy from the roots where it is needed. Deflower them as soon as the petals fade, though it is permissible to allow one fruit only per tree or bush for identification purposes.

Training methods For the least effort try to grow most fruits as trees; either standards, half standards, or bushes. Pruning is minimal with only ingrowing, rubbing, and diseased growths needing to be removed. Big trees do take up a lot of space and are slightly slow to start producing, so for small areas or where many varieties are desired then go for dwarfed and trained forms of fruit. However, these require much more work and need permanent supports. They give large early returns and the quality of fruit is higher, but they cannot be as neglected without dire results.

Cordons are effectively one branch of a fruit tree grafted onto a dwarfing rootstock. They are trained at an angle to make more efficient use of space, but need posts and wires to support them all their life. They can be planted at close intervals allowing many different varieties in a short run, say, along the side of a path. Though each cordon produces much less than a bush or tree, they produce more per acre and the quality can be much better. Apples and pears are very suitable for cordon training as are red and white currants and gooseberries.

Espaliers have a vertical main stem off which are trained several horizontal tiers. They make very attractive forms for enhancing a wall or

It is possible to force a tree into almost any strict shape or form, but it is gentler and just as productive to train it more in the direction it wishes to grow. Use pruning to remove surplus congested young growth in summer, not to force some ideal onto the bare winter framework.

Fall-sown *Limnanthes douglasii* grown under gooseberries (above) protects the soil, feeds beneficial insects, and dies down as the fruit ripens. Scented herbs (right) confuse plant pests and feed beneficial insects, but are not too competitive to be grown under apples.

used as a screen. Step-over espaliers have only one low tier running parallel to the ground and a foot or so high. They are of most use in the smallest of gardens. Espalier treatment is suitable for most apples and pears, but many other tree fruits are more difficult to train this way and are easier as fans.

Fans have all the branches radiating from the top of a short trunk and can look very attractive, they are most suited to the stone fruits, which are difficult to train as espaliers. There are many other trained forms and shapes, such as gridirons, but these are rarely seen—so reading an old book on pruning is always interesting.

Forming the initial framework of trained fruit is not difficult and if left to the nurseryman will cost you more than buying unformed maiden trees. It is more satisfying to do it all yourself, but does take time and some thought. Generally, once the shape has been established, pruning is fairly simple. The main exception is trained stone fruits, which need serious reworking almost every year.

Winter pruning Usually done initially to form the shape of a tree as it stimulates replacement growth, but too often excessive winter pruning is done in place of summer. Remove crossing, rubbing, and dangerous, dead and unhealthy growths as soon as they are spotted—usually when the branches are bare. However, winter pruning is best avoided for the stone fruits, such as plums, as these may then be attacked by silver leaf disease. Winter pruning is worth the risk when major surgery is being carried out, because if it is performed during summer the tree may die of shock. Also, when vigor has been lost, winter pruning and feeding may stimulate new growths. Overly hard winter pruning may cause ill-placed replacement growths, such as "water" shoots seen in gardens where the saw and shears are used too often.

Summer pruning Often ignored, this is a far more useful and important method for looking after trained trees and soft fruit than winter pruning. It does not stimulate growth, but fruiting. Summer pruning is simply the removal of half to three quarters of each new shoot once midsummer is past. This allows air and light access and checks growth, encouraging the formation of fruit buds. However, where the plant is still being allowed to expand to fill space available then shoots going in the desired directions are not cut off. These may be shortened in winter to encourage side shoots to develop.

Soft fruit pruning is easier than for tree fruit and the plants are much quicker to respond to training, so they are ideal for gaining experience. Those grown as stools, such as black currants, are the simplest. Immediately after fruiting cut one third of all the branches back to ground level starting with the oldest stems. Raspberries, blackberries, and their hybrids are also normally grown as stools, with young growth being encouraged from ground level to replace the old on an annual basis. The oldest are cut away after fruiting to leave the new—this simultaneously removes most pest and disease problems. Tying these young canes down on either, or to one, side then allows the next year's new flush to grow straight up and keeps them clean of disease spores dropping from the older. I find bicycle inner tubes fitted with wire hooks are ideal for holding back new growth until I'm ready to tie it in.

The stone fruits, when trained, are treated the same way with constant removal and replenishment of young shoots coming from a central core frame. Red and white currants are very forgiving and can be grown in almost any form imaginable, as can gooseberries, which make for easier

left

Grapevines need both summer and winter pruning if they are to be controlled and fruitful. Fortunately, they are very forgiving and any errors can be corrected within a year or so.

below

If you want only large perfect fruits like this 'Winston,' thin your apples early, hard, and often.

picking when well trained. All of these require their young growths cutting back by half to three quarters in summer and then again by a bit more in winter. They are best pruned to form an open goblet shape, or failing that as bushes on short legs, so that the sun can penetrate and air can circulate, which helps keep them disease free. If you want to grow prize berries, grow them as cordons and feed the soil heavily.

Inducing regular fruiting You may find the situation where your trees are established and growing well, but they fail to flower and fruit. If there are strongly growing vertical branches then attach lines near the tips and pull them gently down from the vertical. This checks the sap flow and induces fruiting more effectively than pruning. The branches can be kept bent by tying on weights. A plastic bottle part-filled with water is ideal because it is adjustable.

If flowers are prolific, but none sets, suspect the lack of a suitable pollinator and "borrow" some sprays in bloom from friends' trees and try pollinating with these. If any of the trials set fruit then graft a branch on.

Some fruit, especially apples, are biennial bearers, cropping only in alternate years. To get fruit every year, remove half or more of the fruits during the "on" years, so that the tree is not exhausted; then it does not need a year off. Indeed, almost all the tree fruits, gooseberries, and grapes will give bigger and better fruit if they are thinned every year. Fruit thinning is also the simplest way of improving the quality as the diseased and pest-ridden fruits can be removed and destroyed before the malady spreads. Thinning is best done after midsummer, but before fruits have started to swell significantly and it should be done ruthlessly. The plants can afford to give us plenty of fruit flesh to eat, it is only sugar and water—it is the seeds inside that exhaust the plant, taking proteins, fats, and minerals. Reducing the number of fruits reduces the numbers of seeds the tree has to produce. It will still give the same *weight* of fruit, but each one will be bigger. Thinning twice is better still. Make the second thinning a month after the first to leave only perfect, well-positioned fruits. Three times thinning is worth the effort because the thinnings are by then large enough to use in the kitchen.

Annual maintenance Visit every staked tree and check the tie regularly, at least twice a year. Also firm the ground around each new tree after hard frosts. Hygiene is essential, remove all diseased material as soon as it is spotted and burn or compost it, especially diseased fruits. Also inspect the fruit store and remove any infected material. All fruit trees and bushes benefit from being banded with sticky tree bands to catch the wingless pests that climb trunks to lay eggs. You need to band the stakes, posts and wires as well. Top up mulches as fruit trees and bushes benefit immensely from these, and at least every third year they should be given sieved garden compost. During the winter, occasionally rake mulches

and compost aside for a day or two so that birds can get at pests overwintering underneath. I find a monthly spraying of the orchard and fruitcage with seaweed solution from early spring to midsummer is beneficial because it promotes vigor and disease resistance.

Watering This is absolutely vital for fruits in containers which need watering three times a day in hot summers. Generally, watering is not as necessary for fruit as for vegetables, but it is always advantageous in dry years, especially for soft fruit, because two crops are threatened—this year's fruit and next year's buds. Fruits growing in borders next to walls or in dry corners will benefit the most from watering.

The critical thing with any plant is to water before it suffers or wilts. Fruitlets often drop in late spring as the soil dries out, so apply mulches early and water well before the plant shows any distress. Warm water will soak into dry soil better than cold, and ice cubes melt so slowly they will wet even really dried out peat. Never water in dribs and drabs; give an occasional good long soaking instead. However, take care not to waterlog plants, especially when growth is slow, since this can starve their roots of air. Water well before the fruits start to swell—do not leave it too late or the skins harden as growth slows and then the fruits split when growth resumes. Given the choice, water early in the day rather than later, and rainwater is much better than water from the tap. This is more important for fruit growing in containers, as rainwater contains less dissolved salts which tend to build up in container compost as the water evaporates.

Plums overcrop and need ruthless thinning. Make sure heavy crops receive heavy watering! This is that old favorite, 'Victoria.'

Cultivation for perfection

Here is my fruit-by-fruit guide to producing perfect crops. I have noted any significant pests, diseases, and treatments; the best methods of harvesting and storage; and my recommended, tastiest, most luscious gourmet choices.

Fruitcage fruits

Black currants Black currants are one of the easiest fruits to grow successfully, though sadly they are banned in parts of the U.S.A. as they are host to white pine blister rust. They are quite distinct from the other types of *Ribes*, though often bundled in with red currants. They fruit on young wood, not old, and have dark purple, almost black, berries with an unforgettable aroma, similar to that of the foliage and stems.

Black currants are self-fertile, but it is worth having several varieties to spread the flowering and ensure a crop even when there are late frosts. Having several varieties also spreads the cropping and picking through summer and fall. Although closely related to redcurrants, blackcurrants need a much richer, moister heavier soil to do really well. Nonetheless, they are easy and will crop in even quite adverse conditions and in moderate to heavy shade.

Black currants are unique in that they must be planted deep. They are grown as a stool as they fruit best on young wood—much like raspberries. Plant them at least two paces apart. Pruning consists of cutting out the wood that has fruited leaving the younger shoots, this can be done brutally with one third to half of each bush being razed to the ground each year. Make sure they are well mulched with copious amounts of compost or well-rotted farmyard manure. Seaweed sprays will also be of great benefit and help ward off mildew attacks.

Mildew is more common in dry years and prevented by heavy watering and thick mulches. Many of the newer varieties, such as 'Alder' and 'Tisel,' are almost completely resistant. Black currants do not suffer as quickly as many fruits from bird attacks, but need to be netted. Aphids curl the tips in early summer, but cause no significant damage. Big bud is a more serious problem. Inspect the plants in midwinter and pick off

A fruitcage is more necessary for strawberries than for blackcurrants.

any big round buds you notice. Burn them to reduce reinfection by the microscopic mites that cause the disfigurement. However, it is not the mites themselves, but a virus they carry called reversion which really devastates black currant crops. So if yields from your plants drop for no apparent reason and will not return after heavy feeding, grub up all the bushes and grow new ones. Stinging nettles grown nearby may benefit black currants.

Epicurean attentions Black currants hang well on the plant for several weeks if the birds cannot get at them. They have very high levels of vitamin

C, freeze well and the jam is the easiest of all to make. I pick the bulk roughly, complete with sprigs, and make a jelly to which I later add the best berries.

Bob's gourmet choices New varieties such as the large berried 'Ben Sarek' (midseason), 'Ben Lomond' (late) and the tasty 'Ben Nevis' (late) are numerous and generally more productive with better disease resistance than old favorites. 'Laxton's Giant' (midseason) is still one of the biggest, 'Wellington XXX' is reputed to be the best flavored and 'Seabrook's Black' (midseason) is supposedly big bud resistant. The 'Jostaberry' is a much larger hybrid, more like a thornless gooseberry. It bears heavy crops of large black currant-flavored berries, see Gooseberries. And if you like black currant jam a lot then try the chokeberry, *Aronia melanocarpa* 'Viking,' an ornamental shrub which produces black currant-like fruits rich in vitamin C, and with a delicious piney taste once jellied.

Red and white currants These are very productive and easy fruits to grow, but are often neglected because they are too sharp to eat many raw—though I see they are currently making a comeback as garnishes. Red currants respond best to a cool, well-mulched soil. They do not need as

Red currant juice adds a delicious tartness to jams, jellies, juices and summer drinks.

rich conditions as black currants or raspberries and will grow in partial shade and quite happily on cold walls—even cropping well on a shady wall. Although highly productive, the birds love them, so they must be netted. They often get apparently disastrous attacks of leaf blistering aphis which puckers and colors the shoot tips and leaves, but it never affects the yields and is cleared away with the summer pruning. Fortunately, these currants are very amenable to pruning and training and can be fitted in anywhere, though, as bushes, they need to be at least two paces apart. Red currants may benefit from stinging nettles grown nearby, but the picker will curse, and *Limnanthes douglasii* is beneficial groundcover once the bushes are established.

Epicurean attentions A bit sharp raw, red currants are delicious cooked with other fruits and the juice makes other jams and jellies set. Their jelly is often preferred because they are pippy. They ripen early in summer, but if protected from pests and wet weather will hang on and remain usable and become sweeter until late fall.

Bob's gourmet choices 'Jhonkheer Van Tets' is my favorite, but all red

currants are amenable and productive and vary little in taste, acidity or season—though this may cover three months in a good year. 'Red Lake Red Currant' is the most hardy. The fruit on 'Wilder' are well spaced, so hang well. 'Primus' and 'White Imperial' are white currants which are sweeter, but generally poorer croppers than the reds.

Gooseberries Homegrown gooseberries are different to the green marbles sold in stores. If well grown, the berries can be as big and sweet as plums and eaten as dessert. It is said "God gave us gooseberries for where grapes will not grow" and it is true. A good gooseberry, well ripened, is a huge drop of nectar in a skin—available in red, green, white, or yellow, each with a different flavor. A very forgiving crop, gooseberries can be trained in any form imaginable, but are easiest as goblet shaped bushes on a short leg. They need moisture and a rich soil and will tolerate some shade, but detest hot, dry spots. Tomatoes and broad beans growing nearby are reputed to aid them and I always grow them with *Limnanthes douglasii* as groundcover.

They can get American gooseberry mildew on the tips in dry conditions, which may spread onto the berries leaving them suitable only for jamming. Avoid this happening by keeping the plants well pruned, mulched, and watered. Sodium bicarbonate sprays and sulfur-based ones (which burn the foliage on some varieties) are available to organic growers. Occasionally, often in the third or so year after planting, gooseberries suffer damage from sawfly caterpillars. First appearing as a host of wee holes in a leaf, they move on to stripping the bush. Vigilance and early action prevents serious damage—the caterpillars can be killed with a spray of derris. Better still is to put a sheet underneath, and shake the bush—the caterpillars simply fall off and are easily collected. You can grow gooseberries without nets, but once they ripen they need protecting from the birds, which will also attack the buds in winter. So when you are pruning, leave the gooseberries until last.

Epicurean attentions When you pick a dessert gooseberry, suck the contents out of the skin and then discard it. Birds, mice, and especially wasps steal the fruit once they're ripe. If protected, the fruit mellow and hang on till late summer becoming sweeter and fruitier, but only if the weather stays dry. Green gooseberry jam is exceptionally good—collect young green fruits in early summer, thinning them at the same time, and cook them at a low temperature or the jam will turn red. Gooseberries freeze well and are easier to top, tail, and de-whisker once frozen.

Bob's gourmet choices Grow them as cordons and try a dozen different ones. The best varieties are still available from specialists. I love 'Jahn's Prairie' a large red, 'Captivator' an early yellow and most of all 'Hinnomaki' a superbly sweet white. 'Poorman' is reputedly the best dual-purpose, and a new culinary variety 'Invicta' is probably worthwhile where one can be fitted in, with 'Colossal' a close second.

Jostaberries and Worcesterberries are both very similar to gooseberries, but are larger, needing to be spaced three paces apart. Their fruits resemble a cross between a gooseberry and a black currant. Jostaberries have a drooping habit, crop heavily, and are thornless, so a good choice. Coastal black gooseberries are very mildew resistant, but have vicious thorns which make them excellent for boundaries. They sucker wildly and the trailing stems root at the tips, making an impenetrable thicket that means the fruit is practically unpickable—though it makes delicious jams and pies.

Strawberries These are probably the most rewarding of all fruits—there is nothing like the taste of your own first fresh-picked strawberry, or the second, or the third . . .

Strawberries need a very rich soil, full of humus, and benefit from slow-release sources of phosphorus, such as bonemeal. The site must be free of

A good gooseberry is impossible to buy, yet very easy to grow.

weeds and prepared well with additions of well-rotted manure or compost. To get the heaviest crops, give them seaweed meal dressings, too. Strawberries can be grown in the vegetable plot, which also helps give that soil a clean break in rotation. The more space you give them the better they do and the less work they will be! A stride each way is the sensible minimum. Strawberries must have bird protection—use nets or jam jars if a cage is not available. Slugs and ground beetles can also eat quite a few fruits. The worst problem, though, is wet weather when the fruit is ripening which not only causes mold (botrytis), but lowers their sweetness. By growing several varieties you can spread the cropping and minimize this risk. Cloching once the fruits are green is an alternative or, if used from late winter, will bring the crops forward by several weeks. Strawing up once the fruits are swelling helps keep the berries clean and infections to a minimum, as does removing and

destroying any moldy fruits that do develop, preferably before the mold goes "fluffy." Regular spraying with seaweed up until flowering will make them sturdy and help prevent infections.

After fruiting has finished, tidy the plants, shearing back surplus runners and dead leaves. In winter, tidy them again removing old straw as well. Aphid attacks can be controlled with soft soap sprays. Any sickly, mottled or odd looking plants should be pulled up and burned to prevent virus problems building up. It is necessary to replace one third of your plants every year with new ones on new ground to get continuous and consistent cropping year after year. Ideally, grow replacements from your own stock for about five to ten years, and then buy new virus-free stock and start again. Choose quality plants for propagation and remove all flowers. Root half a dozen good runners from each plant. The first plantlets on early runners are best.

Everyone ought to grow some strawberries, and the more sun they get the tastier they will be.

Start new beds in late summer or early fall to allow them to establish, and then they can crop well the next summer. Late fall or spring plantings should be deflowered the first summer, to build up their strength for a massive crop the next.

I do not like those vertical growing containers with many holes—they have too little compost and need far too much watering to be worthwhile. Strawberries can be grown in walls built of hollow concrete blocks or car tires filled with compost if given sufficient watering. This works well, especially for early crops if facing the sun. The most ingenious method is to grow them in pots or troughs up in the eaves of a greenhouse. They get full light, fresh warm air, are away from the slugs, and easy to pick as they cascade.

Seed-raised strawberries are generally poor fruiters, apart from alpine strawberries. These do not runner, are easy from seed, but only live a few years and have tiny fruits. Alpine strawberries are very tolerant of soils and sites and will grow almost anywhere, the birds do not eat them as readily and when ripe the flavor is divine. They give only a few fruits at a time, but carry on fruiting from early summer till late fall. Pick them weekly and freeze the fruits until you have enough to make jam which tastes too good to be true, or use them as garnishes.

Epicurean attentions Strawberries freeze easily, but lose their texture on thawing. However, if they are partially thawed they are delicious! Of course, they make wonderful jam. To make the jam set, add red currant, white currant or lemon juice. If you want strawberries to keep fresh for longer, pick them carefully in the morning once they are dry, leaving a bit of stem on and without touching the fruit.

Bob's gourmet choices 'Earliglow' is the standard by which others are judged but 'Sparkle' is different and very tasty. Many modern varieties have fair flavor, but avoid those which are claimed to freeze or jam well! Most varieties fruit at much the same time in early summer, but fall fruiting strawberries continue to the first frost. Their fruits tend to be less sweet from lack of sun, but are delicious anyway. The best variety for flavor is 'Raritan' which will fruit heavily if the first flower trusses are removed. 'Tristar' is another good fruiter with exceptional flavor.

Raspberries Despite being the easiest fruit to grow, raspberries are little grown as garden fruits. They are not common in commerce predominantly because the fruits perish so rapidly. Raspberries vary considerably in size and are usually red, with yellow ones now on sale again. In good varieties the conical fruit pulls off the plug easily, leaving a hole. Some are less easy and have soft, thin-skinned berries which may be damaged.

Raspberries are very productive and the flowers are loved by bees. They prefer cool, moist conditions, so do wonderfully in Scotland. Although they can be grown in most soils, they do best if given a moist, rich, neutral or acidic soil, or at least copious quantities of compost and very thick mulches. They do not like the dry conditions against walls, but can be grown on cool, shady ones with a moist root run. With hot, dry summers and wetter falls, the fall-fruiting varieties are more productive than the common summer fruiters, especially if grown on drier sites.

Summer raspberries are pruned after fruiting by cutting out the old canes leaving the new to grow on. It helps to have thinned these by mid-summer to a hand breadth or so apart. Fall fruiters are simpler still, all canes are cut to the ground in late winter and again the young canes

Raspberries are productive, and easier to pick if the canes are bent down.

benefit from thinning before midsummer leaving the strongest to fruit later. Raspberries produce canes between three and six feet long which can be trained almost horizontal, so they do not need tall post and wire supports. Weeding must be done carefully because of their shallow roots, so thick mulching is almost essential.

As with most fruit, birds are the major cause of lost crops—no protection means no fruit! The raspberry beetle can be controlled with mulches raked aside in winter to allow birds to eat the pupae, or if necessary by using permitted sprays such as derris just after most of the flowers have finished but before the fruits start to swell. These maggots are rarely a problem with fall fruiters. Virus diseases may appear, mottling the leaves with yellow and the plants become less productive. Replacing these with new virus-free stock on a new site is the only practical solution. Intervenal yellowing is caused by alkaline soils—it goes if you use monthly seaweed solution sprays with added magnesium sulfate. Adding compost and a deeper mulch will also help. Raspberries reputedly benefit from tansy, garlic, marigolds, and strawberries grown close by, but not underneath them.

Epicurean attentions Pick gently leaving the plug, if it won't come easily do not force it! They do not keep for long if they are wet and less still if kept warm. If you want to keep them longest, cut the fruiting stalks with scissors and do not touch the fruits. They must be processed or eaten within a matter of hours as they are one of the least durable or transportable fruits. Those sold commercially are the toughest and obviously not homegrown! Raspberries make tasty jam, especially mixed with red currant juice, and freeze well.

Bob's gourmet choices New varieties of raspberry are almost the only ones available and they are soon replaced by others at a great rate. I still like the almost obsolete but tasty 'Latham.' The 'Boyne,' 'Canby,' and 'Caroline' have all been rated as well flavored.

I also love the yellow raspberries— these are less vigorous, with paler leaves than the red types and naturally tend towards fall fruiting. Among the yellow varieties, 'Golden Everest' is superb with richly flavored soft sweet berries that lack the sharpness of many reds. 'Anne' and 'Kiwi Gold' are other fall fruiters. Seedling raspberries are often poor performers, but have excellent flavor.

Blackberries and their hybrids Wild blackberries vary enormously from plant to plant; there is no single native bramble or blackberry but hosts of them. Certainly any blackberry found near enough to people to be picked is a hybrid and you have to select carefully to get the best tasting ones. Grown in the garden, blackberries are productive, but never seem as tasty or as good as the wild ones—so don't waste the space when wild bushes are accessible.

More worthwhile growing are the various crosses made between blackberries and raspberries. All of these different berries prefer the same rich, well-mulched soil of the woodland edge, but can often fruit well on poor soils—even in moderate shade or on a north wall. All are

pruned much the same as raspberries, cutting out the old and tying in the new canes each year. Obviously the more vigorous growers need more wires for support, which must be strongly attached to a wall or stout posts. Vigorous and self-fertile, the only common problem is birds and this is particularly true for tayberries which never even get halfway to ripe unless netted! Modern thornless versions of these berries are often less well flavored and poorer croppers than the thorny originals, but they are much more comfortable to live with in small gardens.

Blackberries benefit from tansy or stinging nettles nearby and they make a good companion and sacrificial crop for grapevines.
Epicurean attentions All these berries rot very quickly once picked, so jam or freeze them as soon as possible. Don't eat the fruits after the frosts arrive as they taste poorer. Blackberries stewed with apples, strained and sweetened make a delicious syrup for diluting as a refreshing drink.
Bob's gourmet choices Few compare with 'Illini Hardy,' the biggest and toughest—it could stop a runaway tank! It is ideal for keeping out

Loganberries crop well and are good for jam.

unwanted visitors when planted along boundaries or trained over a fence and is highly productive. However, it needs a lot of space—at least three or four paces each way. 'Kiowa' fruits earlier and tastes better, but the canes are not as thick or prolific, so they are more controllable. 'Triple Crown' is probably the best tasting thornless blackberry but crops rather too late for colder regions. 'Chester' is a new variety that is thornless, tasty, and early.

Boysenberries are large, well-flavored blackberries, but tend to make a lot of growth with disappointingly light crops.

Loganberries are crosses between raspberries and blackberries, the only one still worth growing is called LY654 which has a good flavor, unusual with a thornless variety.

Tayberries are like improved, sweeter loganberries, but with a much richer flavor—definitely the best of the family. They do better in light shade than full sun, and will even do well on a north wall.

Japanese wineberries are orange-red

and tiny, but the flavor is delicious and thirst quenching. Children love them, and they are best eaten fresh. The canes are bristly, not thorny, and a lovely russet color, and the leaves are attractive, making Japanese wineberries eminently suitable for an ornamental area.

Blueberries, bilberries, cranberries, and cowberries Long popular in the United States, the blueberry (*Vaccinium corymbosum*) is now widely cultivated. The cranberry (*V. oxycoccus*) is closely related and similar apart from the color of the berries. These need no pruning and rarely suffer much from pests or diseases but need moist acid conditions and although self-fertile will fruit better if different varieties are grown nearby. They need to be planted about a pace or two apart. They are all ericaceous and make excellent groundcover between rhododendrons and azaleas. But do not even think about growing them for crops unless you have genuine acid soil and almost waterlogged conditions, say by a pond or stream.
Epicurean attentions The purple berries of blueberries are delicious in tarts, muffins or made into jelly. Cranberries are invariably used as a sauce for turkey.
Bob's gourmet choices 'Berkeley,' 'Blue Crop,' and 'Earliblue' are the easiest blueberries to source. 'Northblue' is reckoned best. For cranberry fruit grow the American *V. macrocarpon* 'McFarlin' or 'Ben Lear' which have better flavor than *V. oxycoccus*. The cowberry *V. vitis* 'Idaea' has even less merit.

Grapevines These are among the most ornamental and decorative of all plants and easily trained to fit into almost any sunny place. Especially attractive leaf colors in fall make the crop almost a bonus. Yet grapevines are highly productive and tolerant of most soil, except very wet ones, and should not be overfed as this

'Riesling Sylvaner' (left) is reliable for white wine and Seibel 13053 (right) for red.

produces growth instead of fruit. They do best against a wall or on wires over a patio, but where space is short they can be grown in large pots which can be stood outside most of the time, just moved under cover during hard frosts and while in fruit. Earlier crops can also be gained by taking pot-grown grapevines into a warm place in late winter, which brings their fruiting forward by months. Grapes can be used to cover almost any sized or shaped area inside or out with formal training, or just left to ramble over trees and sheds—though then the fruit is all eaten by the birds.

Vines are so vigorous they need hard summer pruning to control them even if in pots. The method of pruning under cover is given on page 181 and applies to most vines indoors or out. Grapevines have many other specialized pruning methods, such as Guyot, many of which are more akin to pruning cordon raspberries or black currants and these are more applicable outdoors in warmer climates than the U.K.

Grapes are self-fertile and no problem—even under cover I've never seen a bad set, but they are supposed to need hand pollination. Thinning will prevent grapes overcropping, especially in the early years. Thin out the number of bunches to one every couple of feet or so before they swell, but do not bother to thin out the grapes in the bunches as this is tedious.

The most troublesome pests are birds, flies, and wasps. They are defeated only by netting or covering the ripening bunches with stockings, paper or net bags. However, in wet years this may cause the fruit to rot. The best protection is to grow the vines in a cage or in containers that can be moved under cover when the fruit begins to ripen.

Some varieties are prone to mildew aggravated by dry conditions at the roots and stagnant air. This can be relieved by more open pruning, mulching, and with preventative seaweed sprays. Where outbreaks occur you can also use sulfur or copper spray if necessary. Where permissible, sodium bicarbonate solution may be used to stop mildew. Other diseases are rare in the U.K., though the fruit is prone to rot in wet years.

What is most important is to get a suitable variety of grape. 'Black Hamburg,' commonly on sale, is completely unsuitable outside in the northern U.S. but is excellent in a heated greenhouse or conservatory, or out of doors in warmer parts of North America or Australia and of course southern Europe.

A warm wall will always produce better grapes than the open garden, but even in the open you can grow some grapes in most of the U.K.—and anywhere warmer. These can make good juice for drinking, even if they are poor eating. The time of ripening varies from year to year, but usually from late summer under cover and early fall outdoors.

Grapes have been thought to be inhibited by laurels, radish, and cabbages since classical times and aided by blackberries, hyssop, and mustard. Outdoors, many pests are controlled through good garden hygiene and very effectively by keeping chickens underneath—except when the fruit is ripening. *Epicurean attentions* Without doubt grapes are best eaten fresh. Although the bunches look nice cut off entire for the table, the season can be extended by picking the ripest fruits from each bunch, which are thus judiciously thinned and the later grapes left to ripen till all are used up. When frost is likely, bunches can be cut when ripe with a stem which is inserted in a bottle of water. This will keep them fresh for many weeks if left in a cool place. Trim back the stem and change water weekly. Grapes will jam or jelly, but do not freeze well—they juice easily which can be frozen. Of course, they can be turned into wine.

Bob's gourmet choices 'Canadice' is a light cropper of rose-colored berries which are superb. It needs a wall to be grown north of southern England or can be grown in a pot or under cover. It dislikes lime-rich soil, but is so tasty it's worth it. 'Villard Blanc' and 'Swenson White' are dual-purpose whites, that crop reliably for juice or wine. The hybrids are by far the best croppers and most disease resistant, 'Beta,' 'Freedonia,' 'Prairie Star,' and 'Valiant' produce masses of bunches which make good red wine or juice. The muscadine grape 'Mortensen' crops well and easily, but its distinct texture and flavor is not to everyone's taste. 'Jupiter' is the best outdoor dessert grape, a consistent bearer of large, luscious, sweet black grapes good for juice or wine.

Orchard fruits, top or tree fruits

Apples are easily stored for many months and can be eaten raw, cooked in many ways or turned into juice or cider. However, every fall enormous quantities of apples are left unwanted to rot. So if you have a small garden, think about scrounging apples from other people and grow other fruits. The apples that will be most valuable where space is limited are the extra early varieties, late keepers, and those with exquisite flavor.

Most apples can be grown as cordons at a pace or less apart to squeeze many varieties into a small space, and as espaliers at five paces apart to give high-quality fruit. However, some known as tip bearers, such as 'Jonagold' and 'Northern Spy,' are better grown as rarely pruned dwarf bushes.

Apples are not fussy and do well most anywhere, though very wet sites may encourage scab and canker. Pollinating partners are best provided by growing several varieties because many are incompatible. A crabapple will pollinate most others in flower at the same time. Apples suffer minor infestations of many pests and diseases, but as they crop so heavily there is nearly always plenty of good fruit especially if the poor ones are removed during successive thinnings.

Apply sticky tree bands at the end of summer and keep them touched up all year. Holes in the fruits are usually caused by one of two pests: codling moth or apple sawfly. Codling moth generally makes holes in the core of the fruit, pushing frass out the flower end. Control them with corrugated cardboard band traps, pheromone traps, permitted sprays as the blossom sets, and good

Apples, like most fruits, color best where the sun reaches them. This 'Blenheim Orange,' one of the best dual-purpose apples, is a prime example.

garden hygiene. The other hole maker is apple sawfly, which bores narrow tunnels, emerging anywhere; they may then eat into another or even a third fruit. They are best controlled through good hygiene—removing and destroying affected apples during thinning. Permitted sprays may be used after flowers set, and running poultry underneath an orchard is also effective.

Most newer varieties are scab resistant; old ones get scabby patches on the fruit which are related to blisters and blotches on twigs and leaves. Prune these out to allow more air and light inside the tree canopy. Mulch and feed to stimulate growth, and spray monthly with seaweed solution. This will also discourage the canker "ulcers" often found on poor growers.

Brown, rotten patches on apples are caused by bruising or damage that is infected by spores that overwinter on stems and in the soil. Remove all mummified apples left on the tree after leaf fall, as these are the worst source of reinfection. Hinder these by mulching and give the tree seaweed sprays. White woolly patches are just a type of aphid and can be killed with soft soap or brushed off. It is believed that nasturtiums growing around the tree eventually persuade woolly aphids to depart. Fireblight appears as brown, withered flowers and leaves, prune affected stems out and burn them to prevent it spreading. Apples are strongly affected by replant disease, a symptomatic reluctance to grow near where an established tree is or has been—so replacements must be planted somewhere else.

Apples are benefited by alliums, especially chives, and penstemon growing nearby which are thought to prevent sawfly as well as woolly aphids. Stinging nettles nearby benefit the trees and when dried to make hay mats they help stored fruits keep longer. Remember, though, that despite all their apparent woes most

apple trees just go on giving crops year, after year, after year.

Epicurean attentions 'Early McIntosh' keeps a week or two, but most early apples will not keep a day and are only a pleasure eaten off the tree. The windfalls can be juiced, puréed, and frozen, though. Midseason and late keepers should be left until they just start to drop, unless hard frosts are likely or bird damage becomes too severe. Pick them carefully on a dry day. The fruits must be perfect and the wee stalk (pedicel) must remain attached for them to store. Use a cupped hand and gently lay them in a tray—traditionally padded with dry hay and nettles. As this goes moldy in the damp, use crumpled or shredded newspaper instead. However, if the apples are individually wrapped in paper they keep much longer. Do not store early varieties with lates nor near pears, onions, garlic, or potatoes.

The kumoi, juicy like a pear, crunchy like an apple.

Bob's gourmet choices For the earliest to eat off the tree, choose 'Milton' and 'Early McIntosh,' for late keepers you must have 'Ashmead's Kernel,' 'Bancroft,' 'Sweet Sixteen,' and 'Tydeman's Red' (the last pair need hard thinning to grow fruit to any size). For outstanding midseason flavor, choose 'Joyce,' 'Norda,' 'Egremont Russet,' 'Purdy,' and 'Davey.' 'Bramley's Seedling' grows too large, and I reckon 'Parkland' and 'Redwell' are much better cookers anyway.

Unless you are willing to endure the scrappy growth and poor crop to get the quality, flavor, and texture, then never grow 'Cox's Orange Pippin.' Very similar and much more successful are 'Sunset' and other Cox derivatives. True Cox's have loose seeds that you can hear when the

apple is shaken. Some of the newer varieties also have taste—I'm impressed by 'Empire,' 'Jonagold,' 'MacCoun,' 'Gala,' and 'Spartan.' Even a 'Golden Delicious' doesn't taste "old and suspicious" when grown organically at home. It's a bit prone to scab, though.

Pears Growing the finest pear is a more demanding and worthwhile task than for most other fruits, but they are beautiful in blossom so they enhance any area, especially when trained. Pears need a fairly rich soil, but it is moisture that is most important. They will not fruit well, in terms of quality or quantity, if dry at their roots, so always mulch them heavily and don't allow grass underneath because pears cannot cope with the competition.

As bushes at four or five paces apart on Quince A rootstock pears are compact and will crop with little attention. In the North late frosts often damage the blossoms and young fruitlets, so most varieties are best grown as espaliers on a sheltered wall. 'Flemish Beauty' and 'Herman Last' will crop well, and they also respond well to cordon training on a Quince C rootstock. Growing several varieties in this way will ensure pollination and spread the eating season. After all, there's not much you can do with a big tree full of ripe pears. Most pears need pollinating partners, though some such as 'Manning Miller' are self-fertile, but give better crops if cross-pollinated. 'Nova,' 'Seckle,' and 'Honeysweet' are also partly self-fertile.

With pears there are fewer pests and diseases to worry about than with apples. Leaf blackening in spring is usually from harsh winds, but if the flowers and leaves wither and go brown it may be fireblight which must be cut out and burned before it spreads. Leaf blistering is caused by tiny mites. This pest was traditionally controlled with a lime sulfur wash, but this is no longer available. I find soft soap sprays work instead. Sometimes the fruitlets blacken and drop, if these have maggots inside it's pear midge.

A fine pear like this 'Improved Fertility' is a gourmet treat that needs careful ripening.

Collect the fruitlets up and burn them and lay heavy mulches which can be raked aside in winter to expose the pests' pupae to birds, or run chickens underneath to eat them.

Epicurean attentions Early- and mid-season pears are best picked just as the first start to fall. If left on the tree too long they go woolly. Pears can be picked more underripe than most fruits and will ripen slowly if kept cool, faster when warm, but keep them humid or they'll shrivel. Don't pick unless they come off easily, and handle them more gently than explosives. Watch them carefully while ripening because they go over in a matter of hours.

Late pears need to be left until bird damage is too great, then picked *with a stalk*, and kept in the cool and dark for a few months—they will then ripen up rapidly when brought into the warm.

Do not wrap pears with paper as with apples and never store the two fruits near one another because the flavor of each will be tainted. Pear juice is difficult to press as they are sour underripe and like toothpaste once ripe. Good pear cider is much more difficult to make than apple and really requires the proper perry pears, so be warned.

Bob's gourmet choices Many old and interesting cooking pears can be found, but I don't recommend them because dessert varieties can be used for cooking too. 'Bartlett,' also known as 'Williams' Bon Chrétien' (early/midseason), was widely grown for preserving and is an excellent table fruit, though prone to scab. Without peer, the best dessert pear is 'Beurre Gifford' (late season). No other is as sweet and aromatic—just dissolving in the mouth. It can reach a large size and weight, but only if trained on a warm wall.

Excellent midseason choices are 'Clark,' 'David,' 'Golden Spice,' and 'John.' 'Jubilee' is very hardy and crops heavily and regularly.

Other superb pears for late in the

season are 'Flemish Beauty' and 'Potomac,' which keep into the New Year. There are hundreds of old and many new varieties of which 'Magness,' 'Moonglow,' and 'Buerre Bosc' have good flavor and are worth considering.

Quinces and medlars These all form very decorative, compact trees with big apple-blossom like flowers. There are two sorts of quince: *Cydonia*, which are ancient fruit-trees producing rock-hard fruit; and *Chaenomeles* or Japanese quince, which have smaller and even harder fruits on bushy, spiny shrubs, that are frequently seen in the flower garden for their brilliant red blossom in late winter. Medlars are pretty wee trees with contorted branches, large leathery leaves that color well in fall, and a strange fruit that looks like a huge rose hip or a distorted pear.

All these odd fruits are self-fertile and suffer virtually no pests or diseases. They are tolerant of most soils and sites, though do best on moist ones and benefit from a wall or shelter in the north of Britain. One tree will produce enough fruit for a family; plant any more three or four paces apart and they will need almost no attention other than harvesting.
Epicurean attentions Quinces cannot be eaten raw though they make very tasty jellies. They will store well and give off an aromatic scent that will fill a kitchen, and taint other foods. Included with apple or pear dishes, they impart a delicious spicy aroma and add texture as they keep their shape when cooked. The medlar fruit is only eaten once "bletted." This involves picking the fruit as ripe as possible and storing them in a frost-free place. When they go soft, almost rotten, the pulp is mixed with cream, liqueurs, and honey as a treat—since trying this delicacy I've dug up my tree and burned it.
Bob's gourmet choices 'Boyer's' and 'Harran' are the best *Cydonia* quinces, others are very similar. 'Van Deman'

The medlar is an odd fruit, but the tree's fall color is superb.

and 'Royal' are reckoned the tastiest medlars.

Cherries Years of breeding have produced the modern sweet cherry, which is a triumph of hope over experience, as the birds always get them first. Morello cherries are more successful—the birds leave their sour fruits for a while longer, so you can grab at least some of them. Sweet cherries require a rich, well-aerated soil with plentiful moisture at the roots. However, they don't like waterlogging or heavy, acidic or badly drained soil. Historically, cherries were often grown as big trees on strong roots through a grass sward, which ameliorated poor soil conditions and combined well with livestock running underneath.

Cherries can be trained, but sweet cherries (even on the new dwarfing rootstocks) tend to make far too much growth to be grown in most

Cherries can occasionally be grown successfully despite the birds. This variety, 'Governor Wood,' is particularly delicious.

fruitcages. They can be grown as fans against large walls, but require skillful maintenance and pruning, remembering that they have a tendency to root along the surface, which can damage a lawn or drive. They are therefore most successful grown as half-standard trees at ten to fifteen paces apart in an orchard. Any pruning must be done early in life, and early during the growing season, to avoid silver leaf disease. Only remove dead and diseased growth.

Morello cherries are much more amenable to soil and site, and more confinable, as they respond to hard pruning after fruiting. Remove much of the old wood so that the new can be tied in its place. Morello cherries will even crop on a cold wall, but do take quite some attention—which is amply rewarded if they can be netted (which a wall facilitates). Probably the best way to have some cherries is to grow them in large containers. They can then be moved indoors or into a cage when they are in flower and fruit. Many cherry varieties need compatible pollinators, but some are partly self-fertile. Morello cherries are not only self-fertile but will pollinate almost any late-flowering sweet cherry.

Rain at any time during flowering causes mold on the flowers, and heavy rain while the fruit is ripening will cause it to split. So cherries tend to do best in areas with dry springs and summers. Waterlogging, especially on acid or heavy land, may promote gummosis—oozing from the branches which may lead to an attack of bacterial canker. Treatment requires remedial pruning and restoring vigorous growth by feeding, liming, and draining. Attacks of black aphid can look devastating but do little real damage even though the shoot tips look pretty bad. An aphid attack soon means lots of ladybugs to guard the rest of the garden, and after all it's really the birds who are stealing the crop. Where no netting is possible, pull old stockings over the branches of fruit, though the birds will still eat through them. Be thankful cherries escape the wasps by fruiting early in the year!

Epicurean attentions Cherries can be picked and kept for several days if picked dry, while still on the sprigs and laid on paper in the cool. They can be frozen, but are fiddly as they need stoning to prevent taint. They do jam well especially mixed with redcurrant jelly which makes them set and adds bulk.

Rain on the cherry blossom spoils the crop.

Bob's gourmet choices The Morello is dark, sour and suitable only for cooking, jamming or freezing, but for this it is supreme. For dessert, sweet cherries that have some Morello "blood" are nicely acidic— particularly the 'Duke' or 'Royal' cherries. The earliest self-fertile variety 'Early Berlat' will even fruit on a north wall. 'Stella' is more vigorous and has better quality dark-red fruits a month later. My favorites, 'Emperor Francis' and 'Ranier' are mutually compatible—the first has delicious red fruits, the second sweet yellow ones. 'White Gold' and 'Sweetheart' are new self-fertile cherries worth trying.

Apricots ripen from early summer and are a gourmet's delight grown at home—plucked ripe enough to drop, they are magnificent and nothing like bought ones. The trees are tough, but the flowers come so early they are nearly always damaged by frosts where I live, so without some protection I get good crops only about one year in five. In the northern U.K., apricots will crop reliably only against a warm wall where they prefer to be fan trained at about five paces apart. In sunnier

areas, like mine, they succeed as bushes in sheltered spots. The soil should never be waterlogged, so if you have a heavy soil choose an apricot that has been budded on to St. Julien A rootstock. For lighter, drier soils, like mine, choose one on a seedling peach or apricot rootstock.

The major cause of lost fruit is frosts damaging the self-fertile flowers or fruitlets. Apricots also suffer from ants farming scale insects on them and occasionally caterpillars and aphid attacks may be a bother. More serious are dieback and gummosis. The twigs die back and sticky gum oozes out of cracks in the branches or, fatally, the trunk. The disease is symptomatic of poor growth and every effort should be made to improve the conditions. Fewer weeds, more compost, more mulches, better aerated roots, liming, seaweed sprays, and hard pruning are called for.

Pruning is not otherwise required for bushes, but fans should be done early, after the flowers have set and again when the fruits start to swell. Remove half to three quarters of each young shoot and eliminate any shoots growing inwards towards the wall from the main framework. As they can fruit very heavily in good years, thinning out the fruitlets is as beneficial as is regular watering! *Epicurean attentions* Pick apricots only when they start to drop, they do not keep well, but are easily dried and heavy crops can be frozen. Apricots make a delicious jam and can be preserved in spirits or syrup; unlike most fruits of the *Prunus* family, their kernels are sweet, edible, and used for ratafia biscuits.
Bob's gourmet choices The most reliable variety is 'Moorpark.' 'Alfred' is good, but I rate 'Harglow' as the tastiest.

Peaches, nectarines, and almonds
Peaches are one of the choicest fruits to grow at home almost anywhere in the world and can be successfully grown in most of the U.K. on a warm

'Moorpark' apricots are reliable grown on a wall in much of the U.K. and are even easier in frost-free areas.

wall and in the southeast in the open. The fully ripened peach is a balloon of juice waiting to burst all over you. Nectarines are like slightly more tender peaches without the fuzz, and they will not crop in the open in most of the U.K.: they need the warmth of a sunny wall. Almonds need exactly the same conditions as peaches, but with less rigorous thinning and pruning. All the trees are very beautiful in flower and in leaf—especially almonds—so they can be planted in a flower garden with impunity. They need to be planted five to eight paces apart in a rich, well-aerated piece of soil. They loathe waterlogging, so prefer open soils to heavy ones, but then they need heavy mulching to keep the soil moist. When they are planted against walls, the fruits will often split unless they are watered consistently throughout the season. Peaches should not be planted near to almonds as they may cross pollinate causing the nuts to be bitter.

All three benefit from companion plantings of alliums, especially garlic and chives, while stinging nettles nearby reputedly help prevent the fruit turning moldy. Peaches grown as bushes are easy, self-fertile, and fruitful from early in their life.

As peaches fruit on young shoots, replenish these continually by pruning them harder, and more like blackcurrants, than like most other trees. The tops of higher branches are removed to encourage more young growth lower down, and to keep the bushes within easy reach. On walls, especially under cover, peaches are usually fan trained. Fruiting is then guaranteed because of the frost protection, but flavor may be poorer and pruning must be carefully and regularly done. Selected young shoots are allowed to spring from a main framework and then tied in to replace the older shoots that have fruited. Fortunately, if the pruning of peaches is temporarily neglected, healthy bushes respond to being cut back hard by throwing up plentiful young growths. More important than pruning is thinning, because peaches are prone to overcropping, breaking branches and exhausting themselves. Thin the fruits hard—removing those that are touching or anywhere near

each other. Do this twice: very early and then again later.

Peaches, nectarines, and almonds grown on the dwarfing rootstock Pixy (which makes them even smaller than the usual St. Julien) can even be grown as small bushes in large pots. This means that over winter they can be taken indoors, where they are protected from peach leaf curl, though spider mite can be more of a problem. However, moved outside again when in leaf they will avoid spider mite to a great extent, and can fruit quite well if kept well watered. Peaches suffer great losses from birds and wasps, so use paper bags to protect the fruits. Earwigs get inside the fruits and eat the kernel out, but are readily trapped in rolls of corrugated cardboard tied around the branches.

The main problem with all these fruits is peach leaf curl. This puckers the leaves turning them red and yellow and they cease to work properly. Severe attacks weaken the tree and after a couple of years can even kill it. Spraying with Bordeaux mixture prevents attacks if sprayed

> With peaches, if the flowers miss the frost, the leaves avoid the leaf curl and you thin the fruits well— then you reap the reward!

twice or more as the buds are opening in late winter. Peach leaf curl can also be avoided if the buds are kept dry. Container-grown specimens can be overwintered indoors, while wall-trained trees can be protected with plastic sheet hung from the top of the wall. This will also help provide frost protection.

Frosts will kill the blossoms and fruitlets most years in the U.K., so the trees must be protected while in bloom and for several weeks after they have set. Dieback and gummosis are symptomatic of poor growth, and are best treated by heavy mulching and hard pruning in very late winter. *Epicurean attentions* Peaches are best eaten sun-warm, straight from the tree—you should then need a bib! If picked underripe, peaches never develop the full flavor or the juiciness. Peaches will keep a few days if handled with absolute care and kept cool, but the slightest bruise

and they will rot. Peach stones are ribbed or "perforated" with small holes in their shell. Varieties can be grouped into two types: clingstones, where the flesh sticks in the holes; and freestones where it doesn't, and the fruit is easier to eat. Peaches can be dried, jammed or frozen. When almond crops drop, peel and dry them. Do not crack them until required, then they are best blanched to give a clean and tastier nut. Unhulled they will store in dry salt or sand for years.

Bob's gourmet choices 'Babcock' is an early semi-freestone with white flesh ripening in July. Ripening choice fruits every year for me outdoors as a bush tree is 'August Pride,' which bears sweet, well-flavored fruits with yellowish white flesh and it's supposedly a freestone. 'Bonita' is similar, but with darker yellow flesh. 'Canada Harmony' comes later, has excellent flavor with sweet pale flesh, but is a bit miffy. 'Santa Barbara' is a heavy freestone cropper of beautiful red fruits, but needs a sheltered wall or growing under cover. All nectarines are exquisite, 'Double Delight' most of all. Almond varieties are hard to find. Reliable almond is still grown, but for roasting nuts choose 'Hale's Hardy.'

Plums, including greengages, bullaces, damsons, and cherry plums In general these are all very much alike and, although they can be trained, they are least effort grown as trees at five paces or so apart. Plums like a heavier, moister soil than most other fruits except black currants. They do not like cold, damp sites, though some such as 'Victoria,' 'Ptitsin,' and 'Waneta' have done well trained on a cold wall. Liking richer conditions than most fruits, they can be very favorably sited next to chicken huts or compost heaps.

Grown as trees they are best left unpruned, any pruning is always done in midsummer. Plums wait several years before starting cropping, this can be speeded up by pulling the branches down—though if patiently grown as unpruned standards the fruiting branches will weep and bring the fruit down to picking level. Some plums are self-fertile, but benefit from having pollination partners. Even so, cropping is rather hit and miss, as the blossom is so frequently frosted. Irregular cropping makes them overdo it in good years and then be exhausted for the next couple. So thinning exceptionally heavy crops is necessary—and often expediently done by cutting off half of each overburdened truss with shears. There is much maintenance pruning required for plums trained on walls because the rootstocks still do not control them enough, and traditionally they prefer a herringbone to a fan shape. Better quality fruits can probably be had more easily by growing plums in pots on one of the new dwarfing rootstocks such as Pixy or Colt.

Plums suffer from a host of minor pests, though most seem to barely affect the crop. Maggots in the fruit can be almost eliminated with pheromone traps, and earwigs by banding the trunk. Mealy aphids often coat the leaves, but it is birds and wasps that destroy most fruit. Protect prize fruits with bags. Birds also damage the buds in winter. I find winding black cotton over the trees really worthwhile as soon as there is snow or hard frost. Plum rust affects the leaves and damages future crops, so avoid having anemones nearby as they are an alternative host. Silver leaf disease is prevented by not pruning except during summer, and keeping the tree vigorous. This also helps prevent gummosis, an oozing from the bark on trees growing in badly drained or acid soils.

Epicurean attentions To enjoy the bloom and the sun's warmth eat a plum off the tree—go for the ones the wasps choose if you want the most sweetness. Many varieties will peel and this avoids the well-known side effects of too many plums. I make gourmet jams of the same variety with and without skins, and with double the skins—what a difference this makes, try it! All the plums make good jam fairly easily, use slightly underripe ones for the bite of acidity. They freeze well, but need pitting first to prevent taint. Surpluses can be juiced by simmering in water, straining, and freezing. Or they can be fermented to make wine and, where legal, distilled to make the devastating fluid, plum brandy.

Bob's gourmet choices 'Victoria' is ubiquitous, dual-purpose, fully self-fertile, pollinates many others and reliably produces large yellow-fleshed, red-flushed fruits. 'Stanley' is dual purpose, self-fertile and late cropping with purple fruits. 'Golden Gage' is dual-purpose, self-fertile and delicious, believed to be a plum, but of gage quality with its slightly acidic flesh, fine texture, and pronounced gage scent. It is a late flowerer, useful where frosts are a problem. 'Mirabelle' may also have plum ancestry and makes the most delicious jam.

The true greengages have lightly scented flesh and I prefer them for dessert. 'NY10' is my favorite, but a shy cropper and needs a warm spot or a wall even here in Norfolk. 'Severn Cross' is a delicious seedling more reliable and self-fertile. The transparent gages are hybrids with pale, translucent flesh and fine flavor. They ripen late and benefit from a wall or sheltered site.

Bullaces are small and generally too acid to eat raw, but make some of the most superb preserves. Varieties are scarce. Damsons are closely related to bullaces, but larger and resemble blue black plums distinguished by a delicious spicy flavor once cooked. Damson trees are compact and usually self-fertile. 'Italian Prune' which ripens late has the best flavor, but is a light cropper. The cherry plum or myrobalan is often used as a windbreak because it is tough and more shrublike, and its growth makes good hedges. They are self-fertile and bear almost spherical fruits which have an insipid, but juicy, flesh which makes good jam. 'Onuka' is a new, tastier variety.

Mulberries If you want to eat these you'll have to grow them. They are generally slow to come into fruit, but I have had them fruit a year or two from planting. They are traditionally planted as large specimens with a seat underneath in the middle of a lawn, but can be fruited earlier and easier in pots. Mulberries are self-fertile, have few diseases or pests other than birds, and require no regular pruning.

Epicurean attentions The fruits, which are a bit like black raspberries, are best shaken off the tree onto the grass or a sheet. Take care with clothes and fingers as the color stains everything. Delicious fresh, mulberries also make a good jam and potent wine.

Bob's gourmet choices There are black, red, and white mulberries, all can be eaten, though the white form is usually grown for its leaves to feed silkworms.

Figs have big leaves that add a tropical look. They must not be given too rich a soil or they make too many leaves and soft growth with little fruit. They need a well-drained, chalky soil and traditionally were grown against a wall with their roots restrained by planting them in a sunken brick box. Nowadays, a woven sack of man-made fiber that won't rot or the drum from an old washing machine will do the job. Both will prevent the roots from getting too big, but will still allow fine roots as well as air and water to get through.

Figs will crop in the open, but produce much better quality fruits trained on a wall, preferably a warm one at least four paces wide and as high. Where space is limited, they can be grown in containers. Figs are pruned during late winter just before growth is about to restart. Sturdy, short-jointed wood is the most fruitful if well ripened. Long jointed green shoots are unproductive and should be removed. To ensure crops, remove every fruit and fruitlet larger than a pinhead in early winter, as these sap the plant's strength if left and rarely succeed, usually dropping off just after they have swelled, and preventing a spring flush from forming.

Other than birds and wasps, figs suffer few problems except for spider mite under cover and on walls in hot, dry conditions. Figs may benefit from rue growing nearby.

Epicurean attentions Do not eat figs straight off the tree, but keep them for a day or so. When they start to soften and darken, they are supreme. Figs can be also dried or turned into syrup.

Bob's gourmet choices 'Brown Turkey' and 'Kadota' are reliable, very similar and ripen from high summer. 'Kadota' produces the larger fruits,

but 'Brown Turkey' is the heavier cropper. More than forty varieties are available for the enthusiast varying widely in size, color, and somewhat in taste.

Hazel, cobs, and filberts These are remarkably easy to grow successfully and a rich, storable source of fat and protein. The wild hazels have the best flavor, which the bigger cobnuts lack. Filberts are the ones whose husk or beard encloses the nut and are also reckoned to have a fine flavor. All make big bushes which form excellent windbreaks and need to be planted at least three or four paces apart. Hazels, cobs, and filberts will grow anywhere, but crop badly on heavy, damp sites. They do surprisingly well on poor, stony, and sandy sites.

Traditionally, hazels were trained to a flat wheel-shaped frame with a framework pruned back to spurs, but that's hard work. Nowadays, they are

Figs are tasty and their leaves are very decorative.

probably best formed as goblet-shaped bushes on a single trunk. However, they will still crop if left as thickets, though it is always worth keeping clumps uncongested and removing suckers to prevent too many nuts being lost within the tangle. Apart from thieving wildlife, they seldom suffer many problems.

Growing wild, these nuts are found in association with bluebells and primroses, with truffles growing on their roots—but my supposedly inoculated trees have never produced any.

Epicurean attentions Like many nuts, hazels taste quite milky and sweet when fresh, so start eating them before they fully ripen. As they ripen and fall off, they can be dehusked and dried then stored for years, unshelled, in dry salt or sand. Filberts are stored in their husks, but last nearly as well. Hazelnut macaroons are devilishly good, especially if the kernels are blanched and peeled first.

Bob's gourmet choices 'Turkish Tree Hazel,' 'American Filbert,' and 'Chinese Filbert' are much bigger

than native hazels, but tend to lack the flavor. Red-skinned filberts are tiny, but delicious, and I much prefer them.

Sweet or Spanish chestnuts As far north as the U.K. these fruit well only after hot summers. Individual trees reach a huge size and, because they are rarely self-fertile, several are needed to get a crop. Thus they are seldom planted in our gardens. They do not like thin, chalky soils, preferring a light, well-drained loam or light, dry sandy soil. To produce nuts, they are best sited on the sunny side of woodlands or windbreaks.

Sweet chestnuts are generally problem-free in Britain—the nuts ripen after a hot summer or two, and then the only problems are from thieving wildlife. But in the U.S. chestnut blight has wiped out their best species (see below under *Bob's gourmet choices*). Chestnuts are considered healthier if grown near oak trees.

Epicurean attentions Chestnuts are inedible raw, but are traditionally roasted in their shells. They can be used sweet and sour, made into flour and all sorts of baked goods, and are the basis of the glorious French *crème de marron* and *marrons glacés*. They will store for a year or so if kept cool and dry.

Bob's gourmet choices Better varieties exist, but normally you can only get unnamed seedlings. Look for *Castanea sativa* 'Marron de Lyon,' from France. In America *C. dentata* was the native sweet chestnut and had smaller, better flavored nuts, but this has almost been wiped out by chestnut blight and is being replaced by various new, improved hybrids.

Walnuts These are very slow to grow and to fruit. After fifteen years my 'Franquette' is only just starting to give respectable crops, though now they're coming the nuts are very tasty, large, and nutritious. Walnuts prefer a heavy, moist soil, but detest

Cobnuts and filberts are best fresh, but will store for many years.

waterlogging. They are not really self-fertile, so they are best planted in groups. Collect catkins to put on a stick and hand pollinate the female flowers, which come later.

Not much grows under walnuts, which are generally bad companions, especially the American varieties, so they are best planted at least ten paces apart along drives or in meadows and orchards rather than grown in the garden where they will become too large.

Walnuts need little pruning. Any that is needed must preferably be done early in their life and early in the year. Generally, they are remarkably pest- and disease-free. The old adage "A wife, a dog, and your walnut tree, the more you beat them the better they'll be" is hardly politically correct advice and may puzzle some. The reason behind it is that if you damage the bark of the walnut it then produces the much more prized burred grain in the timber. As to the dog and wife, I suspect attention and treats probably win over either better than an

unsound thrashing.

Epicurean attentions Fresh walnuts can be shelled then skinned. Skinning makes them much sweeter and removes all bitterness. The unripe nuts when soft enough to be punctured with a needle can be pickled or used to make liqueurs, after the manner of sloe gin. Cleaned, dried but not shelled the nuts can be stored for a year or so in salt or sand.

Bob's gourmet choices Named varieties of walnut such as the 'Franquette' are scarce, but worth searching for. One French variety was called the titmouse because the shell was so thin even a titmouse could break in to eat the kernel. American black walnuts are usually offered as the species here, but there are several named varieties also difficult to find. *Juglans ailanthifolia* 'Cordiformis' is the Japanese heartnut, which may be worth growing. It is quicker to fruit than ordinary walnuts and produces strings of small, easily shelled nuts.

chapter seven

FEAST ON FRESH HERBS, SALADS, AND DELICIOUS VEGETABLES

Growing for flavor, health, freshness, and quality using the easiest and most effective means

The value of any homegrown produce is many fold—you know not only that it's really fresh, but that it's simply better than anything you can buy, which is chosen for high yields rather than flavor and vitamin content. In practice, the majority are annuals and require us to be fastidious in our timing and in maintaining their growth without check; otherwise many of them will bolt and throw our crop away. Thus the pragmatic gardener looks to the few perennial crops where possible to minimize the workload and avoids wasting efforts on crops that are uneconomic or just plain unwanted. There is no work as hard as wasted work, and twice is too often for a crop to be left to rot unused and to no one's benefit except the slugs'. Do not waste time or space, and where the latter is very limited, culinary herbs are the sensible plants to grow. With only a slightly larger area it becomes possible to grow many tasty leaves for adding to salads, and only when space and time are generously available should you consider growing many of the vegetables which are less expensive to purchase and more time-consuming. Of course, feel free to concentrate on anything that takes your fancy. Specialize in one thing and you will soon become an expert, and produce first-grade specimens; do a bit of everything and it will rarely be so easy to show off your triumphs.

Summer squash or zucchini can never be sold as fresh or as tender as you can grow them yourself.

Cultural requirements for gourmet crops

Herbs, salad greens, and vegetables need different conditions depending on their nature. The classic herbs such as rosemary, sage, and thyme are perennials from the Mediterranean and require a warm, dry, sheltered spot and not overly rich soil to do well. Herbs grown as annuals, such as parsley, dill, and borage, need a moister richer soil and will tolerate light shade, while the true vegetables require the best conditions of all: full sun and rich, moist soil. Although it may be necessary to grow these all squeezed into one place through lack of space, it is a good idea at least to separate the aromatic perennials from the vegetables, as many of the former inhibit the germination of seeds. Perennial herbs, especially rosemary, make excellent low dividing hedges. Most are also useful in various parts of the garden as companion plants to fruit trees and bushes, and as borders round other areas, especially vegetable beds. Ornamental areas can be made solely from perennial herbs and then need very little maintenance, yet are productive. If borders next to warm walls are available, use these for aromatic perennials; also plant them by brick and stone pathways, ornaments, and low decorative walls, which all retain the warmth these herbs love. Effective herb gardens are designed with brick or stone paths radiating from a central ornament or birdbath. Where space is very short, most perennial herbs will grow in pots or containers, but don't expect them to flourish as they would in the ground. In pots they can be stood under cover, in a coldframe or greenhouse, to extend their season. Don't move them indoors, however, as they soon expire in hot, dry, centrally heated rooms, especially shady ones. Pots are ideal for mints, which are invasive and not easy to control when grown in a bed with other plants. Do not over-enrich the ground for perennial herbs as many then produce rank growth and poor flavor.

Those herbs grown as annuals do not generally need very rich soil either. A good start is essential, some must be sown in situ, though most are better sown under cover in pots or multicelled trays. Growing annual herbs to maturity on the seedbed after the vegetable seedlings have been planted out elsewhere utilizes the space efficiently. You can also plant out annual herbs to intercrop amongst vegetables on the main beds. Wherever you plant herbs, they should be easily and quickly accessible from the kitchen, or they will often be omitted because of the inconvenience. If the main supply has to be far away, make a duplicate planting of the most important herbs right next to the kitchen door.

A salad bed is one plot worked extra intensively for a few years and then best moved on, leaving rich conditions for following crops. Where space is limited, making a bed specifically for salads and concentrating on these is a good strategy. If much salading material is required, then a separate salad area is more productive than growing these succulent crops in with the main vegetables. Work in as much organic material as you can spare into a salad bed. Use deep digging and extra dressings of

above
Fake stone (concrete) paths make my herb bed warmer and drier, and the access is easier.

right
Always have a few French marigolds by even the smallest salad bed, as they discourage so many pests.

seaweed meal to raise the fertility which is aided by copious watering. This is in order to promote the rapid, lush growth that makes for sweet succulent salads. If a permanent site is chosen, then it is hard work but worthwhile to create a sloping bed by raising the north end (in the northern hemisphere) and grade the whole bed down towards the south. This sun-facing slope increases the amount of sunlight falling on the soil, and gives faster earlier starts in spring and longer cropping in the fall.

For any sized vegetable garden to be a productive area, it needs careful planning so that it functions efficiently. Although ornamental areas can look reasonable most of the time despite a little neglect, a vegetable plot will rapidly become a weedy eyesore and little of value will come from it. Vegetables require the best in soil, sun, and situation to crop at all, let alone well. One reason is that many of them are extremely overbred plants. They are the Olympic athletes of the plant world. Many, such as onions and carrots, are naturally biennials that store up nutrients so they can flower and set seed the following year. However, we eat them before then. Given the very best conditions they grow fat for us, but the slightest check to growth or poor growing conditions leads them to bolt, which simply means they flower too soon. The vegetables we grow for their fruit or seed, such as peas and beans, are more forgiving, but still need good conditions to produce any amount of crop.

Hardest of all are the highly unnatural cauliflower and broccoli. The part we eat is an enormous multiple flower bud which we want to stay immature and succulent while the plant wants it to open up into blossom and be pollinated. Similarly, a cabbage is an enormous swollen terminal bud, and Brussels sprouts are overgrown buds in the leaf axils so these also require optimum conditions.

Some crops, such as tomatoes and corn, come from hotter climes with longer growing seasons. Although they can just about ripen in the warmth of our summers, they must be started off early if they are to do so in time. We need to give them protection and warmth, mimicking spring in their country of origin, so that they start into growth early enough to catch all the summer's warmth. Most vegetables, therefore, need the very best conditions to give us good results. We must give them rich soil so they can draw on sufficient nutrients, plenty of sunlight as this provides the energy, copious water which is the basic raw material, and enough unchecked growing time to finish the job. A common failing is crowding too many plants in together which makes three of the four vital ingredients rapidly dwindle into short supply. It makes little difference if the crowding is from crop plants or weeds as they all compete to the death.

It is better to grow a few plants well rather than many poorly. This applies to each and every sowing, *and* to the garden as a whole. Certainly for the less experienced, it is always a good idea to concentrate initially on just a few vegetables, adding to the range in following years. I have seen enthusiastic new gardeners become despondent having spent a fortune on seed for every vegetable in the catalog and then fail to produce crops from most of them. So, plan just which crops you really want and leave the others for later years.

COMPARATIVE VALUE OF DIFFERENT CROPS

There is no point in growing anything you don't like or more than you need. Yet many crops are grown just because they are always grown. Look round any allotment site and see rows of leathery beets, rotting cabbages, and withered beans hanging by bolted lettuces. So before wasting time, effort, and money decide why you are growing vegetables. If it is for the fresh air and exercise then fine, grow anything, but if it is to save money, produce pollution-free food, fresh salads or get maximum nutrition then you must select carefully what you are to grow.

Time is often more limited than space. A large town garden or allotment can feed a family all year if unlimited time is available, but will provide very little if few hours are spent on it. Growing a few crops

below
Garlic is probably *the* most valuable crop, both for its taste and for its companion effects.

above

A large vegetable garden gives you the luxury of growing as many crops as your labor will run to.

in quantity takes much less time than growing a little each of many. A good plan is to list the vegetables you already buy each week, which you could grow yourself and how much these cost you in a year. If you think you might like a vegetable but have never tried it, buy some before going to the effort of growing it.

Many books offer tables of expected yields, but these cannot be taken as more than guidelines, as yields can vary enormously. Some years all of a crop fails, and another year you are eating it till it comes out of your ears. Still, some comparison of expected yields does help with initial planning, so you can decide roughly how much ground to give to each crop. In most good soils, in an average year, with a careful gardener a ten-foot row might produce the amounts shown in the table below. This is a very rough guide, so when you find that there are just not enough carrots, far too many peas, or whatever, you can plan to devote more or less ground to that particular crop the following year. The table also indicates whether a crop is hard, moderate or easy to grow well and cleanly to the same quality as store-bought produce. This varies enormously with soil and situation. For example, it is unlikely any plot will grow both carrots and cauliflowers well, because the former needs a light, sandy soil and the latter a heavy rich clay. However, I have assessed each crop according to whether or not it is usually easy to produce a crop, bearing in mind their needs and common pests and diseases. I have further indicated how much work is involved with each crop. The final columns are an indication of whether that crop costs more or less to grow than to buy. The biggest expense is the cost of seed, so the total costs will vary much more if home-saved seed or expensively promoted "own brand" seeds are bought instead of standard varieties.

It is pointless to judge which crops are best to grow for saving money

KEY

GROW

Degree of difficulty to grow well and clean	□ Easy
	☑ Moderate
	■ Hard

TIME

Amount of time needed to grow well and clean	□ Quick
	☑ Moderate
	■ Lengthy

COST

Cost compared with buying equivalent crop	□ Cheaper
	☑ Same
	■ More

VALUE

Ease and cost of growing from saved seed or offsets	□ Cheap
	☑ Moderate
	■ Difficult

Comparative values of vegetable crops

CROP	YIELD	GROW	TIME	COST	VALUE	CROP	YIELD	GROW	TIME	COST	VALUE
Beans, broad	8 lb.	□	□	☑	□	Kohlrabi	9 lb.	□	☑	□	■
Beans, French	13 lb.	☑	☑	□	□	Leeks	8 lb.	■	☑	□	☑
Beans, runner	20 lb.	□	■	■	□	Lettuce	5 lb.	☑	☑	□	☑
Beets	12 lb.	☑	☑	□	■	Onions	10 lb.	☑	■	■	■
Broccoli	6 lb.	■	☑	□	■	Parsnips	9 lb.	☑	☑	■	☑
Brussels sprouts	8 lb.	■	■	☑	□	Peas	6 lb.	□	■	■	□
Cabbage	10 lb.	□	☑	□	■	Potatoes, new	15 lb.	□	☑	□	□
Cauliflowers	8 lb.	■	☑	□	■	Potatoes, main	24 lb.	☑	■	☑	□
Carrots	11 lb.	■	■	□	■	Radishes	6 lb.	☑	□	□	☑
Celery	10 lb.	■	■	☑	☑	Spinach	8 lb.	☑	■	□	☑
Courgettes(Zucchini)	10 lb.	□	□	□	■	Sweet corn (Corn)	5 lb.	□	■	☑	■
Cucumbers, ridge	10 lb.	☑	□	■	■	Tomatoes	20 lb.	☑	☑	☑	☑
Garlic or Shallots	7 lb.	□	☑	☑	□	Turnips and Rutabaga	10 lb.	☑	☑	□	■

because you cannot give them a fixed value: the price fluctuates, with the earliest of any crop being the most expensive and the price dropping as main crops mature. Local scarcities and gluts can change the cash value by ten fold. Generally, though, crops such as zucchini, broccoli and French beans, are very expensive to buy compared to the cost of growing them. Most root crops and main crop potatoes, on the other hand, are incredibly cheap to purchase, even organic ones. Peas and corn are expensive and time-consuming to grow, but nothing you can buy is as good as your own. Similarly, bought lettuce and other salad crops are never as crisp. Ultimately, real quality—especially freshness—is obtainable only from your own garden. In many ways, luxury crops and salads are the best vegetables to concentrate on, while onions, roots, and main crop potatoes could perhaps be left out unless time and ground are amply available.

Nutrition from vegetables is affected by their variety, treatment, and freshness. Anything grown organically at home of a good variety will always carry more nutritive value than store-bought produce, as well as fewer residues. However, to get the maximum vitamin value from a small space concentrate on carrots, spinach, and chards for vitamin A, peas, onions, and potatoes for vitamin B1, broccoli for vitamin B2, potatoes and peas for vitamin B3, and broccoli, Brussels sprouts, and kale for vitamin C.

Where space is at a premium, the best all-round value comes from carrots, saladings, and climbing peas and beans. If time is very limited then zucchini and squashes, beans especially drying haricots and broad beans, and early potatoes can all be grown with little work or attention. Onion sets, garlic, and shallots are equally easy and take little time providing the soil is not very weedy.

ALLOCATING SPACE, PLANNING AND LAYING OUT

Having decided what you want to grow you can then decide how much space you need for it. Alternatively, work it out the other way round and fill whatever space is provided by proportion. Either way, the vegetable plot needs careful positioning and laying out if any choice is possible. Preferably, it should be in full sun with no overhanging trees and as far away from trees, walls or hedges on its sunny side as practical. Wet boggy sites and low areas should be avoided as they will cause winter losses and frost damage in the spring. However, they may be ideal for summer salad crops, leeks, and celery. The plot should be kept well away from big hedges—especially leyland cypress and privet which will steal any goodness and moisture from the soil. Competition from any nearby trees and hedges can be reduced by digging a hip-deep slit trench parallel to them, cutting out and removing their roots and preventing them from returning by setting in a continuous plastic sheet before refilling the trench.

A vegetable plot should not be too far from the kitchen, a water point,

left
When I was laying out some of my forty raised beds the turf was incorporated by carpet mulching and the paths dug out as seen here. The beds have never been dug or walked on in the fifteen years since.

below
Cabbages and garlic have grown on all winter. Behind them, cloches with straw and grass-clipping mulches protect squashes and potato plants.

and the tool/potting shed or much time will be wasted going to and fro. The most frequently used path will be best hard surfaced or graveled to make it more pleasant to use in wet conditions. Grass paths dividing up a plot are a serious error. They look nice initially, but are difficult to keep cut and edged, encourage slugs and other pests and soon get smeared by wear and mud. One easy way to get more from less space is if paths are replaced by stepping stones.

The shape of a plot is best square or rectangular as others make harder work, and it must be designed so that rows or beds run north-south so that the sun can shine evenly and not cause dense shade behind taller crops. For this reason, a long rectangular plot is best running east-west, with short rows or beds going north-south. If this means the plot is best aligned askew to the main garden then surround it with triangular borders and screens of fruit or low hedges to disguise it. Do not make the hedges too tall or dense as air must be able to circulate freely. Borders and beds around the main vegetable plot will be useful for the perennial crops, such as asparagus or artichokes, and for seed, nursery, and salad beds which need even more intensive care than the main plot.

In the smallest garden choice is rarely possible and the best use has to be made of what is available. Of course with less area to deal with then time and money can be applied more intensively. Thick mulches, deep digging, heavy feeding, and cunning cropping can be used to squeeze more out of the smallest sunny space.

Rotation Provision for rotation is important, as explained in Chapter Ten (see page 205), but it is not necessary to divide the plot up into four quarters as shown in many books then religiously following the potatoes, legumes, brassicas, and roots cycle. What is critical is that you do not grow the crop or its near relations on the same ground year after year, but move it around or abandon it entirely for a year or two. It is not that important which you follow with which, though some combinations can be less satisfactory. For example, potatoes do not happily follow brassicas or legumes if the soil was limed for them. So roughly sticking to the traditional rotation cycle makes sense, but it is not gospel. What you need to take most care with is ensuring that potatoes are not returned to the same spot for as long as possible, that brassicas are similarly kept away for as long as possible and that the other vegetables do not return to their previous site from the year before. Of course, the more elaborate your rotation and the longer the gaps then the better the results. This is made easier if you grow a range of different crops in smaller amounts and if you include break crops such as flowers, strawberries, or artichokes.

Rotation is greatly facilitated if you keep accurate records of what is grown where and when. The fixed bed system lends itself to this, though it is not difficult with rows if you use permanent markers on the plot. Keep a book or a card file and record not only the crop and its position, but also its variety, sowing dates, and performance, as this information aids future planning.

Blocks, rows, fixed and raised beds Block and row planting are alternative ways of laying out crops. For those that need support such as peas, rows have the advantage provided they run north-south and don't shade other crops. Peas and beans can also be grown up strings tied in a circle round a central pole. Rows are more wasteful of space and the paths between each row get compacted and require digging. For most crops, especially those that are closely planted such as carrots, block plantings are advantageous. Apart from saving space, block planting helps with weed control because once the plants are half grown their foliage meets and excludes light from the soil, choking out seedling weeds. This also forms a favorable microclimate and prevents moisture loss. Where netting or fleece is used to prevent pests reaching the plants, then rectangular block planting is obviously convenient. Although row planting is easiest when very large areas are being cultivated, block planting in small beds is much more suitable for most crops in most gardens.

Raised beds are becoming popular, but their main advantages accrue from their being fixed beds. They are simply permanent subplots surrounded with narrow paths (packed soil is sufficient). Since the beds are not walked on they need digging only every seven or eight years and they make block planting easy. Rows can still be run down the middle if they run north-south. The ideal width is about four feet, as it is comfortable to reach in two feet from either side, and make them no longer than say sixteen feet or there is temptation to walk over rather than around them. Having permanently fixed beds makes record keeping and rotation simple, with each bed considered and treated as a separate little plot. Fixed beds slowly become raised beds naturally as mulches, compost, and root residues build up.

Being raised has several advantages. It reduces the need for bending, increases the surface area which provides extra planting space, and improves aeration and evaporation. Raised beds warm up sooner, too, which gives an earlier start in the spring. In winter, cold air runs off the bed like water so giving slightly warmer conditions. However, raised beds also dry out more quickly in summer and mulches tend to slide off or be pulled off by birds. Still, on the whole, their advantages outweigh their drawbacks, especially if their shape is kept to the natural sine curve formed by slumping soil. This then gives several useful microclimates. The south end is a hot slope suitable for early cropping and tender herbs, while the north end is permanently shaded and suits saladings and leaf crops. The sides are protected from the wind and so keep moist, suiting leeks, roots, and saladings. The top is open ground, but especially well suited to onions, shallots, brassicas, legumes as row crops, and to overwintering vegetables.

Raising the beds artificially with planks, bricks or whatever reduces the

above
Raised beds suit potatoes and corn. The former can flop out into the alleys and both love grass-clipping mulches.

right
Corn needs to be planted in blocks, as the wind distributes the pollen from the male flowers on top to the female tassels on the cobs.

area available, removes many of the useful microclimates, adds to costs with the materials required, and provides hiding places for pests. Paths of packed soil are sufficient, but get muddy in the wet. Straw and other mulches harbor pests and are hard to weed. So sharp sand or crushed gravel are much the best option, and it doesn't matter if some gets mixed into the soil. I have gone over to straw for paths and mulches because I am suffering from drought summers and have forty raised vegetable beds, which would be too expensive to cover with preferable materials.

Extending the season Using a seedbed makes it easier to spread the harvesting period because when a crop is transplanted it receives a slight check—the bigger a crop has grown the greater the check. For example, if one sowing of Brussels sprouts or lettuce is divided into three portions and then each portion is transplanted to its final position at ten days apart, each portion will mature at a slightly different time. Of course, for most vegetables successive crops can also be ensured by sowing in several batches over weeks or months and by sowing different varieties that mature at different rates. The fastest are usually called earlies and tend to produce less than the slower main crops. Of course, cloches and growing under cover can greatly extend the season (see Chapter 8, page 170).

Intercropping, catch cropping, and companion planting These are ways to get more out of a small plot, and are made easier if you raise as many plants as possible in seedbeds or in pots (though remember that some crops, such as root vegetables, have to be sown in situ). The idea is that many crops, especially the slower growing ones, do not need all the space allocated to them all the time. Catch cropping means using the quickest-growing crops, such as radishes, baby turnips, and saladings, to fill the space before another crop has grown very big. Intercropping is similar and refers simply to growing crops together. Also, when the main crop has finished growing and is standing waiting to be used, as with cabbages, intercropping means starting off the next crop in between so that when the latter is removed, the follow-on crop is already established and grows rapidly to fill the space made available. Do not overdo this, however, as crowding will give poorer results. Crops will compete as fiercely as weeds unless the spacing and timing are well controlled.

Companion crops are those which can be combined together most successfully and give added benefits over simple intercropping. Again great care must be taken not to crowd plants, but provided that sufficient air, light, nutrients, and water are available, some combinations of crops do particularly well together, while others do not (see chart overleaf). For example, instead of three beds growing peas, potatoes and corn respectively, I find that growing three beds with all three crops on each I get a higher yield overall. I put the peas in a thin row down the middle and flank it on either side with alternate corn and potato plants. The peas provide shelter for the tender young shoots, the

Corn and squashes prefer to be grown together.

potatoes keep the soil covered and moist which the corn and peas enjoy, while none shades out the others.

Further and most importantly, combining and mixing up crops significantly reduces the damage from pests and diseases. For example, I have found that beets grown between rutabaga and parsnip do not get attacked by the birds, and brassicas surrounded by French beans suffer far fewer pests. Most useful of all are French marigolds which should be planted in every plot and by paths and gates so you brush against them releasing their pungent, pest-confusing smell. Similarly, some annual herbs, such as chervil, dill, and summer savory, are beneficial when grown amongst crops as their strong scents help hide the plants from their pests. Perennial herbs, such as rosemary, thyme, sage, chives, southernwood, hyssop, and lavender are beneficial when confined to the edges of the vegetable plot, where their scents are effective pest deterrents and their flowers bring in predators and pollinators.

right

The scent of lavender confuses
pests and delights us.

Good and bad companions for vegetable crops

CROP	DOES WELL WITH	DOES BADLY WITH
Beans, broad & field	brassicas, carrot, celery, cucurbits, potatoes, summer savory, most herbs	onions & garlic
Beans, French	celery, corn, cucurbits, potatoes, strawberries	onions & garlic
Beans, runner	corn, summer savory	beets, chards & kohlrabi
Beets & chards	most beans, brassicas, onions & garlic, kohlrabi, parsnips, rutabaga	runner beans
Brassicas	French beans, beets & chards, celery, dill, nasturtiums, onions & garlic, peas, potatoes	runner beans, strawberries
Carrots	chives, leeks, lettuce, onions & garlic, peas and tomatoes	dill
Celery & celeriac	brassicas, beans, leek, tomatoes	
Cucurbits	beans, corn, nasturtium, peas	potatoes
Leeks	carrots, celery, onions	
Lettuce	carrots, cucurbits, radish, strawberries, chervil	
Onions & garlic	beets & chards, lettuce, strawberries, summer savory, tomatoes	beans, peas
Peas	beans, carrots, corn, cucurbits, turnips, potatoes	onions & garlic
Potatoes	beans, brassicas, corn, peas	tomatoes, cucurbits
Sweet corn (Corn)	beans, cucurbits, peas, potatoes	sunflowers
Sweet & chili peppers	basil	kohlrabi, radishes
Sunflowers	cucurbits, nasturtiums	potatoes, runner beans, grass
Tomatoes	asparagus, basil, carrots, brassicas, onions & garlic, parsley	kohlrabi, potatoes
Turnips & rutabaga	peas	

Culinary herbs and saladings

Perennial herbs are the most valuable crops, not demanding, yet attractive and useful. Thus the herb garden is ideal for the lazy perfectionist, needing little labor to maintain a good appearance. Herbs are the easiest of plants to grow organically as most are little bothered by pests and diseases. Although we rarely use them for medicinal purposes, herbs are still health giving and many are bactericidal. Indeed, most herbs are packed full of vitamins and minerals and are tasty additions to salads and cooking. What cuisine is complete without fresh herbs?

Although expensive and sometimes difficult to buy, most are so easy to grow and many of the perennial types even suppress weeds. Herbs have pleasant if not strong scents—after all, that is why we use them—so grow them where you can smell them, near windows, at corners, and on patios. Most also have attractive foliage, so are easy to incorporate in ornamental areas. Many are good companion plants with beneficial effects on other plants as well.

Sweet cicely has edible aniseed-flavored leaves and flowers, wonderful in salads or just nibbled fresh.

Furthermore, in summers with droughts and sprinkling bans it is possible to pick a cool succulent salad almost solely from herbs growing in soil that would be too dry for most vegetables (see page 137). Lettuce is certainly not the only salad base, many mild herbs and annual leafy crops are more tasty and succulent and these are well worth cultivating.

I have divided the culinary herbs and saladings into two groups: perennial and annual, as these really benefit from being grown apart. Most perennials are happiest grown in their own sunny bed, as edging companions to fruit plots, vegetable beds, or as permanent features in ornamental areas. The annuals are mostly best used fresh during the summer and better grown as salad vegetables on their own bed or planted out amongst sturdier vegetables. Some gourmet saladings I rate highly are thus dealt with early on in these lists, with the annual herbs and salads amongst which I suggest they should be grown, rather than later with the vegetables, where they are usually found in both the garden and the tome. Latin names are given only where these may help you find the right plant.

Perennial herbs Most perennial herbs will tolerate—indeed often prefer—drier, poorer soils than annual herbs. Many of the perennials come from the Mediterranean region and need some shelter or a cloche to come through our worst winters. It is the combination of damp and cold which kills them, so growing them against a wall is usually sufficient help. In well-sheltered or town gardens most perennial herbs will last for many years.

Almost all are good at suppressing weeds, suffer from few pests and diseases and need little maintenance apart from cutting back dead, overgrown and excessive growth. The majority are best bought as young plants rather than grown from seed—though most will come true from seed, it will cost as much as a plant, and cuttings from that will produce many more plants more quickly and for free. Many are very easily propagated from cuttings or dividing existing plants, so visit your friends' gardens with something to trade. Do not divide or move most herbs during fall or winter. In particular, buy and plant up a new herb bed during spring, so that if there has been a hard winter the nurseryman lost the plants not you. It is the tender young tips and leaves we use for the most part, so cutting back most herbs each spring removes withered growths and produces a flush of new shoots. Leave pruning till spring, so that the old growth protects the new against bad weather. Care needs to be taken not to cut back too far or the plant may die; go no further than the point where live green shoots emerge from older wood.

ESSENTIAL PERENNIAL HERBS

The following are used mostly for their leaves.

Bay *(Laurus nobilis)* is a rather tender shrub especially suffering from harsh winds while small and is easily lost, but once established it becomes a tough medium sized tree. It can be grown in tubs and taken under cover in winter, but is then more prone to pests, especially scale insect. Bay is difficult to propagate and expensive to buy—you could have several packets of the leaves for the cost of one plant. Use the leaves in savory dishes especially with tomatoes and garlic. I find carefully dried leaves taste better than the fresh. The leaves preserve grains and seeds from weevils and the burning leaves are poisonous to us and insects. They can be attractive as specimens if trimmed neatly, so it's worth having one if you can protect it while small.

Chives can be started from seed, or any bits from the side of existing clumps. They benefit from being divided every other year so can be multiplied rapidly and used as edgings. Left to flower, they attract beneficial insects and are pretty but self-seed and give less useful leaves—I cut back alternate plants hard every other year. Being an allium, chives are probably the best herb to grow to reduce the incidence of fungal diseases. Use them to ward off blackspot on roses and scab on apples by planting in large patches underneath. You'll need to be patient, though, as it takes three years to have effect. Chives discourage aphids on chrysanthemums, sunflowers, and tomatoes and benefit carrots. Chive sprays have been used against downy and powdery mildew on cucumbers and gooseberries. Add chives to savory dishes especially with cheese, and put loads in salads. Grow plenty of them and have some under cover as well!

Bay is not very hardy when small—protect it from strong winds until it is well established.

Horseradish crowns ready for digging.

Fennel is a large herbaceous plant with an aniseed flavor which goes well with savory fish and cheese dishes as well as in salads. The seeds are used with baked products. The plant is upright and stately growing to shoulder height. It is ideal for ornamental areas and the bronze form is particularly attractive.

Propagate the green from seed or both by division in the spring. Keep fennel away from tomatoes, caraway, and dill. It self seeds viciously unless you deadhead in time!

Garlic is the most pungent of the onion family and a most effective accumulator of sulfur which may explain its very ancient reputation as a fungicide. Garlic emulsion has also been used against aphids, carrot rootfly, onion fly, codling moths, and snails, and peach leaf curl. Garlic is a good companion for roses and fruit trees, but keep it away from beans and peas—though it may follow them in rotation.

Plant the cloves in fall in zones 5-9 for the biggest yields, and be careful to plant them neither too shallow nor too deep. The planting holes should be between one and two inches deep, and up to a foot apart. Fill in afterwards with gritty sandy compost. Garlic can be planted till late spring, but the earlier the better. Dig the crop up before the leaves totally wither and blow away. Dry them in a warm airy place. Any garlic bulbs left in the ground will show their position when they start to sprout, and can be dug up, split and replanted for the next crop. Garlic can be fitted into any spare site and can be used to mark the corners of beds. Rocambole is similar, smaller bulbed and more disease resistant, producing an edible cluster of bulbils in place of seeds.

Horseradish *(Armoracia rusticana)* is hard to eradicate once established: any bit of the root will grow vigorously anywhere. Horseradish accumulates calcium, potassium and sulfur. In the U.S.A an infusion has been used against brown rot in apples and against blister beetles and Colorado beetles. Horseradish is traditionally grown with potatoes, both in the U.K. and in China, but as it is almost impossible to get rid of it is best confined in a container. I use a perforated stainless steel drum from an old washing machine buried to its rim in a bed.

The root is grated for use in sauces and even in minute amounts for salads. Mixed with garlic, chili, mustard, and cider vinegar, horseradish makes a warming sauce.

Lavender *(Lavandula spica)* is rarely used in cooking nowadays, but is such a lovely flavor everyone should try a little once in rice pudding—and lavender biscuits are heavenly. There are large and small varieties to suit any garden with a sunny spot.

Lovage *(Levisticum officinale),* love parsley is propagated by root division or seed. This monster of a plant is not for small gardens as it towers way above head height. It needs moist soil and is believed to aid most other plants by its presence, though not too close! The leaves are used moderately in salads and for giving a rich flavor to savory dishes and it adds "body" to vegetable stocks. It is also claimed to be a substitute for salt. The stems can be eaten raw if blanched tender like celery, and the seed used with baked products and in salads.

Lemon verbena *(Lippia citriodora/ riphyla)* has an exquisite lemon-sherbet scent that stays with the dried leaves for many years. A lovely flavor for salads, fruit salads, sweet dishes, and teas. It is not very hardy and gets killed above ground by hard frosts, so plant against a warm wall, protect the roots from damp and cold, and it may sprout again the following spring. Easily grown from cuttings, it can be kept in a pot under cover over winter. It can even be used as a house plant, but it is then prone to aphids and spider mite.

Marjoram and oregano have many varieties, all of which are similar to oregano and essential for Italian food. The leaves can be added to salads, but the flavor goes exceptionally well with savory dishes. Marjoram has good flavor fresh, dried or frozen and can be grown in a pot under cover for winter use. Grow as annuals and propagate by seed to get the best flavored plants. Perennial forms can be propagated by root division, are nearly as tasty and tend to form low mounds which make them useful as informal edging or to go under fruit trees and bushes. There is a particularly attractive golden form that turns a butter cream yellow during summer and reverts to green in winter. In flower these attract many bees and butterflies.

Mints love rich, moist soil. They detest wood ash and are more than somewhat invasive. Any bit of root grows almost anywhere anytime. Never put mint in with other herbs, as their roots interpenetrate everything. To minimize their expansionist tendency grow them in containers plunged to the rim in the soil or in beds surrounded by concrete or regularly cut grass.

Mint is one of the few plants to grow under walnuts and they thrive near stinging nettles. They make good companions for cabbage and tomatoes before they overwhelm them. The odor can be used to repel rodents, clothes moths, fleas, and flea beetles. Spearmint also discourages aphids by putting off ants.

Mints are famous for sauces and teas and go well in salads. Best used fresh, they can be potted up for winter under cover. Cool, refreshingly scented forms such as 'Eau de Cologne' and 'Spearmint' suit ornamental areas, as do golden and silver variegated, yellow, gray, and curly forms which are mostly less vigorous. Mints make cheap, low-maintenance groundcover for large areas, especially under trees, and their late flowering is attractive to bees and beneficial insects.

Rose petals are wonderful in salads! They can also be used with apple, milk dishes, and baked products. Highly recommended especially the thornless 'Zéphirine Drouhin' which flowers longer than most and smells and tastes divine.

Rosemary is not very hardy, but usually survives to be had fresh all year if given a warm spot against a wall in zones 6-9. It will grow in a pot under cover. Easily propagated from cuttings in the spring, it is loved by bees. Delicious in moderation with almost all savory dishes, the leaves and the flowers go well in salads.

Sage is the traditional stuffing herb but also goes well in moderation in salads and with savory dishes. The red form has a finer flavor, the more compact multicolored sages are not very hardy. Easily grown from cuttings or seed, sage needs replacing every few years as it gets straggly and resents pruning.

Sweet cicely *(Myrrhis odorata)* has aniseed- or liquorice-tasting leaves like chervil and is excellent in salads. The stems, seeds, and roots can also be cooked. The plant is very decorative; I use it freely, and chew it for refreshment on drying days.

Winter savory Summer savory tastes better, but winter savory is shrubbier and survives hard weather. Small amounts improve salads, the flavor of beans, and the smell of cooking brassicas. It grows easily from seed; small and compact, it will crop most of the year, and longer in a pot under cover.

Tarragon Do not confuse the real French with the poor Russian version. Taste the leaves, the French is sweet and piquant, the Russian rank and sour. Unfortunately, the Russian which is hardier, comes from seed and root division and is more common. The French needs a warm spot and extra protection from cold and damp. It is propagated only by root division—which must be carried out every third year or it dies out! Tarragon flavors vinegar, is wonderful with eggs and fish, and in salads I use it liberally.

Thymes are wonderful, they all smell divine and can be used in salads and savory dishes. The bees love thyme and it is low-growing so is ideal under fruit trees and bushes if it's sunny enough. Different thymes offer varied scents, colors, and forms and will thrive in poor dry, sunny situations and lime–rich soils. Try the caraway-flavored 'Herba Barona.'

PERENNIAL HERBS TO GROW IF YOU HAVE THE SPACE

Angelica is a tough, tall, short-lived herbaceous plant which likes shady,

Bergamot prefers a moister soil if it is to do any better than this.

Red sage, lovage, and fennel with lavender behind.

rich, moist soil and is attractive enough to be planted at the back of ornamental borders where it will self seed. The stems can be preserved candied in sugar syrup. Adding angelica and sweet cicely stems to rhubarb removes the tartness and makes it sweeter, but angelica is only worth having in larger gardens.

Bergamot *(Monarda didyma)* is a neat, knee-to-waist-high herbaceous plant with beautiful scarlet or purple flowers well suited to ornamental areas. The aromatic leaves and flowers make a calming drink once sold as Oswego tea. A few petals can add vibrant color to salads. Divide the clump to propagate the variety— it is worth doing this and replanting every third year anyway. Bergamot thrives on moist soil.

Dandelion is a maligned plant, surprisingly health-giving when

eaten and does not necessarily cause nocturnal problems. Since it is bitter, it is best blanched first: cover the heads with a flowerpot a week or so before you want to use them.

Good King Henry, Lincolnshire asparagus *(Chenopodium bonus henricus)* is a vigorous self-seeder and highly nutritious, but little grown. The leaves and shoots can be eaten as asparagus or spinach or used in moderation in salads. Early to grow each year it can provide a good standby crop and is worth having by a pond.

Hyssop is a sun-loving perennial herb and a superb bee plant that gives honey a lovely flavor. It is said to benefit grapevines and help to deter cabbage white butterflies, but radishes do badly near it. The young leaves were added to salads or eaten with any rich savory food, but the flavor is strong, bitter, and hot, so use it with care. Propagate hyssop from cuttings, root division or seed.

Lemon balm *(Melissa officinalis)* resembles a mint with the same tendency to spread, though not by root but by seed. Compact and dense growing it excludes weeds wherever planted and will flourish almost anywhere. There is a cheerful yellow variegated form especially useful in ornamental areas. Both have a refreshing clean lemon scent, once used in salads, soups, and teas, but lemon balm is much better smelt than eaten. In flower, it is beloved by bees.

Sorrel *(Rumex acetosa)* is easy to grow, spinach-like and can be used as spinach or in soups and salads if you like sour flavors. It likes moist, lightly shaded soil and tends to spread. Grow it from seed or root divisions and replant every few years.

Watercress is surprisingly easy if you have clean running water in

Variegated lemon balm adds color to the herb bed.

quantity, though it is possible to get excellent crops with only a trickle running down a water trough. It can be grown in mud but then is much poorer stuff and is best in a clean gravel with sparkling aerated lime rich water. The watercress sold in shops can often be rooted. It bolts and reseeds itself, and is best when regularly replaced by cuttings.

Annual herbs and salads

Most annual herbs are best started off sown in situ during midspring. They resent transplanting and will not make as much growth though they will be easier to manage if started in small pots or cells as for the vegetables. Pot them up if necessary then harden off and plant out after the last frost. If sowing direct, mark out and station sow as for vegetables (see page 91), but for most herbs there is no necessity to sow or thin to one plant per site.

Sow most annual herbs fairly shallowly. I press a cane into the surface to make a drill and, after sowing, cover the seed with clean potting compost and firm down well. It is important to mark the site as many are slow to germinate. A label aids later identification.

With most, the flavor is ruined

by the onset of flowering, so successional small sowings are a good idea, spreading the cropping. Cut them back often. The younger shoots and leaves are the more tender, and most herbs become more succulent with adequate moisture. They all grow lusher in a richer soil though this may spoil their flavor—see individual entries for details.

ANNUAL HERBS USED MOSTLY FOR THEIR LEAVES AND BEST SOWN FREQUENTLY THROUGHOUT THE YEAR

Arugula *(Eruca sativa)* Italian cress leaves are spicy and peppery and the flowers add interest to salads. It is very easy to grow, but tastes best when grown quickly in moist conditions. It can be cut back for new flushes. Sow often and sow thickly. Arugula is prone to flea beetle but otherwise no problem. Sow this instead of radishes, because it is the best salading. Arugula was banned from monastery diets as it allegedly inflamed lust!

Chervil will grow in shade, needs moisture and loathes transplanting very much like parsley. Yet it's easier to grow with a milder flavor so much more can be used in salads. The root was also once cooked as a vegetable. It may keep aphids off lettuce. Sow thickly in situ from late winter till fall. Chervil will self-seed if left to flower, but you may prefer to cut it down before flowering to produce a new crop of fresh foliage. A subtle flavor, chervil enhances other flavors best when raw or only slightly cooked, very highly recommended.

Dill has a pleasing, fresh, clean flavor. The leaves and seeds are added to pickles, sauces, cheese, and fish dishes. The fresh leaves can be added in quantity to salads. Sow dill thickly direct or in pots and in situ. If left to grow waist high, it flowers and attracts hoverflies. Dill allegedly attracts bees, though I find otherwise.

It's not liked by carrots, but aids cabbages and may help lettuce, onions, corn, and cucumber as it repels aphids and spider mites. It appears to hybridize with fennel!

Purslane *(Portulaca oleracea sativa)* is an infuriating plant as it is hard to grow from seed, but self-seeds happily. Useful as a salad crop it needs to be grown quickly and kept cut back hard for flushes of the young, succulent shoots. Get fresh seed, sow it on the surface of a layer of sterile compost on top of the soil where it is to grow. If you succeed, let it flower and seed, then it will appear of its own accord everywhere.

Radishes can be sown in situ anywhere you like, a few seeds at a time every week from spring to fall. Very quick, but need to be eaten young and tender as they get more fibrous and hotter with age. If ordinary radishes are allowed to go to flower, they are good for beneficial insects and then produce pods which are tasty and nutritious while still small and tender. 'Munchen Bier' was developed for that purpose. The 'Black Spanish' and Japanese radishes are sown after midsummer and are more like turnips than radishes so treat them as such. They are almost pleasant grated raw in salads.

Land cress resembles watercress, but grows almost anywhere, even in windowboxes, if kept moist. It gives a peppery flavor to salads. Surface sow in situ and keep cutting it back.

ANNUAL HERBS AND SALADINGS SOWN ONCE OR TWICE A YEAR

Basil is one of the tastiest herbs in the garden—it is a shame it needs so much warmth. It goes so well with tomatoes, with which it also grows happily, and these make a trio with asparagus, but basil dislikes rue. It has been sprayed as an emulsion against asparagus beetle and used as a

Claytonia is a most useful salading, even in flower, and makes a good winter green manure under cover.

trap plant for aphids. There are a purple-leaved, a tiny-leaved and a lemon-flavored version as well as the familiar sweet basil. They are all delicious, though their final heights vary from dwarf to shoulder level— given time and heat. Use basil leaves in salads, with cheese, and in quantity with garlic in every tomato dish. Freeze or dry any surplus for winter, as this is sadly a very tender plant. Start basil off in pots in the warm and grow alongside tomatoes or peppers as they like similar conditions. Watch out for aphids, and cut the plants back before flowering.

Claytonia *(Montia perfoliata)*, winter purslane, miners' lettuce, is a potential weed as it seeds prolifically and comes up everywhere. However, it grows really well, even in mid-winter under cover, on any soil. It is very tasty in salads and all the leaves, stalks and flowers are edible. Surface sow anywhere and thin if you wish. Let it self seed because you will want perpetual supplies and give it shady, moist, rich conditions for lush growth. You'll like it, chickens love it and children will eat it.

Corn salad, lambs' lettuce, is a very useful winter salad crop, best grown

under cover to keep the weather and dirt off the leaves. Corn salad can be sown direct or in pots from spring till midfall and spaced a finger or so apart. Left to flower it resembles small forget-me-nots and self-seeds. Pick individual leaves rather than the whole plant.

Iceplant *(Mesembryanthemum crystallinum)* is an ornamental and makes excellent groundcover for barren, hot, dry sites. The leaves can be used in salads or cooked like spinach. It will grow in hot, dry conditions when all else fails. Sow in pots and plant out in early summer. It's well worth trying though a peculiar texture and strange taste.

Lettuces and endives are among the easiest crops to grow well and yet are often badly grown. Never sow a lot of seed at once, instead sow in small batches in a seedbed. Better still, use multicelled packs. Sow a few cells each of several varieties every few weeks through most of the year. Thin to one plant per cell and plant out as catch and intercrops putting them in as you pull other plants out. They do best among cucumbers, carrots, radish, and strawberries, but may not prosper near broccoli. Lettuce can be partly protected from aphids with chervil nearby. Their root aphid over-winters as eggs on poplar trees, later infesting the leaf stalks and forming galls which split in midsummer when the aphids move on to lettuce. Anthocorid bugs destroy these galls and reduce the pest numbers.

If it is hot, sow lettuce in the shade as the seeds will not germinate if they are very warm. Lettuce is one of the plants that has been shown to take up natural antibiotics from the soil. Birds need keeping off, and slugs controlling. The biggest problem is slow growth caused by lack of water which makes them bitter, so keep them well watered. Salad bowl and cutting varieties make the best use of the ground because they are not uprooted at harvest time, but eaten on a cut-and-come-again basis. Romaine lettuces are tall and need tying up to blanch them or they may be bitter.

Over winter, lettuce need to be grown under cover not so much for the warmth as for protection from the weather and hungry creatures. There is a tremendous range of lettuce varieties, so try many different ones to see which you enjoy most. I grow dozens, but only a few of each. Endives are grown just like lettuce, but must be blanched or they are too bitter. They can also be cropped on the cut-and-come-again basis, so are economical on the ground. Sow in situ from early summer or, better, start them in cells like lettuce.

Mustard and cress are the easiest of all saladings and quicker than arugula. Just sow them densely in short rows on the flat any day of the year. Spray gently with water, then cover each batch of seed with a clean cardboard mat. Once the seed has germinated well, remove the mat. Cut with scissors when two inches high, they don't regrow.

Bok choy, leaf mustards, and Chinese greens are fast-growing, pest- and disease-resistant additions to other dishes, occasionally used raw in salads but usually cooked, especially stir-fried. Sow in pots or direct, and thin to just less than a foot apart from early summer to fall. Late crops need a cloche or coldframe to protect their appearance and growth. They benefit from a moist rich soil and slugs may cause problems. Well worth growing under cover in winter as it is very easy and productive—and especially if you like Chinese food.

Parsley is very nutritious and is used in countless dishes as well as a garnish and salading. It is biennial so flowers in its second year. Leave to seed, as self-sown plants are always best. Sow soaked seed on the soil surface and barely cover them. Sow once in spring and again in fall for two years then use self-sown seedlings. Thin plants for seed to one per foot. It will revel in rich, moist conditions and will stand moderate shade. Parsley freezes and dries well and plants can be dug up, potted and moved under cover or cloched for fresh winter leaves. The bigger, continental flat-leaved variety has more flavour than our common curly-leaved form. Both are highly recommended.

Shungiku is an edible, highly decorative chrysanthemum which is rich in vitamin C. It is a good companion for keeping pests away from other plants. Used like bok choy and as chop suey greens, it has a very strong flavor and gets bitter once it has started flowering. (The flower petals are good in salads, however.) Very tough and easy to grow, it can be sown direct or in pots from late winter to fall and under cover.

Summer savory is traditionally grown and used with broad beans and the tips are tasty in salads. It adds a lovely flavor to all savory dishes. Do not allow it to flower or the flavor goes. Sow shallowly in pots or direct in the soil. It can be dug up and potted for winter use under cover, but dries perfectly well anyway.

VEGETABLES SUITABLE FOR SALAD BEDS

Celery is difficult to grow, so unless you have a rich, constantly moist soil and really desire celery for the sticks grow celeriac instead. Celery must never dry out, is prone to bolting, suffers from slug damage and needs careful blanching. Swiss chard gives a similar and superior stem for braising and is easier to grow, so substitute this for celery and add other flavorings. Celery does well with beans, tomatoes, and benefits brassicas by deterring cabbage white butterflies, but grows best of all with leeks. If left to flower, the celery and leeks will attract many beneficial insects especially predatory wasps and celery seed is good in baking.

Celery and celeriac need careful tending and a permanently moist, if not boggy, rich soil to grow at all well. Ideally, sow thinly on the surface in tiny pots or cells in early spring in a propagator. It is difficult to sow individually so thin early and pot up into bigger pots, before planting out at about a foot apart in trenches under plastic bottles or cloches in early summer. They must never be allowed to dry out. Once the plants are three quarters grown, remove poor leaves, surround each plant with newspaper collars and earth them up to blanch them. Take precautions against slugs and do not believe the claims of self-blanching types, which have a tougher texture.

If you only want celery flavor from the leaves, sow it direct and thick like chervil or parsley. Or grow celeriac instead. Sow in the same way as for celery and give it the same moist, rich soil when planting out. Celeriac is more forgiving and can be persuaded to produce its swollen root by most gardeners. No blanching is ever needed. The peeled root is used grated raw, braised or in other ways where celery flavor is required. Strip off the lowest leaves as the root starts to swell, and store once mature in a cool, frost-free place. Celery rust may be discouraged with a tea made of nettles and *Equisetum*.

Chicory produces big heads that are like a bitter lettuce and are grown just the same. The heads may be solid, or round and looser. The popular radicchio ('Rossa de Verona') is dark red, adds color and a subtle bitterness to salads. This is sown direct or started in cells like lettuce and planted out in early summer. However, some varieties of chicory such as 'Brussels Witloef' can also be left unharvested till late fall when the roots are lifted, their foliage cut off before being stored in a cool place. Then, when wanted, the roots are packed in sand in a box and kept in a warm, dark place where they produce solid shoots, called chicons. Finely sliced chicons are a superb addition to winter salads. If not lifted, chicory may overwinter and produce early leaves for cutting before bolting. The root can also be roasted and ground to make a coffee substitute.

Chinese cabbage is better known than most related oriental vegetables and is a valuable crop in its own right. It must be sown in situ, a foot or so apart in rich moist soil, or it will quickly bolt. In dry conditions, Chinese cabbages suffer from flea beetle before they bolt, and in wet conditions they are eaten by slugs. New varieties may produce a crop if sown before midsummer, but most only do well sown just after midsummer till midfall—though the later sowings need cloching.

Florence fennel is similar to celery with an aniseed flavour and is considerably easier to grow. It is best sown early or in the middle of the summer in situ or in cells. Plant out when very small a foot or so apart. Do not let the plants ever dry out otherwise they bolt as will many early sowings. The leaf can be used in the same way as fennel. If the swollen bulb is cut off above the root it resprouts.

Kohlrabi A tough and disease-resistant crop much like a turnip but easier and not as hot. This should not be grown with brassicas, tomatoes, strawberries, sweet peppers, or runner beans, but can be mixed with onions, beets, and ridge cucumbers. Though rarely grown, this odd-looking vegetable is very easy, highly nutritious and immune to most pests and diseases. It can be cooked,

It may look alien, but kohlrabi is a tasty, versatile vegetable.

but is best used raw, grated or as crudité sticks.

It will grow in relatively poor conditions and, unlike turnips, can be transplanted from seedbed, cells or pots. Sow it in succession from mid-spring to midsummer. Eat kohlrabi before they get large and tough, and use them instead of grated cabbage for Kohlslaw! (see page 196). Look out for 'Gigante,' from Czechoslovakia, which, if given space, can get very big and yet still remain crisp, tender, and good for crudités.

Spinach For those who want the real thing, sow in situ from early spring till late summer. However, spinach can be started in cells or pots if planted out while still very small. It is worth feeding the soil beforehand with ground seaweed or sieved compost as spinach needs moist, rich conditions otherwise it bolts. Protect the plants from birds, use slug traps and never allow them or the plants to dry out. One of the crops most deserving of being grown through a plastic sheet mulch, which keeps the soil off the leaves as well as aiding growth. Round seeded spinaches are the best for summer. For winter and early spring use prickly seeded spinaches—sow them in the same way, but during late summer. Cloches will keep the weather from messing up the leaves, but may encourage mildew. New Zealand spinach is a non-spinach that is used and grown in the same way. It's far better in hot, dry conditions, can be started in pots, and is more reluctant to bolt. However, it needs twice the space at about two foot apart.

Sunflower seeds make tasty snacks for us, chickens, and wild birds.

ANNUAL HERBS USED MOSTLY FOR THEIR FLOWERS

Borage is one of the best bee plants, a good accumulator of minerals for compost and grows well with strawberries. The flowers add color to beverages and tender leaves can be added in small amounts to salads. Borage tends to sprawl, so is best at the back of borders. Sow in situ, thin to a foot or so apart and allow to self-seed thereafter. Kept renovated, with occasional trimming, borage can be in flower most of late spring and summer.

Pot marigold Do not try French or African marigolds. It is the flower petals of pot marigolds (*Calendula*) that are edible. Use their petals freely in salads and with seafood; they are also surprisingly good in stews. Sow in pots or direct any time of year at a foot apart each way and allow to self-seed.

Nasturtiums are edible in all parts—the flowers are colorful additions to salads and the young leaves add piquancy. The seeds and pods can be pickled and used as a better substitute for capers. Sow nasturtiums after the last frost in a moist place or in pots and grow at a foot apart. Do not overfeed the plants or there will be few flowers.

Sunflowers are usually grown for their seeds but the petals are bitter sweet and the young heads can be eaten while they are in bud like globe artichokes. For good heads sow in early spring and give each plant at least a foot each way.

ANNUAL HERBS GROWN FOR THEIR SEEDS

All of the following will give bigger crops per plant if given enough space, say a foot each way. However, the total yield is higher if they are crowded a bit, so sow three inches or so apart.

Anise *(Pimpinella anisum)* is a pungent annual herb often used in ointments against insect bites and stings. A host to predatory wasps, it also deters aphids. The flavor of the herb goes well with both sweet and savory foods; the leaves are used fresh and the seed dried. Sow in warm soil after the last frost.

Caraway can be difficult to establish and takes one and a half years to crop. It is best sown in situ in early summer, or fall if fresh seed is available. The feathery leaves and tiny pungent seed are used in salads and savory dishes and the seeds are really good on baked products. The roots have been boiled as a vegetable.

Coriander seeds are often added to bread or baked dishes to give them a warm, spicy flavor. The leaves are also popular in some cuisines. Coriander repels aphids and has been used as a spray against spider mites. Sow in situ in late spring.

Cumin seeds are the real curry flavor and need to be well dried to keep. If you acquire the taste, they can be used like black pepper and in almost every dish. Station sow (see page 91) in early summer a finger or so apart. Support the plants with sticks to stop the seed heads falling over and getting dirty. Black cumin comes from the seeds of *Nigella sativa*; the seeds of the closely related *N. damascena* are also edible. Both have a spicy, aromatic flavor that is pleasant, especially with sweet, sticky buns. Sow in spring in situ.

Poppies *(Papaver somniferum)* have been grown for their seed for use on baked products for as long as they have been grown for opium. They are a weed and self-sow wildly. For the best seed give them full sun and pick the heads before they open.

Growing poppies for opium is, of course, illegal, but I believe you may still grow poppies for seed in the U.S.—and the number required for home baking would only be a few dozen heads, whereas for the drug you would need a small farm for serious production. I doubt the average English summer would make for a good crop anyway.

Vegetables

This section deals with the individual needs and uses of each vegetable to help you to produce organically and with the least effort crops that are suitable for household consumption, not to give record yields or win prizes at shows. I have found the methods I recommend satisfactory for producing reasonable crops with least work. I have given sowing periods, but these are only guidelines as they will vary for area and season. Depths for sowing are maximums, planting distances are for vegetables grown in blocks to optimum size, but again these may vary tremendously depending on whether you want small young specimens or larger-growing ones. Seed packets carry sufficient instructions for larger and smaller varieties and distances for row planting.

Fresh asparagus is sweet and fit for anyone's table.

Despite the loss of most old varieties, there are still many to choose from and although I recommend those I have found exceptionally good for flavor, you may find that they are not to your taste. However, new varieties come along constantly and it is always worth trying different ones to see what suits your soil, situation, and taste. Where I have a strong opinion as to whether or not a crop is worth growing, I have said so, basing my judgment on its culinary value, reliability, effort required, and space taken.

Perennials are given first, as they proffer the best value all round. The legumes are rated next most valuable, as they also create fertility, followed, in my estimation, by alliums, roots, brassicas, cucurbits, and others—with main-crop potatoes last as they are a lot of work compared to the cost of buying a sack of organic ones. . .

Perennial vegetables

Asparagus is a real luxury crop. It is expensive to buy and the home-grown is so much sweeter. Being a member of the lily family, asparagus takes time to build up large enough resources to throw up good, thick spears—it is usually three years before it becomes productive. The attractive foliage means asparagus can be planted in ornamental areas, but yields are best in a permanent bed in full sun—and it takes a lot of space to yield any quantity. Asparagus rarely suffers from pests and diseases, though the asparagus beetle can be temporarily troublesome. It's the small, slug-like larvae which do the damage, but they are easily killed with derris dust.

Asparagus can be grown under fruit trees and grapes to save space—it was traditionally grown in the vineyards of Beaujolais as the berries fob off the birds. It grows well with tomatoes which helps hide it from the asparagus beetle, and a root secretion from asparagus kills Trichodorus, a nematode that attacks the roots of tomatoes. Both like basil and together they make a happy trio. Parsley does well with asparagus, onions are disliked.

Sow in situ, or plant one-year-old crowns as early as possible in spring. Plant the fleshy roots carefully on a mound in a trench at a good stride apart each way. Do not take a spear till three years from planting, and then never after the start of summer. Likewise never remove the ferny foliage till it's dried up. Darken the soil with soot and do not mulch if you want the earliest spears. You can also force plants with cloches.

Epicurean attentions Green asparagus has more flavor than white, blanched spears, but may be bitter if not fresh. Steaming is best for fresh, home-picked asparagus—if it's store-bought, boil it with salted water to remove any stale bitterness.

Bob's gourmet choices New hybrids are offered that are all male and do not waste energy producing seed. Otherwise there is very little to choose between varieties, and personally I prefer female plants anyway as they give bigger, thicker, more succulent spears. 'Jersey Knight' produces very thick spears. (Asparagus addicts read Kidner's book on asparagus and seek out seed from his Regal strain, which gave half-pound spears!)

Seakale is rarely grown in Britain, despite being native to the country, practically unaffected by pests and diseases, and producing a tasty, nutritious crop in early spring. It is attractive enough to be grown in ornamental areas. Ideally, get planting "thongs" of a good, long-selected local variety. Sadly, only 'Lily White' is usually available. The alternative is to sow in a seed bed and grow the best plants on for a year, before transplanting them to their permanent position. Plant them a stride apart in late winter, and grow

Rhubarb is one of the easiest and earliest fresh crops each year.

them on till fall. Put bottomless buckets over the crowns during dry weather and fill a foot deep with a mixture of peat or leafmold and sand. When the shoots appear in spring, remove the bucket and filling, then cut off the blanched shoots and head at ground level. Left to sprout and grow the root and crown will crop for many years.

Epicurean attentions Steam the cleaned shoots for three quarters of an hour and serve with a Hollandaise sauce or butter for a luxury treat. If the bitter flavor is too much, boil instead of steam and change the water twice.

Rhubarb is early to crop and reliable and, although hard to find, there are a surprising number of varieties. It will grow in between other fruits, in ornamental areas or as groundcover at a good stride apart. Rhubarb is not too fussy about shade, site or position and rarely suffers pests or diseases. To force for earlier crops, simply cover the crowns with a bottomless bucket, barrel or stack of tires lined with a little loose straw. Do give the crowns

some compost every year or two to keep up their productivity. It is worth buying certified virus-free plants initially, as these produce much more freely. You can also grow some varieties from seed.

Epicurean attentions Pull the stems with a twist rather than cutting them. Stop at midsummer, as the sourness becomes too much. Rhubarb can be eaten in desserts, frozen or made into jam and wine.

Bob's gourmet choices 'Timperley Early' is best for forcing, and 'Victoria' is very good. 'Glaskin's Perpetual' can be pulled for longer before it gets too acid, and all old varieties such as 'Holstein Blood Red' and 'Early Champagne' are worth searching for.

Globe artichokes and cardoons
Artichokes are very large attractive plants that can be used in an ornamental area. They have beautiful blue flowers that attract bees. They do better given their own bed of rich soil and rotated every third year or so. Rarely affected by pests and diseases, they are easy but may be lost in hard, wet winters unless protected with straw or a cloche. Ideally, procure offsets from good clean stock in·early spring, as they do not come true from seed. They can be sown in pots in spring, later to be transplanted out a good stride or two apart. Select from this stock after a couple of years of building up the plants to tell their worth.

Cardoons look much the same but are grown annually. They have their leaves bound up and wrapped in late summer to blanch the hearts for winter use. Cardoons are always grown fresh from seed—the skill lies in keeping them growing without check, so you need a rich, moist soil to make a succulent heart for blanching.

Epicurean attentions If aphids or earwigs get in the artichoke heads, soak them in salt water before cooking and the pests float off. The hearts can be frozen for winter use and are scrumptious on pizza and in patés.

the oysters, which grow on wood, straw or sawdust and are worthwhile for the fun of it. Surpluses are easily dried or frozen.

Epicurean attentions The stalks of mushrooms are tough, so save them up, dried or frozen, for making stock or soup. Gently fry mushrooms in butter with salt, freshly ground black pepper, and lemon juice. Keep them at a low temperature to avoid scalding.

Bob's gourmet choices Shiitake mushrooms are so expensive to buy their kits almost look good value, and the fresh mushrooms are fantastic, almost garlicky, and delicious.

Legumes

These enrich the soil by fixing nitrogen in nodules of bacteria on their roots. In some soils, the first few crops may be poor as these bacteria are not present. Inoculate your soil with the bacteria, available from commercial seedsmen for use with alfalfa. Alternatively, acquire a little compost or soil from the garden of a friend (without brassica clubroot) who grows peas and beans well, and add this to the water for your first seed drill.

When clearing these crops, cut off the stems at ground level to leave the root systems to enrich the soil. They all enjoy lime in the soil and it can be applied during their rotation. Mulching with a thin sterile layer after sowing these large, strong-seeded crops will suppress weeds among them without risking their own emergence.

Broad beans are very nutritious and easy to grow, they freeze well, and can even be dried for use in soups. Extra early crops of long-pod varieties may usually be had from early winter sowings in mild years. Broad beans can be planted with potatoes both in the fall for the earliest crops if the winters are mild, or in the spring. The young beans protect the early

Bob's gourmet choices 'Green Globe' and 'Imperial Strain' are excellent. Purple artichokes can taste better than the green, but have small thorns on the bud scales; try 'Purple Globe' and 'Violetta di Chioggia.'

Jerusalem artichokes are a good standby crop for when the potatoes fail, not much loved by anyone as they save wind up all season to release once you've eaten them! These tall plants make useful, quick and easy windbreaks. Being related to sunflowers they get on well with corn and their dense growth will suppress ground elder and even *Equisetum*. Plant the tubers one to two fingers deep a foot apart in early spring. They are difficult to eradicate, so are best confined to wild corners. The tubers are not easy to clean, but are nutritious. They keep well only if left in the ground and are immune to pests and diseases. Straw over their beds in late fall, so you can dig them unfrozen in deepest winter.

Epicurean attentions Try them peeled, sliced, and deep fried and as a soup with anchovies and shallots.

Bob's gourmet choices 'Fuseau' has golden, chocolate-vanilla-scented

Globe artichokes are beautiful and edible—well, a very tasty little bit is.

flowers and longish tubers. 'Stampede' is shorter, flowers more freely, and has thin-skinned tubers.

Mushroom kits are available which are very expensive per mushroom produced and are unreliable unless you follow the instructions religiously. Starting with fresh strawy horse manure and mushroom spawn is a lot of work for risky results. The critical thing is to get the ambient conditions perfect. Without a cellar or similar, success is rare as mushrooms prefer a fairly constant temperature. I believe my lack of decent yields is due to the low humidity where I live. In wetter climes more success is likely. My best crop came years ago from a kit that I kept down in the bilges of a houseboat I was living on.

Mushrooms are probably less irksome grown as a perennial. Pare back rich, lush turf by a shady, damp hedge base and mix the spawn in with the soil, then re-cover with turf. If you are lucky you will get a harvest, if not. . . There are many other different edible fungi, such as potato shoots from wind and frost. Grown with gooseberries, they discourage sawfly caterpillars. Broad beans are also a good crop to follow with corn as they leave a rich, moist soil and the stumps give wind protection to the corn's young shoots. I sow them almost a hand's breadth apart and nearly a finger deep. Pinch out the tips once the beans have flowered as this prevents black aphid attacks, or use soft soap later. Growing summer savory nearby helps discourage the pest. Black ants protect the aphids from predators, so destroy their nests.

Epicurean attentions Broad beans go well with summer savory, and if they are deskinned they make a base for a most delicious pâté.

Bob's gourmet choices 'Aquadulce Claudia' is the hardiest, 'Express' is quick and productive, but not as tasty as the tenderer 'Windsor' sorts. For small gardens, the dwarf 'The Sutton' is handy, but for us gourmets it has to be 'Red Epicure.'

French and haricot beans came originally from South America and are variously known as waxpod, snap, string, green or just dwarf beans. These are a nutritious crop which freeze well and the seeds can be dried for winter use. They are prone to late frosts, cold wind and

French beans are expensive to buy, freeze well, and are very productive.

slug and bird damage, so benefit immensely from plastic bottle cloches. Mulches after sowing with grass clippings keep the soil in better condition, but encourage slugs. These beans do well with brassicas and celery when planted in rich, moist soil. Sow under cloches from late spring till late summer, an inch or so deep at a foot each way. If you are hungry enough, almost any home-grown dried French beans can be boiled and eaten, but for gourmet haricots of the best texture, grow suitable drying sorts. Give the plants a warm, dry site so they ripen well—cloches may help towards the end of the season. There are several climbing varieties that grow much like runner beans but have the finer texture and flavor of dwarf French beans. These are much the same to grow, but obviously need supports and are the best for growing out of season under cover.

Epicurean attentions Keep the green bean varieties well picked or they soon stop producing. The pods are finest when you cannot see the bean seed shape from outside and the flesh snaps crisply when bent. Store the dried beans in the pods in a very dry, rodent-proof place and remember to start soaking them the night before they're wanted for cooking.

Bob's gourmet choices 'Slenderette,' 'Tendercrop,' and 'Venture' are my favorites for squeaky greens, as I call them. For beans 'Jacob's Cattle' and 'Soldier' are reliable—and wind-producing. 'Blue Lake White Seeded' and 'Fortex' are good climbers.

Runner beans are highly productive climbers, but have a coarser texture and flavor than French beans. They need to be well mulched and watered to do very well and kept picked. They need supporting on poles, wires, or strings—netting is better and wire netting best of all. All of these can be suspended from posts, walls or fences. Runner beans can be a problem late in the season when they tend to shade out other crops. This may benefit some, especially celery

and saladings, but only when enough water is available. Brassicas, especially Brussels sprouts, also benefit. They are sheltered by runner beans while small and then grow on once the beans die back, flourishing on the nitrogen left by them. Runner beans dislike kohlrabi, onions, and often sunflowers, which is a shame! Try sowing the shorter varieties to grow up and over corn. Runner beans are perennial and can be protected or overwintered as dormant "tubers" for an earlier crop. Sow the seed in late spring in situ two or three inches deep and the same apart in rows. An easy crop to grow loads of, and varieties with colored flowers and purple beans look good in ornamental areas.

Epicurean attentions Usually best picked small. Surpluses can be frozen, salted or pickled and the dried seeds can be used in stews.

Bob's gourmet choices Grow 'Desiree,' 'Achievement,' 'Merit,' 'Scarlet Emperor,' and the nearly stringless 'Lady Di.' Dried 'Sunset' seeds are as good as lima beans.

Peas are more work than most vegetables, but are so delicious fresh that I can never give up growing them and, being legumes, they enrich the soil for other crops. They are one of the few crops better grown in rows. I have modified the way they are usually sown and supported to save as much work as possible. First grow short varieties; although they produce less they do not need as much or as strong support, nor do they shade out other crops. Do not use pea sticks, as these take a lot of time to put up and take down and get in the way when picking. Instead use galvanized chicken netting on strong canes or metal stakes; it's quick and easy to erect and in fall the dried haulm can be stripped off, the roll wound up and any haulm left on can be burned off, destroying spores and pests. And if you have enough, you can bend the bottom edge of the netting back and over the row, making a guard to keep off birds.

I sow peas an inch or two apart and the same deep in a well-watered and drained slit trench made with the edge of a spade instead of digging out a wide drill. After sowing peas, infill with soil and firm down. I use a thin, sterile mulch over the row to keep weeds down. My peas come through grass clippings, but in wetter areas peat or similar and sand is safer. It is expensive to buy pea seed and self-saved seed comes true. It is not even necessary to shell out the seed—I've laid the pods end to end in the slit, watered really well and had complete success. In dry conditions, peas germinate quicker if soaked for an hour or so before sowing. Adding a dash of seaweed solution helps disguise their smell from mice.

As peas need support, grow them down the middle of a bed with potatoes, brassicas, carrots or corn on either side. For succession, peas can be sown from late winter till late summer. Some can even be sown in late fall for overwintering, though these rarely do very well unprotected. The early crops miss most problems, though. Pea guards keep birds from eating the seeds and young leaves—but not mice, so use humane traps if these are a great problem. Don't worry about mildew: if the soil is quite moist, the plants won't suffer. One good watering when the flowers are just finishing will improve yields substantially. If maggots in the peas bother you, use barriers of fine netting, or spray with derris once most of the flowers have just finished, but wait till the bees have gone home in the evening, or use the tip below.

Epicurean attentions Pick peas early not late! Pod them immediately, blanch and freeze or cook and eat soon after, with joyous haste and lots of butter and mint jelly.

Tip: I cook the peas in the pods and serve them whole, so one can eat them like asparagus by putting the pod in the mouth, gripping it with the teeth and withdrawing the pod

The scent of rows of leeks and onions helps keep carrot root flies from their lunch.

leaving the succulent peas within. Surplus peas can be dried on the vines and saved for use in winter soups and stews, though they need soaking overnight before use.

Bob's gourmet choices The round-seeded varieties are the hardiest but not as sweet. 'Meteor' is probably most reliable but 'Alaska' is sweeter and 'Dakota' is best for early harvests. The wrinkle-seeded varieties are sweeter so for later sowings grow 'Wando,' 'Little Marvel,' and 'Progress #9.' Petit pois are small, very sweet, wrinkle-seeded peas that take a lot of podding, so use the tip above. Grow 'French Citadel,' 'Waverex,' and 'Carouby Maussane.'

Mangetout (snow) peas have edible pods, so podding is not necessary when they are young and tender, but they are usually very tall and rapidly get too tough to eat.

Sugar-snap peas are similar, but much improved with thicker, sweeter edible pods. They also tend to be tall. Asparagus peas are not really peas—they are more like a vetch. The pods can be eaten when very small and tender. The best that can be said of them is that they will grow in poor conditions and have pretty flowers.

Alliums

Easy to grow and store, valuable in the diet alliums have to be grown by every gardener. They accumulate sulfur and impart some disease resistance to plants near them, and their flowers are good for beneficial insects.

Shallots are the easiest vegetables to grow; simply put healthy cloves in very shallow depressions and fix in place with a dollop of sand, at about a foot apart from midwinter on, and even during the prior fall in mild areas. They are soon pulled out of their holes by birds and worms and need replanting, but otherwise rarely suffer any problems. When the leaves have withered, lift the crop and store them in a dry, airy place selecting the best clumps for next year's "seed." New varieties such as 'Prisma' can be grown from true seed. Shallots can be planted almost anywhere convenient, even in the ornamental garden.

Epicurean attentions Pickled shallots are much better than onions.

Bob's gourmet choices 'Matador' and 'French Demi-Long.'

Leeks are a very hardy crop, take up little space and rarely suffer any problems in a rich, moist soil, but they do not do well in hot, dry conditions. They can be grown mixed with onions, celery, and with carrots where they will decrease attacks of carrot root flies. They hide brassicas from pigeons, and unused leeks should be left to flower as they are loved by beneficial insects. Sow them shallowly indoors in mid-winter and in a seed bed in mid-spring. Transplant them in late spring to about a foot apart. When transplanting make deep holes, insert the leeks and align them so their leaves hang out of the way then water them in well with dilute seaweed solution.

Epicurean attentions Surround leeks with paper collars and be ultra careful not to let grit in the middle. Invert them for trimming and careful washing for the same reason.

Bob's gourmet choices For fall leeks sow 'Fall Giant' or 'Toledo.' For winter use, 'Musselburgh' is hard to beat and 'Winora' will stand and grow larger until the end of spring. The latter has blue foliage and looks good in ornamental areas.

Onions do suffer a few pests and diseases, but most years they still produce good results if the weather is favorable. They can be grown in several different ways which splits the risks and also extends their season of availability. Easiest of all is to buy organic onion sets. These are not cheap, but usually avoid many of the problems and give good results. Onion sets are planted from late winter to midspring, but the earlier the better if the ground is ready. Plant them in very shallow holes a hand's breadth or so apart, and keep putting them back as the birds and worms pull them out or fix them with a handful of sand. Onions are convenient for intercropping where space is available especially between brassicas, but keep them away from beans. They are also useful in ornamental areas where they discourage pests and diseases. Onions

Onions store best if the tops are allowed to wither naturally. *Never bend them down "to help."*

can be sown direct but are best sown under cover in mid- to late winter in pots or cellular seed trays. Do not worry about getting more than one plant per cell, as two or three grown together will produce smaller, harder onions that will keep longer than big ones. Plant the seedlings out in mid-spring. Use closer planting—down to one every three inches—for small long keepers, and much more space for big ones and clumps. In late summer, mid-August in southern Britain, you can direct sow Japanese onions for overwintering. These crop before midsummer when onions are expensive to buy, but do not try to store them as they go off easily.

If onion fly is a problem in your area grow sets which rarely suffer or grow under netting or horticultural fleece. The spring sowings can be mixed with carrots as an intercrop which helps hide them from the fly. If the leaves get a gray mold, dust them with wood ash, which checks the attack. Be careful never to break or damage the leaves or bulb when cultivating—it is best to weed round onions by hand.

Once the bulbs start to ripen, let the weeds grow, as they will take up nutrients and help the ripening process. Never bend the leaves down

to help ripening, as this lets in disease. Loosen the soil underneath the onions with a fork or sever the roots with a sharp knife. Dry them off under cover in an airy place, and store on open trays rather than tie them up in bunches.

For small pickling onions, just sow thickly so that they crowd each other. Escallions are the slender ones you want for salads, but are never ready in time, they need to be sown the year before in fall or winter for spring use and again every few weeks for succession.

Epicurean attentions Peel onions under water; slice them in both rings and segments as these cook differently.

Bob's gourmet choices 'Sturon' and 'Turbo' are excellent, 'Giant Zittau' is good for pickling, 'Bedfordshire Champion' is a good keeper and 'Southport Red Globe' a lovely change for the kitchen. 'Shikuro' and 'Tokyo Long White' are the best Japanese onions, and 'Barletta' is the ultimate pickling variety, especially good in piccalilli.

Roots

These are often highly nutritious as their deep roots tap levels of soil further down than most plants. Thus they are soil breakers and improvers, leaving behind fine roots and foliage enriched with minerals, particularly the beets and chards. The soil does not need digging because the fine taproot will go straight down into the hardest ground if it is moist and the seed has a firm covering of soil to push against. They are mostly biennials building up their reserves to flower the following year. If they get stressed, bolting into flower early is a common problem. Remove bolters to prevent them encouraging others. I use a two-prong fork made from the middle of a four-prong digging fork to lift out roots with minimal disturbance and greatest ease.

Carrots are probably the most worthwhile crop, but they must be grown under an old net curtain, horticultural fleece or similar to prevent root fly damage. Perpetually plagued by this, I have tried many herbs and strong-smelling remedies with some success, mostly from intercropping onions, chives, and leeks. Carrot root fly can be stopped by a simple barrier of anything thigh-high around small beds. This stops the adult fly which will go round rather than over such barriers. But the very best preventatives are crop rotation and a physical barrier of fleece to stop the fly laying its eggs by the seedling carrots.

Carrots need a stone-free, light soil to do well. Heavy clay soils need lightening with organic material and sharp sand well mixed in. Do not overfeed or use fresh manure as these will cause poor flavor and forked roots. Heavy soil may be improved the year before sowing with a green manuring of flax. I find carrots will follow onions well on a light soil. Do not disturb the soil deeper than an inch and the seedling carrots will grow straight down. Sow successively and shallowly from early spring through till midsummer. Station sowing (see page 91) at three or fewer per foot apart is best if you want large carrots for storing, but for handfuls of baby carrots I prefer broadcast sowing. Rake the soil, then water it heavily and let it percolate away. Mix the seed with sand and then sow this from side to side, back and fro. Cover the seed with a half inch of used sterile potting compost, sharp sand and peat or similar, pat it down and cover with fleece well pegged down at the edges.

Unwanted carrots left to flower attract hoverflies and beneficial wasps. I keep most of mine in the ground over winter just covered with straw and a plastic sheet. Geese love them!

Epicurean attentions Carrots keep best once dug with the dirt left on them

Carrots grow easily in a light, sandy soil.

and only washed when needed. Carrots stored near apples may acquire a bitter taint.

Bob's gourmet choices 'Coreless Amsterdam' is the best quick carrot and is excellent grown in a coldframe. Surpluses freeze well. 'Earlibird' is nearly as good and can be sown from late winter under cover and right through to late summer for little ones for winter. 'Mokum' and 'Nigel' are good summer carrots with sweet crunchiness rivalling store-bought apples and a better flavor. 'Fall King' is superb if a bit coarse for winter storage. For shallow soil or containers in the greenhouse 'Parmex' is useful as it grows short

and round like a radish. For maximum vitamin A 'Juwarot' is superb, having double the average amount. It is worth trying many different carrot varieties.

Parsnips, Hamburg parsley, salsify and scorzonera are all similar root crops that are not difficult to grow but occupy the ground for a long time and so are not recommended where space is short. Hamburg parsley produces a parsnip-like root and is grown and used like parsnips, but tastes of parsley and the leaves can be used as parsley. Salsify and scorzonera are like long, thin parsnips with a much better flavor. These all rarely suffer from pests or diseases other than the usual soil pests and carrot rootfly. Protect them with cloches or

Turnips with roots, Hamburg parsley, and scorzonera are gourmet vegetables you will rarely find in shops.

Swiss chard is exceptionally good value, with chunky stalks for braising and the leaves good for "spinach."

fleece. If left to flower, they are good for beneficial insects and are best intercropped with peas or lettuce. They all keep well in the ground, though it is wise to dig some up to store in a shed when hard frosts are likely. These all need sowing in early spring three seeds per station at about a foot apart and protecting with a small cloche as germination is slow. The seed does not keep, so use fresh every year. Thin to one seedling once they emerge and forget about them till harvest.

Epicurean attentions Parsnips taste better after the frost has got to them—try them parboiled, then made into French fries. Salsify and scorzonera do not store well, so dig them just before use, parboil without peeling, then slip the skins off and fry the roots in butter. Young scorzonera shoots can be eaten in salads.

Bob's gourmet choices Among the parsnips, 'Avonresister' is reliable but

small, 'Gladiator' makes a flavorsome large one, and 'Dagger' is a tasty mini variety. There is little choice with the others.

Turnips and rutabaga can be started in cells if planted out while still small, but do much better sown direct, half an inch deep at up to a foot apart, from early spring right through to late summer. Other than flea beetle, they rarely suffer from pests and diseases, but if grown in dry conditions become tough and hot. They grow well in the shade of peas or intercropped with French beans. The leaves of turnips can be eaten as spinach. Rutabaga are very like turnips, but are sown in late spring either direct or in cells and transplanted while small for fall and winter use, as they stand and store better than turnips.

Bob's gourmet choices 'Tokyo Cross' is the best all-round turnip and will store reasonably well in a cool place. 'Snowball' is quick to grow and more succulent but 'Purple Top Milan' is the best-flavored turnip. 'Acme Purple Top' and 'Joan' are both reliable rutabagas. 'Gilfeather' is sweet and 'Best of All' is the hardiest.

Beets and chards Red, yellow, and sugar beet are very closely related to leaf beet, perpetual spinach and Swiss chard. Originating from maritime regions, they need trace elements more than most crops. They thrive on seaweed products but do poorly in impoverished chemically fertilized soil. Good mineral accumulators— one quarter of the mineral content of their leaves is magnesium, which is extremely valuable when added to the compost. They do well growing mixed with French beans, onions, and brassicas, especially kohlrabi. The most troublesome pest is birds eating the seedlings and young leaves. Use wire-netting guards or plastic bottle cloches. Sow in pots or cells under cover in early spring, then plant out in the open from late spring to mid-summer. The beets do well sown one seed capsule to a pot, cell or station and left unthinned at a foot or so apart to give clumps of smaller beet for pickling. Sown direct and thinned, they can be grown larger for winter storage. Chards, leaf beets, and perpetual spinach are effectively beets grown for their leaf and stems instead of their roots. They are treated similarly, but must be thinned to almost two foot apart. These are one of the most productive crops for small gardens, as they will produce till hard winter frosts come, and often sprout again in spring.

Epicurean attentions The stems of Swiss chard braised in a cheese sauce are delicious. The green leaf can also be used as spinach—keep pulling the stems and it comes again.

Bob's gourmet choices Especially recommended are 'Red Ace,' the yellow 'Burpee's Golden,' and for pickling and slicing 'Detroit Dark Red' or 'Cylindra,' which have barrel-shaped roots. For winter storage, grow 'Crimson King'; if bolting is a problem, try 'Boltardy.' Ruby chard is brightly colored and looks good in the ornamental garden, but 'Fordhook Giant,' 'Lucullus,' or 'Orea' taste better.

Brassicas

Members of the cabbage family are highly bred and very specialized, needing rich soil and plenty of lime. They are all prone to clubroot disease so if you do not have it in your soil *never bring in any brassica plants*. Once present, clubroot is almost incurable. If you must buy brassica plants, choose only those grown in sterile compost. Wallflowers and stocks can carry the disease and it may be introduced with muck, so compost it thoroughly before use. Clubroot can be decreased in virulence by liming the plot very heavily. And you can give your crops a head start by raising them in pots filled with sterile compost, so that the infected soil does not touch the young roots.

Although brassicas are best sown direct, they can be started in small pots. The most reliable crops are sown in a seed bed, thinned to three inches apart, lifted and planted back again when they are about three inches high. They are then transplanted to their final site when they have a couple of pairs of real leaves. All brassicas suffer badly from bird damage, so use black cotton or cloches while they are small.

They benefit from herbs such as chamomile, dill, peppermint, rosemary, and sage nearby to help confuse their pests. One old companion idea was to plant wormwood or southernwood with the cabbages to drive away the cabbage white butterflies. It worked, but the leaf exudations poisoned the soil, lowering yields significantly.

Generally brassicas grow well with peas, celery, potatoes, onions, and dwarf beans, but not near rue, runner beans, lettuce or strawberries. Cabbage rootfly attacks them when they are transplanted, so make collars up to a foot square out of cardboard, old carpet underlay or roofing felt. With a slit to the center of the collar, they can be pushed round the stem of the seedling brassica and laid flat on the ground to prevent the fly laying its eggs in the soil by the stem. The loathed caterpillars can be hand-picked or sprayed with *Bacillus thuringiensis*, or the adults can be kept off with nets. Whitefly, which are different to the ones in greenhouses, are not much of a problem but can be controlled with soft soap if they start to increase as can aphid attacks. Flea beetle makes little pinholes in the seedling leaves, keep the area wet to discourage them.

When planting out brassicas, mix a handful of sieved garden compost, seaweed, and calcified seaweed in with the soil you return to the planting hole. The brassicas are exceptionally good for our health and are the most reliable over-wintering crops available in the spring. They all need sowing in spring and transplanting a couple of feet apart or so by early summer. Read the packets carefully. It's very hard to save true seed.

Cabbages are terminal buds and to get them to swell without opening is a marvel of controlling nature. Constant unchecked growth in rich, moist conditions is required. Cabbages can be produced for use

A good cabbage well grown is as sweet as an apple.

every day of the year—some can be close planted for small heads. In early spring, a liquid feed can be applied to get slow overwintered greens moving again, but don't overdo it as this spoils the flavour.

Epicurean attentions Don't cut all a cabbage in one go. Cut a section out and cover the rest of the head with foil, as it keeps fresher in the garden than in the fridge. All cabbages may produce a bonus crop of little ones if the root is left when the head is cut and a cross made in the top of the stem. However, this is not worthwhile if the ground is needed for another crop.

Bob's gourmet choices For early summer cabbages start 'Grayhound,' Golden Acre,' or 'Spitfire' in pots under glass from late winter and plant out in spring. Then sow 'Pixie,' 'Minicole,' or 'Stonehead' from early spring in a seed bed and plant out in late spring. For early fall cabbages, sow 'Grand Prize,' 'Winningstadt,' and 'Dynasty' from late spring and plant out in early summer. For late fall and into winter, sow 'Multikeeper,' 'Survivor,' 'Arena,' 'Huron,' and 'Ace' from late spring and plant out in summer. When hard frosts threaten, pull the winter cabbages up, roots and all, and hang them upside down in a cool, frost-free shed or cover them in straw and a plastic bag. For spring cabbages in zones 7-9, sow 'Head Start,' 'Dynamo,' and 'Balbro' in late summer, plant out in early fall and protect against harsh weather.

Broccolis Sprouting broccoli are useful spring varieties that throw many small heads instead of one big one. The popular calabrese is an fall broccoli. All these are very highly bred and require rich conditions and heavy soil to form their swollen immature flowerbuds. All of these do best sown directly in situ, but with care can be started off in small pots and planted out well before their root system fills the compost. They need to be at least two foot apart each way

and three for the sprouters.

Epicurean attentions Break the surrounding leaves over the curd to prevent the sun turning it yellow.

Bob's gourmet choices Grow early purple, late purple, and white sprouting broccolis for succession in early spring. All varieties are excellent. 'Green Comet' is very productive, 'Packman' is the most forgiving and disease resistant and 'Romanesco' really delicious with a superb texture and flavor, but it is quite difficult to grow well.

Cauliflowers are really cauliflowers only during the warm months—the winter-hardy ones are botanically broccoli which are tougher than true cauliflowers. They are the most highly bred and the most difficult of the family to grow well. The part we eat is an enormous multiple-flowered head suspended in the bud stage. Any check or damage will lead to "button" heads. There are red and green cauliflowers and dwarf ones that take less space. They all require rich, moist soil to do well; do not expect good results on light soils. Sowing dates are critical, so read the packet! They need to be at least two foot apart each way, three for big heads. With successional sowings of different varieties cauliflowers can be had most of the year but it is much more difficult to get all of these to do well than for cabbages.

Epicurean attentions Subject to the same problems as the other brassicas, cauliflowers need most attention as the shape and texture of their heads makes pest problems more detrimental than for, say, cabbage where the outer leaves can be discarded. When the curd starts to swell, bend side leaves over to keep the light from yellowing it.

Bob's gourmet choices Sow 'All the Year Round,' 'Apex,' and 'Snow Crown' from early spring to early summer, and plant out from late spring for summer and fall. On light soils and in small gardens grow mini-caulis;

Curly kale is a good standby crop for hard springs, and the smallest leaves are delicious in salads.

these are direct sown at six inches apart and produce small heads suitable for individual meals and good for freezing. 'Garant' is the most reliable.

Kale is the hardiest of all brassicas and will feed you with tasty greens, raw or cooked, in spring when all else fails. It is nutritious, fairly resistant to clubroot and cabbage root fly, and rarely eaten by birds. Sow in late spring and plant in early summer.

Epicurean attentions Try the smallest leaves chopped fine with the first chives and parsley in mayonnaise on buttered toast.

Bob's gourmet choices 'Dwarf Green Curled' and 'Vates Blue Curled' are almost the only varieties available. A wonderfully tasty old variety, 'Asparagus Kale,' has been lost to us commercially, which is a shame.

Brussels sprouts One of the hardier brassicas, they have the family tendencies differing mainly in a tolerance for runner beans and a liking for really firm soil. They need to be two to three feet apart and in loose soil are best in threes to later make a tripod tied together at the top ready for the windiest weather.

Epicurean attentions If you want really firm, tight sprouts plant extra deep and extra firm. If you want the sprouts to swell more quickly nip out the terminal shoot—it's a tasty dish on it's own.

Bob's gourmet choices Brussels sprouts can be available from fall till spring if several varieties are grown. Sow successional varieties from early spring till early summer, transplant by midsummer in well-firmed soil and plant them extra deep. Grow 'Vancouver' (early), 'Jade Cross' (mid), 'Oliver,' and 'Revenge' (late). If you love sprouts then try Noisette which produces tiny nutty ones, and 'Rubine' which are red like red cabbage but also small. The tops can be eaten as spring greens.

Cucurbits

Summer squashes, and pumpkins are all closely related. It is not worth saving their seed as they cross pollinate too freely. They all need similar conditions especially rich soil and warmth at the start.

Summer Squash give large numbers of small fruits from each plant which are easy to cook in myriad ways. They need a very rich soil to do well, and flourish on the compost heap. Grow zucchini among corn, peas, and beans, but avoid having potatoes nearby. Sow in pots in the warm in late spring, and plant out three feet apart once the last frost has gone. Or sow direct under a cloche or plastic bottle in late spring. Watch out for slug damage, but otherwise they have few treatable pest or disease problems.

Bob's gourmet choices 'Defender' and 'Goldbar' are the supreme summer squash, the yellow varieties such as 'Golden Zucchini' are poor but add color to dishes. 'Green Bush' is a compact variety more like a zucchini. Vegetable spaghetti is just a marrow with stringy insides, only worth growing if you like it! 'Golden Nugget' is the best storing squash for winter, it has a compact habit.

Old-fashioned (non-F1) sprouts swell a few at a time and can be picked over weeks.

'Uchiki Kuri' is a similar Japanese form and has sweet nutty fruits which can be added to soups and stews or baked. 'Mammoth' grows big, takes even more space and has little culinary value, unless you want to eat pumpkin pie for months on end. Grow zucchini instead.

Cucumbers are often considered the poor relation of the greenhouse or frame cucumbers, but can have fine texture and flavor if grown well. They can benefit from a coldframe or cloches and can be grown in a cold greenhouse or tunnel. In hot summers, ridge cucumbers do well under corn or sunflowers in the light shade. They also grow well among dill, peas, beans, beet, and carrots, but dislike potatoes and most strong herbs especially sage.

Sow the seed, on edge, half an inch deep in individual pots in warmth in late spring. Keep warm and pot up until planted out at least two feet apart with some protection in early summer. Alternatively, sow in situ under cloches in early summer. Most trailing cucumbers can be grown up fences or over trellis once they are vigorous enough to fill the cloche or coldframe. It does not matter if they are pollinated as, unlike indoor cucumbers, this does not make them bitter. Gherkin varieties for pickling are more reliable and can be eaten as small cucumbers anyway and vice versa. The Japanese varieties are the easiest to grow—I find them as generously productive as runner beans can be.

Epicurean attentions Gherkins are best picked small so check them daily. Dill goes exceptionally well with all cucumbers.

Bob's gourmet choices 'Bush Pickle' is good, 'Marketmore' is tasty, the Japanese varieties 'Orient Express' and 'Kyoto' are excellent. 'County Fair' is my favorite gherkin.

Corn Maize is bred for animal fodder and is not good for eating. Corn is almost uniquely Anglo-American and relatively unknown to continental Europeans. Traditionally grown in a hillock covering a dead fish, the modern alternative is incorporating fishmeal, seaweed meal, or compost as corn needs rich, moist soil. It should follow a legume or be sown with them, because it does well with peas or beans. I have grown French runner beans up and over corn. The light shade makes the space underneath conducive to ridge cucumbers, squashes, zucchini, marrows, and even melons in warmer climates. Corn may also be interplanted with brassicas or sunflowers, and I find that potatoes are a good intercrop, keeping the soil moist and providing the young shoots with more shelter.

Corn has few pest or disease problems, but is hard to grow in cold, wet conditions, so it is often started off under cover in deep pots to give it time to crop. I sow some indoors in pots in midspring and sow a second and third lot a week apart direct during late spring, so that at least one lot will do well! Each sowing or

planting hole is dug deep and wide and partly refilled with soil and sieved compost, with extra ground seaweed. The seedlings are planted out deep, but refilled in two stages and then later earthed up to encourage rooting from the base of the stem, as it helps keep them upright. Similarly, when sowing direct, cover the seed with only an inch of soil at the bottom of a deeper hole.

Whether transplanted or direct sown, the hole and seedling are covered with a plastic bottle cloche which is left on until the plant is a foot or so high, to protect it from the cold winds. Corn grows best at two feet apart each way, in blocks for pollination. Do not grow extra-sweet varieties near ordinary ones as they cross-pollinate with poorer results. A good watering once the cobs start to swell is well worthwhile!

Epicurean attentions A real luxury, this needs to be cooked within half an hour of picking or it is not as sweet. I run in with the cobs to plunge them in already boiling water. Corn is bulky but freezes well after blanching, so strip it from the cob for use in soups.

Bob's gourmet choices Grow several varieties to give a succession. The "non-F1" 'Double Standard' is excellent and you can save the seed, F1 'Northern' used to be my favorite early and 'Extra Early Supersweet' the best extra sweet. Recently I've grown mostly 'Gourmet' and 'Black Aztec.'

Potatoes These are easy to grow, but need care to give worthwhile yields. They need a soil well enriched with organic material and can be a lot of work. To make this as little as possible and to cope with dry conditions, I have modified the usual method of growing them.

As potatoes are very prone to diseases spread on the "seed" potato tubers, it is best, but expensive, to buy new certified stock every year. However, to save expense, grow self-

saved tubers for a couple of years and buy new stock before yields drop or after a year with disease. Save tubers only from healthy-looking plants and never from those that yield badly or look poor. Egg-sized tubers are best, green bits do not matter. Organic gardeners are advised to grow early varieties—these give lower yields but crop quickly. They can therefore be harvested before potato blight becomes a problem, as it usually comes after midsummer during a warm, wet period.

Second earlies similarly miss most blight attacks, but the more productive main crops need to grow on into late fall to give full yields. Blight is recognized by blackening foliage which smells bad and all the plants are rapidly affected. Do not confuse it with natural withering as the crop matures. You may prevent blight by spraying with the permissible fungicide Bordeaux mixture, but this is not highly recommended. If blight appears, cut off the haulms before it runs down them and wait a fortnight before harvesting the tubers. Do not worry about blight—it is rarely a problem if you grow mostly earlies and second earlies and these will store almost as well as main crops anyway. I grow main crops as well and have yet to suffer blight badly.

As soon as you can each year purchase your "seed" and chit it. This means laying the tubers in a tray and keeping them in a frost-free, slightly warm place with lots of light so they start to grow short green shoots. Earlies need chitting more than main crops. As soon as the weeds start to grow vigorously it is time to plant the seed. Earlies need to be planted a fist deep and only a foot or more apart. Main crops need to be a little deeper and at least a couple of feet apart. To produce many small new potatoes leave all the shoots on, but for fewer bigger tubers remove all the shoots except one or two. These wee shoots can be potted up in the warm and grown on to produce extra plants. Conventionally the "seed" is planted in a trench with ridges for earthing up, but I prefer to dig individual holes. These can be generous, though I use a small post hole borer. Put the "seed" in the bottom of the hole, then infill with soil mixed with sieved garden compost, but do not fill the hole completely.

Once the shoots appear, add soil around them whenever a frosty night is predicted. Continue to drag soil up around the shoots until you have reached molehill size. From then on earth up with a mulch of straw, leaves, or grass clippings. The latter are excellent, but must be put on in several thin layers when the weather is dry to stop them going slimy. Protect the foliage against frosty nights once it is too big to earth up—newspaper sheets will do.

Once flowers appear (they don't always), search among the clippings and soft soil for tubers big enough to eat, but leave the smallest to grow on. This saves digging up a whole row for the first meal and increases overall yields. If birds continuously drag the mulch aside, the tubers develop green poisonous bits from the light, so tear slits to the middle of sheets of newspaper, push these around the foliage, and replace the mulch on top of them.

If scabby patches appear on the tubers, they only spoil the appearance. You can avoid them by mixing in grass clippings with the planting soil and compost. Incorporating well-wilted comfrey leaves also works and adds potassium, too.

To increase yields significantly, give potatoes heavy waterings when the flowers appear. Remove any poisonous seed heads that come after the flowers. To get the longest storing potatoes, cut the haulm off and leave the tubers for a fortnight before digging because this gives them tougher skins. The most important factor, however, is to dig potatoes up

Dry the skins of your "spuds" before you store them in paper sacks.

in dry conditions. Be careful not to bruise them and take out the smallest and any damaged tubers to use up first. Leave the best to dry in the sun for an hour, but no more. Keep them in paper bags in a cool, frost-free place. An old freezer makes an ideal store for them, but a garage will usually do.

I also force potatoes under cover for early new potatoes (see Chapter 8, page 178).

Epicurean attentions Do not let potatoes freeze or they go sweet and they pick up taints easily. Adding potatoes can "remove" excess salt from a dish. Try steaming potatoes for better flavor—leave the skins on and peel them after cooking.

Bob's gourmet choices There are hundreds of varieties available from specialists and they are becoming more widely offered again. I grow 'Adora,' 'Anoka,' 'Bison,' 'Red Bliss,' 'Caribe,' 'Charlotte,' and 'Early Ohio' for my earlies. 'Irish Cobbler' potatoes are the ones to make home-made chips better than you've ever tasted. For main crops I grow the wonderful but low-yielding 'Nooksack' and for salads the divine waxy 'All Red,' 'Cherokee,' and 'Chippawa.' 'Ida Rose,' 'Kennebec,' 'Pink Pearl,' 'Red Gold,' and 'Katahdin' are best for baking and fries. Try as many as you can!

chapter eight

SHELTER FROM THE WEATHER

Grow more crops and flowers for more months in the year, and be warm yourself

Much of being a naturally successful gardener is about fitting the plant to the microclimate. The most radical way of affecting the microclimate is to grow the plant under cover. In warm countries this may be done to provide shade and/or cooler temperatures or to alter the day length, but in much of the world many plants are grown under cover to keep them warm. Cover allows various degrees of control over the plant's environment depending on the investment. A cloche or two will extend the season, and a coldframe allows a wider range of plants and more successful propagation. But a greenhouse, conservatory or polytunnel, especially if kept frost-free, opens up whole new areas of gardening—if heat can be afforded then you can easily have your own pineapples or bananas!

If you have part of your garden under cover, you'll spend more and more time there because being in the warm and out of the wind makes many more days a year gardening days! As Cowper said, "Who loves a garden, loves a greenhouse too."

left

Passion flowers are lightly scented, set fruit easily, and the vines need only to be kept frost-free.

overleaf

Cover can take many forms, from plastic bottle cloches to walk-in tunnels.

Gardening under cover

Cloches of any size create significant weather and pest protection, and allow the keen gardener to extend the growing season by several weeks at both ends. Their clever use makes possible a wide range of plants; indeed melons and grapes can be successfully grown under cloches even in the north of England. However, the traditional cloche has now been widely replaced by low plastic tunnels, but these are not as warm at night as the old glass ones. In either case, some ventilation is always required on hot days and extra cover at nights, if full use is to be made of cloches. Where they are only used temporarily, cloches cause no problems, but after a time they can cause dryness underneath if rainfall is patchy and not heavy enough to soak sideways under the cloche. Cloches are most useful for getting earlier crops of favorite vegetables, and they are best set in place a week or two early to prewarm the soil. They are then used for protecting young tender plants, such as tomatoes or zucchini, and after can be full with melons all summer. In fall, they can cover crops to keep the weather off and are ideal for saladings through the winter.

Large plastic water bottles with the base cut off and the cap removed make excellent cloches for individual young plants. It is easy to make cloches by using several bottles held together with waterproof clear tape to make a box and a lid of glass or plastic. Do not cut the bottoms off as a little water in the bottom of each will prevent the cloche blowing away and if the lot are filled with water this acts as a heat reservoir. On cold nights, they could even be filled with warm water from the house to give extra protection. Later in the season, making a small hole near the bottom of each will allow trickle irrigation when the cap is removed. Clear plastic bottles full of water can be used piled up just like bricks, to build a sheltering cloche around a treasured plant while it establishes.

Coldframes are the next stage, and these are usually sited in a warm sunny spot. The better ones are snug and well insulated. The better they are made the better job they will do, but the more careful you need to be not to cook the plants by leaving the lid closed on a sunny day. A coldframe can be covered at night with a blanket and kept frost free for longer through the year by popping in bottles of hot water. This then allows you to start off many more of the tender plants and to grow them on before planting out in late spring or early summer. In summer, a coldframe can produce some good crops of cucumbers, peppers, or even a decent melon or two.

A coldframe is also useful for propagating plants from seeds and cuttings and overwintering nearly tender plants. With a soil-warming cable or a compost heap or hot bed underneath, you can achieve great things—even very good crops of excellent melons. However, you are then really better off putting the whole setup under walk-in cover.

Greenhouses and plastic covered tunnels One of the most useful if time-consuming accessories to a garden is walk-in cover. This is much better than using cloches or coldframes for shelter and warmth because the extra volume of air gives a more stable environment, and it allows the gardener to work in comfort! Why should the plants alone have good conditions? A greenhouse or a plastic-covered tunnel, a polytunnel, can be used for giving most plants a really early start and provide protection from pests and the weather. They can also be used for growing winter salads or flowers, for growing plants a little too tender for outside, and for forcing or protecting fruit trees. A greenhouse is lighter and warmer, and usually the frame is easy to use as a support for staging, potting benches or plant supports. This makes a greenhouse more suitable for plants in pots and perennials. Wooden-framed ones are more aesthetically pleasing in a garden, are warmer, but need regular maintenance. Metal-framed ones last longer, but are ugly. A polytunnel is uglier still, much cheaper but colder, may be very humid and is harder to ventilate. The plastic cover needs replacing every few years which makes it poor value ecologically, but does give the opportunity, where space allows, of moving the whole thing making rotation possible. As the frame is unsuitable for fixing benches or staging they are most useful for growing annual or short-lived plants directly in the soil.

Whatever you buy, get the biggest you can afford. The larger they are, the better value and the more stable the environment produced. Site them with their longest axis east–west to maximize sunlight and do not put them in heavy shade. Make sure you have water close by, and electric light and power allows evening work and the use of heated propagation. Make sure everything is securely built and have adequate ground fixings against strong wind. A double-skinned polythene tunnel is a mixed blessing. Although the two layers of polythene keeps plants warmer, it reduces valuable light too much. However, in winter I use triple layers of polythene and add supplementary lighting because it is cheaper than heating a single-sheet polythene tunnel. Ventilation must be adequate for hot weather and automatic unless you are at home all day. Money spent fitting automatic heating, ventilation, and watering systems will be recouped in terms of time and better growth and more than doubles their value.

Conservatories are different. Originally the term was for a plant room which you visited. Now a conservatory is an extra living room attached to the house and you live in it, so the plants cannot necessarily have first call. Your partner may object to a potting bench next to their seat, and guests may wonder as your house becomes a greenhouse-come-garden shed—mine has! However, a conservatory can be easily heated and it is a perfect place to be on most British days! It is nice for you and for early spring sowing and potting up seedlings. Ideal for the small plants, but they do get in the way—and worse. The problem is that the conditions we live in and what plants need are very different; most plants want it much more humid. So humid, that our furniture and household goods tend to mold and rot. So the ideal conservatory subject is a cacti or succulents, or any plant that likes dry atmospheres—pelargoniums can become monsters. Many other plants can be kept in a conservatory, but will appreciate spraying with water regularly to keep them happy. In a shaded conservatory with no direct sun then foliage house plants will be most successful. Ideally grow conservatory specimens in pots, then they can go out in summer—or in winter, as many deciduous plants, such as peaches and grapes, need to go dormant and this is usually during a cold period. If planted in the border of a conservatory, these would never get cold enough for long enough.

Heating The value of any cover is much greater if it can be kept frost free. On the smallest scale, you can get seedtray-sized electric propagators to sit on windowsills. These are very convenient for germinating and rooting, but they are so small the plants cannot grow uncongested for long. Then there is nowhere to put them until the weather outdoors has warmed up. Thus we may want to warm a larger area. This may range from simply adding insulation to a coldframe at night and popping in a couple of cans full of hot water each evening to keep it frost free, to introducing a full-scale automatic system with hot-air blowers. The more heat this provides, the earlier you can start cropping and the greater the range of plants you can grow. However, it is expensive to install and run heat. A kerosene stove is the cheapest option, but it causes damp and fumes, although I use one in the spring for extra heat for a week or four, when planting up my polytunnel with tomatoes and so on.

With electricity available, a fan heater is most useful, especially if it has a thermostat. This is the cheapest way to heat because the capital cost is so low and most heat is needed at night, which can be off-peak cheaper electricity. Gas can be as cheap to run, but is more costly to install and any leaks or fumes may damage the plants. Oil is very similar to gas. Solid fuel heating is also cheap, but a lot of physical effort unless very modern equipment is installed.

Soil-warming cables are very inexpensive to run, often using no more power than a bright light bulb. They heat the soil underneath plants and keep the roots warm which is more important for many plants than warm top growth. They can be used to make propagators, to heat coldframes or to warm an area of floor inside a greenhouse for more tender plants—this can even be in an indoor coldframe.

Passive heating is the ideal. You need much better insulated glazing and a massive back wall that will absorb the energy from the sun during the day and then release it at night as the temperature drops. This system has been used almost unaided to keep homes warm, so why not a greenhouse?

Multicelled trays give each seedling an undisturbed rootball and are economical with space.

A better coldframe or a bigger propagator Falling between the coldframe and the greenhouse, I find the best solution is a dead deep freezer. This is best stood in a greenhouse, but will work against a sunny wall or even sunk in the ground. Basically it is a well-insulated box with a lid, which can be fitted with a ventilated glass or plastic cover for daytime use, and shut at night to keep the warmth in. A false floor is needed to bring the plants up near the light. If this is covered in sand, a soil-warming cable can be run in it to keep it warmer still for use as a giant propagator. It makes a superb coldframe and I find it cheaper to run the warming cable only at night on a time switch, rather than have the temperature controlled by a soil thermostat which corrodes away faster than the cables. Without an electrical heat source, extra warmth can be supplied by putting in bricks warmed on a radiator indoors, or by adding bottles full of hot water. Once the weather is warm enough for moving the plants into a polytunnel or greenhouse, the old freezer can be used for growing melons or even watermelons. If you are really handy, you can cut a panel out of the front of the dead freezer and replace it with glass making the box even better as a coldframe or propagator.

Hotbeds are not often made nowadays. It's not a shortage of fresh, strawy manure because that can be had from most riding stables. I suspect it is that they are seen as ineffective, certainly I thought so. However, when I first saw how hot a big compost heap got I soon learned to put a thick layer of soil on top and cover it with a coldframe. Without doubt this is a very simple and easy way to grow cucumbers and melons of a very good quality. Now on a smaller, but still effective, scale I make little hotbeds for these crops, inside my polytunnel.

Hotbed mixtures are just compost heaps. Traditionally, strawy dung is preferred, but I find grass clippings work well, too. I use stacks of big tires to hold the mixture of three quarters grass clippings, one eighth soil and one eighth straw. As the heat in the tires drops, they can be swapped for new ones, transferring the top one or two over onto the new stack. The topmost tire holds the compost and the plant, which is usually sown in situ under an extra wee cloche.

Ventilation You cannot overventilate if there is sufficient heat. The greater the throughput of air, then the healthier the plants as they consume the carbon dioxide and fresh dry air usually reduces mildews and molds. However, never suddenly chill the plants by completely opening up too soon, or worse too late when they are half cooked. To prevent overheating under cover, automatic vents are indispensable. Always ensure enough area can be opened to allow for those few days when you actually have a heat wave. Automatic fans are another good investment. Just keeping the air moving under cover improves conditions and reduces incidences of under- and overheating. A small electric fan can even be solar powered—just to move air when the

conditions are hot! It is hard to ventilate sufficiently with safety on cold spring days because the vents have to be kept shut. Since there is then little change of air, it is worth fortifying the atmosphere under cover with bottles of fermenting wine or beer which give off carbon dioxide replacing that used up by the plants as they photosynthesize.

Water control Under cover, in pots or borders, and outdoors against dry walls and in sheltered corners, air moisture is very important. Too much encourages molds and botrytis, and too little promotes mildew and spider mite. In general, during the growing season it is better to err on

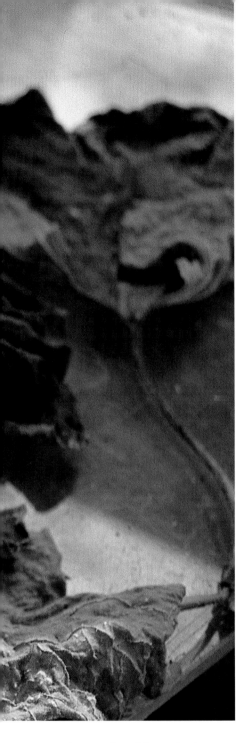

Melons need careful watering but
are worth every effort.

the side of too moist, so spray the walls, plants, and floor with a fine jet in the morning so it can dry before nightfall. It will save time to arrange an overhead sprinkling system for plants under cover. Outside, these are wasteful as much of the water just evaporates and chills the soil. Sprinklers are inexpensive and will soon repay their cost, but for only a little more you can have seep hoses and trickle feeders which use water more efficiently by applying it directly to the roots. In a greenhouse with a larger investment a microchip-operated system can be installed that will control accurately the soil and air moisture levels and the heating and ventilation. Less expensive systems can be run with timers or simple moisture sensors. In a polytunnel, the air conditions tend to err on the too moist side and more heat or ventilation is required.

Light Although all plants need light not all need full sunlight and many need partial shade or they may get leaf burn. In very hot weather plants may cook without adequate ventilation, or even glass shading or blinds. The problem is worst when a period of cold dull weather is suddenly replaced by clear blue skies and nonstop sun. The plants get too much too soon, and effectively get sunburnt just like us.

Generally, though, more often the problem is of insufficient light, made worse in small gardens by overhanging trees and nearby buildings. Pruning may allow more light in and dark walls can be lightened with white paint. In winter, all glass and plastic should be kept scrupulously clean to prevent further light loss. Electric light can supplement weak winter sun; it is especially useful for early sowings and valuable plants.

Ordinary incandescent bulbs are counterproductive as they give the wrong spectrum. Instead, use special fluorescent tubes and discharge lamps made for the purpose, though these are expensive. I now believe it is better to add extra layers of insulation to retain heat, and add extra artificial light to compensate the young plants at the start of the year. It is much cheaper to provide lighting than it is to heat the structure that gives brighter conditions by doing without the extra insulation.

Pest and disease control under cover While a cloche isolates a plant to an extent it is still in the soil and only temporarily covered. Growing under walk-in cover is more artificial and requires more intervention as the natural systems cannot control pests and diseases unaided. The old approach of sterilize and poison everything in sight with chemical fumigants does not appeal to the organic gardener who does not want a "sterile" environment—though in extremes a greenhouse or tunnel can be cleansed thoroughly with a high pressure steam jet.

The natural alternative is to encourage predators for pest control (see Chapter 10, page 206). Supply water in saucers and film canisters, nests made of straw filled pots, sections of hollow-stemmed plants, and rolled up cardboard tied in dry nooks and crannies. Groundcover plants can be included under staging and rock piles in shady corners for beetles, spiders, frogs, and toads. I hang strings just to give my spiders good frames for their webs which soon fill them all in. Companion plants can bring in and feed more predators and pollinators, such as ladybugs, hoverflies, and lacewings. I grow French marigolds in the greenhouse or tunnel especially by the door where you brush against them as these keep whitefly out, but attract bees and hoverflies in. I also find sweet tobacco and wild tobacco (*Nicotiana sylvestris*) beneficial as their sticky stems trap many little insects like thrips. Most effectively bought-in predators can be introduced to control specific pests (see Chapter 10), then refrain from even organic pesticides and the yellow sticky pest traps sold commercially or the predators may suffer.

Soil care under cover In the greenhouse or polytunnel, as everywhere else, it is preferable to grow plants to fruition directly in the soil rather than in containers as it saves considerably on watering and compost. The greater root run in the soil gives plants the most stable conditions and the best chance of finding nutrients for themselves. Even with a rotation and moving the plants around each year and adding copious amounts of garden compost and lime the yields may theoretically start to drop after five years or so as the soil becomes worked out. (I have never found this, but I suppose it is possible.) The answer is simply to dig out the topsoil and replace it with compost and fresh soil dug from a clean part of the garden. This is hard work, but does not need doing more often than one year in five and is much less work than the watering and carrying in and out the compost for containers or "bags" over the same period of time. For the paths I use old carpet and cardboard to cover bare soil because this has several advantages. It prevents weeds and moisture loss, it stops splashing of soil onto crops, it is more pleasant to work on, and rolling the strips back allows me to pick off slugs and other pests hiding there.

Hardening off tender plants the ideal way I start off all my tender plants in a heated old freezer-propagator and move the hardiest out first into a coldframe in the greenhouse, one section of which is heated. As they get bigger and tougher they move to the unheated section of the coldframe, and then out of the frame and into the greenhouse proper. Some of them are eventually hardened off and go outside. As each type of plant moves through this sequence, it leaves space for others so that I can raise many dozens of plants with very little total space or much electricity. The general order is indoor tomatoes and cucumbers are started first, soon joined by sweet peppers and eggplants. As the first of these move on, outdoor tomatoes, corn and indoor melons are sown, then the other cucurbits. Corn, ridge cucumbers, and zucchini move from the warmth then the squashes, leaving the space for indoor cucumbers, melons, watermelons, and okra, the last of which stay all summer because they need the extra heat continuously.

Corn plants being hardened off for a few days before planting out.

Tomatoes keep well into winter just hanging on the plant in a dry, frost-free greenhouse.

Winter salads and flowers, long-season crops, and tropical delights

Winter salads are more valuable than summer ones as there is less other fresh food available. Most perennial herbs such as rosemary, thyme, winter savory, tarragon, chives, and sage, are usable much longer if potted up and taken under glass. Any cover, even a humble cloche, can allow many more green saladings any day of the year. It is the wind and weather protection that helps most, and there are often bright, sunny days in winter. Even under cover these annuals need sowing in fall while the soil is warm. Thereafter, they make slow growth but can be cut, carefully and on a regular basis, to provide lots of tasty and healthy fodder. Of most value in my estimation are arugula, claytonia, parsley, chervil, corn salad, lettuce, escallions, cress, and mustard.

Winter flowers are luxuries you can afford once you have a light, frost-free place. There are so many to choose from but my favorites are: greenhouse cyclamen, gardenias, almost any bulbs, primulas, and pansies. If you want to be impressed, sow *Schizanthus* in mid- to late summer in cells. Pot up under cover, and in the late winter you will have many "poor man's orchids."

177

Bonus crops under cover

Longer seasons are the productive gardener's reason for wanting more covered space. Growing under glass or plastic simply adds weeks to both ends of the growing season. The first advantage comes from having somewhere to raise many plants that will finally mature out of doors. Without such early protection they could not be started in time and would not be ripening before the fall frosts. You can also grow plants that would require a much better growing season by keeping them indoors throughout. This means that many things you just wouldn't dream of can be grown in colder climates, and others become easy. And not just tomatoes.

New potatoes are to my mind one of the most delicious and valuable crops. When most people are only planting theirs on Good Friday, as is traditional in the U.K., I am eating mine. Most of my effort and heated growing space is taken up with new potatoes forced in pots. I plant 'Red Norland' and other very early varieties as soon as the days lengthen after midwinter's day. I grow these first in pots and move them up to black bags of compost. The yields are not terrific, but they are worth it. More batches are started every week or so until early spring when more batches can be started under cloches and in my unheated tunnel. Late crops are also easily had by starting earlies off in big pots after midsummer, these are brought under cover before the frosts and kept dry once the foliage dies, the "new" potatoes are superb for festive winter meals.

Sweet potatoes are actually an easy crop to grow if you start them off in late winter in a propagator and grow them on in a plastic tunnel. However, I find the tubers are hard to get to sprout, and any that do form are then best detached and grown on rather than left on the tuber. From then on, propagate by overwintering young layered plants. They crop at the end of a long season and do best in mounds or in very large pots, so their compost or soil is warm. I prefer the orange-fleshed large varieties, often from North Carolina, to the yellow- or white-fleshed thinner varieties—though these latter are easier croppers. The foliage is a rambling vine with pretty flowers.

Tomatoes can be grown outside under cover. I grow both for safety. In years when the outdoor ones do ripen, they undoubtedly taste the best, but averaged out over the years they crop a fraction as well. Start tomatoes off in individual cells or pots in a propagator in late winter for indoor crops and early spring for outdoor. Pot up twice and keep them warm until hardened off. Plant out a couple of feet apart in spring under cover or early summer outdoors. Most varieties indoors or out are normally grown as single cordons tied to canes with all the side shoots rubbed off. I grow some plants as double and triple cordons, though, as these give bigger early crops. Early removed side shoots can be potted up as they easily root to make more plants. I grow a couple of plants to crop extra early in small pots, these are debudded and deheaded once one truss has set. They then ripen sooner than when the plant is allowed to grow on.

Bush tomatoes produce many sprawling stems and are more often grown outdoors. To keep the stems and the fruit of these off the soil, I place old wire baskets over or around the young plants which grow up through and onto them. These can also be covered with plastic sheet to act as cloches while the plants establish. Out of doors tomatoes always benefit from cloching or at least wind protection from nets on stakes. These can be used later to cover the plants to keep the birds from eating the fruits.

Indoors or out they rarely suffer badly from pests and diseases especially if grown with French marigolds and basil. Grow the tomatoes directly into the ground in the greenhouse or tunnel rather than use pots—the extra watering and feeding for pots can never replace a free root run. The soil may become tired if tomatoes are grown in it year after year; if so, dig it out and refill the top foot with enriched fresh topsoil every few years.

Feeding is not really necessary in rich loamy soil, but is needed by plants in poor soils, pots, or containers. If you are after early crops be careful not to overfeed as this produces growth instead of fruit and I find fruit from slightly underfed plants tastes best though starved ones just do badly. Remember it is tomatoes you are after, not lush tropical looking tomato plants. Comfrey liquid in moderation is ideal for feeding tomatoes, seaweed sprays are also beneficial.

Watering is best done well, but not too often for plants in the ground, without ever allowing the plants to get checked, which causes blossom end rot— a brown blotch on the flower end of the fruit. In pots or containers it is harder to get an even water balance. Water frequently and keep the medium constantly moist once growth starts vigorously.

Pollination is free out of doors, under cover it may help to use a cotton ball, but I plant alyssum and marigolds to flower and draw in the pollinators to do it for me. Pests are few out of doors; under cover whitefly may appear but can be dealt with by *Encarsia formosa* predators or soft soap. Most other problems are caused by poor nutrition, low temperatures, or water stress. Tomatoes ripen best on the plant but these stop others setting. Leave a ripe one or a banana in the greenhouse to help them ripen. At the end of the season pull the plants up and hang them upside down in a warm airy place to ripen the remaining fruits.

Epicurean attentions Tomatoes freeze easily without blanching for use in soups and stews. The skins slip off if they are scalded in hot water for a few seconds.

Bob's gourmet choices Grow several varieties for different uses and flavor. Under cover or out of doors 'Gardener's Delight' is the best, 'Celebrity' is a close second. I find 'Mountain Spring' to be the most reliable early tomatoes for under cover, 'Matador' is reliable for later. 'Dombito' and 'Marmande' are beefsteak-type and produce large fruit, tasty and good for salads. To get really big tomatoes limit them to three or four per plant at a time. 'San Marzano' is a plum tomato which tastes poor raw, but is wonderful cooked, especially fried. 'Golden Sunrise' is yellow and adds colour to salads, but also makes a good jam with lemon juice.

Peppers, sweet and chili are as easy to grow as tomatoes. In very sheltered, warm gardens they may even just succeed planted out of doors in southern Britain. Sow in pots, preferably in a propagator, in early spring, re-pot monthly, plant under cover in early summer at a foot or two apart. Peppers even crop well in large pots under cover. They can get damaged by aphids early on, and watch for slug damage to ripening fruit.

Epicurean attentions Most varieties go red when ripe. Chilis are often hotter the smaller the fruits. Peppers dry and store remarkably easily.

Bob's gourmet choices 'Canapé' and 'Bell Boy' are reliable, 'Jupiter' fruits are big and solid and 'California Wonder' is tasty and sweet. 'Hungarian Hot Wax' is highly recommended; other chili varieties get surprisingly hot! Mini-peppers are not very desirable, but are early producers.

The hotter peppers—these are 'Hungarian Hot Wax'—are fruitful and grow as hot as in the Tropics.

Eggplants are demanding plants, but the fruit's quality makes them worth it.

Eggplants are related to tomatoes, potatoes, and peppers, and often grown with the latter as they like the same warm conditions. However, they should be kept away from tomatoes and potatoes. This is definitely a greenhouse crop and needs continuous warm, moist, rich conditions. Sow in pots in warmth in early spring and repot monthly, then plant under cover in early summer at two foot or so apart. Eggplants need tying to canes to support the crop. They are prone to red spider mite and aphid attacks.

Bob's gourmet choices Try 'Millionaire,' 'Black Beauty,' and 'Black Enorma.' In general, avoid original white egg or mini-eggplant.

Okra is not difficult to grow if a light, warm space is available. Treat it the same as eggplants. Unfortunately you need several plants to get enough to use, so it is not an awfully practical crop. Pick the pods while small to add their peculiar slimy texture to stews.

Frame or indoor cucumbers need continuous warmth and moisture with a really rich soil for the best varieties, though there are some that will crop in warm, sunny frames in good seasons. Indoor cucumbers need sowing in pots in a heated propagator during late winter or early spring. Pot them up regularly until they are ready to plant in their final position. Take care not to let the neck, where the stem leaves the soil, get damaged or wet as it will easily rot. For this reason, they are best grown on a little mound of sterile compost. They trail like squash, so can be grown up strong strings or wires. They must have continuous high temperatures, very high humidity, and are prone to spider mite and mildew. Regular spraying with water and adding seaweed solution or nettle tea may help prevent downy mildew. If indoor cucumbers are allowed to pollinate, the resulting fruits are bitter, so remove all male flowers (those with no tiny cucumber behind them) before opening so that females are not pollinated. All female varieties occasionally produce a male flower, so be vigilant. The seed is expensive but given the warmth and rich

Britain, melons can be planted out where they like to ramble under corn or sunflowers. On the ground, place the young fruit on a piece of wood or tile to stop it rotting. Under cover, melons are usually trained up strong strings and the ripening fruits need supporting in bags or nets.

Epicurean attentions Pick melons when they give off scent and the stalk will start to pull out. Chill for a day or so, then gently warm just before serving.

Bob's gourmet choices 'Ambrosia,' 'Burpee Hybrid,' and 'Sugar Bowl' are worth trying in an unheated greenhouse or frame in a warm garden, but expect really good results only in hot years. 'Charentais' and 'Ogen' are better, but need warmth. For exquisite melons grow 'Edonia,' 'Honey Pearl,' 'Passport,' and 'Galia,' which are divine if grown well.

Watermelons are even more difficult than melons in a cold climate, but I just manage them in a heated coldframe and in my polytunnel. Watermelons are started much the same as indoor cucumbers and need similar conditions, but prefer a more open, gritty compost and need more sun and lots of water. They seem to be the ultimate spider mite attractant! Although not enormous, the homegrown fruit's texture and sweetness have amazed me. Try 'Green Jade' or 'Golden Crown.'

Tender and early perennial fruits

Almost any fruit can be grown under cover to extend the season, or just to keep off the birds. Traditionally, currants and berries sold in the markets were forced months before their season. Cherries are well worth growing in pots and only need moving under cover when in flower or with ripening fruit. Peaches kept indoors all winter escape peach leaf curl, and in spring the flowers are protected from the frosts. The plants can go out once it's warm to return

conditions cucumbers give very quick results and are very productive early in the year, when other things are still weeks away.

Epicurean attentions Pick cucumbers early in the morning before they warm up for maximum crispness.

Bob's gourmet choices 'Telegraph' is well known. 'Niagara', which is tolerant of cooler conditions, has long been popular for coldframes or unheated greenhouses. 'Pepinex 69' used to be my favorite, but 'Carmen' and 'Naomi' are excellent and 'Corona' is superb!

Melons are treated exactly the same as cucumbers, but need even more heat to keep them growing well. As

Compared to its ancestors, the modern all-female greenhouse cucumber is easy to grow—go on, have a try!

with cucumbers, they will rot if the neck gets damaged or wet, so plant on a mound of sterile compost. Ideally, nip out the growing tip after four good leaves to produce side shoots. Later, in one go, pollinate one flower on each side shoot with a brush or cotton-bud to get even-sized fruits. Melons are even more prone to spider mite than cucumbers.

The best melons I grow outdoors are sown direct in a coldframe on top of a freshly made compost heap in late spring. In warmer regions than just for the few weeks when the fruit is ripening. Some fruits merit special attention:

Strawberries are probably the most rewarding crop to have under cover. You can have them planted out in borders under cover but they soon get miffy. Far better to pot up runners in summer, grow these on in big pots outdoors and bring them in from late winter on for very early forced crops. Alpine strawberries force easily, as do most summer fruiters. The fall fruiters ripen fruits better and for longer if they are grown in pots and taken in well before the first frost. For those who strive ambitiously against the greatest disadvantages, the newer day-length neutral varieties may make it marginally easier to achieve that dream of fresh strawberries in midwinter.

Grapevines Grapes are one of the best fruits to grow in a greenhouse or conservatory where they are less subject to rot, frosts, and bird damage. They can be planted inside, but outside gives them a bigger root run with more moisture to draw on and leaves the inside floor area clear for other plants. Bring the vine inside through a hole, make sure the hole can be enlarged as the stem grows and insulate the outside stem. It is considerably advantageous to grow vines in large containers, with the roots confined, because this reduces the pruning and allows for many varieties in the space taken by just one vine growing unhindered. Heat is used under cover so that the vines can be started into growth sooner. Then grapes can be had for mid-summer or earlier, and some of the more tender and luscious, but long-season old varieties, such as 'Ison's Muscadine' and 'New York Muscat,' can be grown.

Less heat is used if you take the vines outdoors after they have fruited to ripen and harden the wood in the late fall. Prune them once the frosts

have come and leave them out until late winter or early spring, when bringing them under barely heated cover will start them into growth. If it's frost-free they will crop much earlier. Once under cover, be careful not to let them get a chill or draft as the sudden change can precipitate mildew attacks.

Prune hard. Grapes fruit best on last year's wood, so in the U.K. a framework is usually formed along horizontal wires. This is because sap always rises, so if any of the canes are significantly lower than the rest of the vine they will get little sap and not fruit. It is better to fill a high wall with two vines, one for the lower tiers and one for the higher than to try and cover it with only one plant. A year after planting, cut back really hard to three buds to get only one or two strong regrowths; these should grow up to the level of the wires. In late fall, cut these back well below the wires; their regrowth in the third year can then be trained up to and along the wires and eventually trimmed back to make the frame.

Once the frame is made, which must take at least a couple of years, pruning becomes more complicated. Select and cut back the younger growths to form fruiting spurs in good places on this framework. This is best done in a couple of stages. All shoots are trimmed in summer to three or four leaves beyond the flower trusses—except any growths wanted to replace or extend the framework. If no flower truss appears by the sixth leaf stop it anyway, and mark those canes for later removal and do not use these for next year's spurs if alternatives are available! Any later regrowths are also cut back to prevent congestion and to redirect energy to the ripening fruit. Then, in winter, every surplus bit of wood is removed, leaving well-placed spurs tipped with one small piece of young wood with a bud or two. All else is removed, except where needed to

extend or replace the framework. Occasionally a strong young shoot from lower down can be used to replace ugly, worn out spurs or a whole limb of the frame.

In pots, grapes are pruned even harder to a stump with only a couple of shoots with a couple of buds on each. Ideally four or five equal and fruiting shoots emerge to be tied together at shoulder height and later trimmed not far above. These are then cut back to a bud or two apiece in winter. Be bold, you can rarely overprune grapes if you leave some firm, well-ripened, medium-sized *young* wood. Especially under cover, thin the fruit bunches down to a reasonable number if you want size and quality and to keep the vine from exhaustion. The vine will set plenty, so remove three out of four bunches in a good year! In a pot three or four bunches is more than ample.

Make sure grapes, especially in pots, never run out of water because if they slow down and restart growth the berries will split. Vines suffer from many common pests and diseases and the usual remedies apply to these (see Chapter 10, page 209). *Epicurean attentions* In my dry, frost-free greenhouse 'Golden Chasselas' ripens the first berries in mid-summer and still carries slightly wrinkled, but eatable, fruits into the New Year. I've found spraying my ripe grape bunches with neat high proof vodka cleans them of mealy bugs and other pests without damaging the appearance or quality. *Bob's gourmet choices* Under cover 'Muscat Ottonel' (black) is supreme and 'Concord' (black) is quite good where some warmth is available, 'Interlaken' ('Chasselas D'Or') (white) and 'Niagara' (white) are both remarkably sweet and reliable. 'Siegerrebe' is exquisite, but dislikes lime-rich soils.

Kiwi (*Actinidia deliciosa*) is an edible-climber which needs a very warm wall or to be under cover to fruit. It takes up a lot of space, but has lovely leaves and attractive bristly stems, so allow it to ramble over a shed or pergola. If it crops in a hot summer look on it as a bonus. Grown this way pruning is not required and kiwis have few pests or diseases. Under cover, they are only controlled by being grown in large pots. You must have a male as well as (several) females, though self-pollinating cultivars are becoming available. *Bob's gourmet choices* 'Anna' and 'Arctic Beauty,' or 'September Sun,' 'Blake,' 'Fifty-five,' and the mini kiwi *A. arguta* 'Issai.'

Citrus trees wait a decade before fruiting when grown from pips, but grafted plants can be obtained which will fruit while small. These need frost-free conditions and are best in an open, gritty, rich, almost ericaceous, potting compost in large containers, preferably of terra cotta or wood slat. The roots need good aeration, so drill multiple breathing holes in plastic pots. Citrus like nitrogenous feeds—I add fresh human recycled liquid fertilizer to their water once a week during the growing season. They should be watered copiously then allowed to drain and must never dry out. Citrus are easy to look after but suffer from aphids, spider mite, and scale insects, so need regular careful inspection. A hard prune in late winter keeps them compact and provides propagation material. They do not like being under cover year round—put them outdoors in summer. Although, not cheap to buy, they can be multiplied by cuttings which fruit more readily than seedlings.

Epicurean attentions Marmalade is easy to make so I freeze all homegrown orange and lemon skins.to add to a jelly made with yellow tomatoes and white currants. The flowers have such divine scent that the plants are worth having for this alone.

Bob's gourmet choices Lemons seem the

Kiwis are worth growing for their beautiful shoots, leaves, and flowers.

easiest and can produce worthwhile quantities of fruit almost year round, 'Meyer's' is most reliable.

Satsumas are easy and produce delicious sweet fruits. Oranges, grapefruits, and others require more warmth and bigger pots to do well but are still possible.

Tomatillo *(Physalis ixocarpa)* is essential for the taste of real salsa and is grown just like greenhouse tomatoes.

Tropical delights you may not think possible

Many of us have started off seeds from an unusual fruit we've eaten just to see what grows and I'm sure the windowsills of most households have had a bonsai date, mango, litchi, custard apple, or tamarind decorating them at some time. All, especially the tamarind, make very attractive houseplants.

But some of these plants can be encouraged to fruit with just a bit more attention. For instance, the Swiss cheese plant, given a big pot and more light, produces large arum-like flowers which ripen into banana-size cerimans which are delicious once ripe—the skin flakes off in little plates. If you want an impressive house plant that also crops try 'Eddoes' or 'Taro,' these are Colocasias and the "tubers" are eaten, especially in West Indian cookery. Watch out for the tubers because they have an irritant skin.

With only a plastic tent inside a plastic tunnel, a soil warming cable and a household fan heater, I have grown and fruited all the following with surprising ease at home in Norfolk. Most of their seeds are widely sold in brightly coloured packets with a free fruit to eat!

Cape gooseberries and other *Physalis* species are surprisingly easy. The seed is best ripened in the fruit till the pulp wrinkles up. The plant is perennial under cover, which flowers and fruits better the second year. It will produce prolifically throughout the summer and fall. They can be hard pruned in late winter or early spring. They need a lot of water!

Peanuts are for the kids, of all ages. You stick them in the soil, not pots, and get compact soft-leaved little plants with yellowish leaves. When you dig them up at the end of the season you have peanuts—simple as that.

Passionfruits are equally easy, but don't survive long, cold, damp winters well even under cover. They are so quick to grow and fruit that you can often have fruits the first winter after an early spring sowing.

Guavas surprised me. The hard object from the supermarket, hardly fit for jam, produced an attractive compact shrub that cropped in its second year with the most lusciously perfumed and succulent fruit I could imagine, as have its sisters. Try these!

Lemon grass is essential to much Eastern cuisine and is expensive to buy, yet grows like a weed in its native habitat. Look for fresh stock in the supermarket which hasn't been cut too close to the stem leaving a tiny bit of the root crown. These will root easily if potted up and given a little bottom heat, or even in a glass of water in summer. Once growing, lemon grass makes magnificent mounds of lemon-scented grass. But beware, it can cut the fingers if mishandled—detach and trim plump new side shoots to use for flavoring.

Guavas make attractive houseplants and when the fruit ripens it perfumes the room.

Ginger is also expensive to buy, yet almost any part of the fresh root with a bud will grow if detached, potted and given some warmth. I grow ginger on in the warm in big buckets which, by winter, produce several pounds of root each.

Pineapples are harder: they need it hot, they need two or three years to crop and must never get chilled.

Bananas are surprisingly easy to produce, even in Norfolk.

However, they will flower and fruit given the time, bottom heat, and a bucket-sized pot of rich, well-drained compost. Choose a good healthy crowned pineapple, cut off the crown immediately above the fruit and let it dry for several days. Then peel away the lower decaying leaves, usually you will see the first roots already there. Pot up, arrange a little bottom heat and a hot sunny position and keep the center dry in winter. Be patient, the reward will be worth it!

Bananas are easy but only if you grow the dwarf *Musa acuminata* 'Basjoo Hardy' or 'Red Leaf Hardy,' and have the roof height because these still need about 10 feet to open their leaves. To guarantee tasty fruits, grow from an offset, not seed—the "bulb" can be brought into the U.K. from the Canary Islands, where they are widely grown. Pot it up, until it is large enough to plant in the ground under cover, then keep it warm. In a year or two it will fruit—honest! After fruiting, cut down the "tree" and allow the biggest replacement shoot to stay, removing all others.

chapter nine

HARVESTING, STORING, COOKING, AND SHARING OUR BOUNTY

Easy and effective ways to spread the enjoyment of our bountiful produce over even more months of the year

In temperate climates we only have a short growing season of about half the year. In most of the U.S. we can sow most hardy crops outdoors in March and April and we have to harvest most of them before the frosts of late September or October. Though in the deep south and Southern California it is possible to garden virtually year 'around. In much of the country,the majority of shrubs and trees have no leaves for the winter and no fruits except in fall. We are forced to grow all our year's supplies in six months to keep us going for the whole year. Of course, we can always go and buy some imported substitute, but these never taste the same. So successful harvesting and storing are as important as growing the crops in the first place, and deserve every care.

Successful harvesting

Harvesting is the most glorious job of the year, whether it is on a grand or a modest scale. Digging potatoes is like searching for buried gold, while jam-filled cupboards and the deep freeze become our treasure chests. While all the cups are overflowing, do remember that soon there will be an almost bare garden and little chance of replenishment for another year.

Fresh cobs from our late summer-
holiday barbecue.

Apple surpluses are easily turned into juice or cider.

So harvest and store diligently, and do not give away all your best to non-gardening friends and neighbors. This may be mean-spirited, but they would not expect you to retain the poorer, misshapen ones for yourself—as most gardeners do. Have them round for a meal and share it with them that way. Store only the best, eat fresh the rest, compost what's left.

While the harvesting time for most vegetables is not often that critical, most fruits are more demanding and only thoroughly enjoyable when perfectly ripened. Melons are improved by chilling first, but most fruits are tastiest warmed by the sun and eaten straight off the plant. A few fruits, such as pears, have to be watched till they are nearly ripe, picked a tad early and brought to perfection in a warm, not too dry, dim room that is inspected daily. Long-keeping apples need careful picking for storage if they are to last ten months. The best date for picking fruit depends on the cultivar, soil, site, and season and can be determined

Garlic (top) needs to be thoroughly sun-dried if it is to keep well. Pears (above) need handling gently and watching if you are to catch them at peak.

only by experience as these factors vary considerably. For storing for home use, fruits need to be at just the right stage. Most store best when picked just underripe. They may keep longer picked younger, but very much at the cost of flavor and sweetness. On any tree, the sunny side ripens first—in the northern hemisphere usually the southeast corner, as morning sun is stronger than afternoon because the air is cleaner.

Fruit will also ripen earlier if extra warmth is supplied—next to a wall, window, chimney or vent, or just close to the soil, are good places for early fruits. Likewise, when the rest have gone, you may find some hidden in the shade. So wait for the fruits on the sunny side to ripen—the rest of the crop is probably perfect for picking to store or process.

Vegetables can usually be picked over a long season and many vegetables are easier to store than fruits as they are less prone to rots. Indeed some, such as parsnips and most roots, brassicas, and leeks, are best left in the ground if they are protected against hard frosts. Some, such as the squashes and the onion tribe, just need careful drying and keeping in an airy, frost-free place. A few crops, such as petits pois, ripen and go over rather rapidly, so you need to plan your harvest carefully so that they can be used fresh on the day and the rest processed in one efficient swoop, otherwise it's tough peas or save them for drying.

Harvesting herbs is best done at the last minute for fresh use. It is not widely appreciated how quickly valuable nutrients diminish in food once it is picked. Time spent wilting in poor conditions can halve the vitamin content as well as spoil the texture and flavor. If herbs are going to be stored, pick them at their peak—often just before they flower. Do not leave them to go over. Crunchy salad crops should always be picked at dawn with the cool dew on them; then they will have maximum crispness and can be kept in the refrigerator till required.

Simple and preferable ways of storing efficiently, ecologically, and organically

Although we occasionally store some crops, such as pears, for a period to improve their condition, most storing is done just to extend the season for as long as possible. On the commercial scale, tremendous advances have been made, so that by careful regulation of gas, humidity, and temperature, many crops can be stored for months, some even a year or more. These conditions are hard for us amateurs to duplicate, but we can keep most crops for longer if we treat them well. To be stored, any crop must be perfect, any blemish or bruise is where molds start. There is absolutely no point in trying to store anything that has any real damage—use it up straightaway or process it into juice, jelly, chutney, purée, etc.

Choose varieties suitable for storing—some early croppers are notoriously bad keepers! Waxing fruits is good for extending their life, but could help shorten yours. Some will keep as well wrapped in paper or oiled-(vegetable) paper. Another early method of mold deterrence was to dip fruits in a solution of sodium bicarbonate, drying it before storing. This worked well, but left a powdery appearance. Common long-keeping fruits and vegetables, such as apples and potatoes, can be stored at home for up to a year. The major problems apart from molds are shriveling through water loss and the depredations of rodents and other pests.

A conventional store is too large for most of us and in the house or garage is too warm, cold or dry. I find dead deep freezers or refrigerators make excellent, compact stores. They are dark, keep the contents at a constant temperature and keep out nightly frosts. Most useful of all, they are rodent-proof, and they can even be locked to deter two-legged pests! Ventilation can be obtained by cutting small holes in the rubber door or lid seal. Condensation usually indicates insufficient ventilation, but too much draft will dry out fruits. The unit can stand somewhere dry outdoors. It is out of sight in a shed and better protected against the cold, but then may get too warm. In extreme conditions, ensure extra frost protection by putting a sealed bottle of warm water inside the unit night and morning. To save space, providing the water table is low, a dead chest freezer can be sunk into the ground and the lid painted over.

When putting crops in store it is usually best to leave them to chill at night in trays or bags and then to load them into the store in the morning when they have dried off, but before they are warm. Similarly, it is helpful to chill and dry off many crops initially by leaving the store open on cool, dry nights and closing it during the day for a week or two after filling. Most fruits are best removed from their store some time before use, so that any staleness can leave them. Care should be taken not to store early and late varieties together, or any that may cross taint.

Vegetables need to be kept separate from fruits! Obviously, do not situate your store in the same place as strong-smelling substances such as paint or creosote! Likewise, although straw is a convenient litter, if it gets damp it taints. Shredded newspaper is safer, but still has a slight whiff. Dried stinging nettles are reckoned good, but dangerous to handle.

Always inspect stored crops regularly—they can go off very quickly. Remember, if only one in ten goes off every month then to have one tray after six months you have to start with two trays just to allow for the rots! So do not store everything for ages merely for the sake of it—be selective, and store well only that which you will use.

Simple and preferable ways of processing efficiently, ecologically and organically

Although many crops can be stored in their virgin state, some will go off quickly, so are best processed to preserve them longer. There are several

ways to achieve success, varying in their complexity, cost in equipment, energy, and time. You must weigh these up against the pleasure from having even more of your own. I now enjoy not only my own fresh crops, but almost every pickle, sauce, chutney, and confectionery is home made. The time taken is great but freely given—especially the eating bit. The most valuable crops to process have to be herbs and fruits; vegetables take more effort and have generally less cash value—but you can never have too much frozen asparagus. It is important to note that badly bottled fruit and moldy jam are rarely as harmful as vegetables which have gone off—these can be extremely hazardous. So if you skimp on instructions and detail when preserving, stick to processing fruits!

Juicing is I find the best way of storing fruit, other than turning it into wine, but that's another book! Not all crops can be easily juiced. Many can be squeezed to express the juice, or heated and/or frozen to break down the texture, then strained. Harder fruits and vegetables need to be liquidized first. Sugar or salt may be added to taste and may also improve the color, flavor, and keeping qualities. Juices may be drunk as they are, drunk as squashes diluted with water, added to cocktails, and used in cooking. Fruit juices take less space in a freezer than the crop they come from and are as good afterwards, until they ferment. I freeze mine in the wax cartons and plastic bottles milk comes in, leaving a wee space for expansion. (Vegetable juices should only be consumed fresh, for safety.)

Grapes are the easiest to press and the most rewarding. You can still ferment the pips and skins afterwards, and the resulting wine tastes no worse than most of my regular brew, though that is slight praise. Grapes are best crushed first to break the skins and most of the currants and berries can be squeezed in the same way. Apples and pears must be crushed first and then squeezed, they will go through the same equipment as the more juicy fruits, but more slowly. Pulpy firm fruits, such as black currants and plums, are best simmered with water till they soften then the juice strained off. Repeating the process and adding sugar to the combined juices is also the basis for jellies. Raspberries, strawberries, and other fruits have such delicate flavors that they are best frozen, then defrosted and strained—a pure juice unchanged by heating is thus obtained.

If your quantities are too large for kitchen tools, many different presses and crushers are sold and hired for home use and small-scale wine-making. Commercially, juices may be passed through microfine filters or flash-pasteurized; at home, they ferment rapidly in the warm, but keep for days in the refrigerator and months or years if frozen. I have two freezers, one for juices and one for everything else, because I want to drink my own apple or grape juice, not the stuff that comes out of my tap.

Jellying and jamming are similar, both preserving the fruit in a sugary jell. The difference is that jelly is made from the juice, while jam contains the seeds, skins, and sometimes whole fruits or pieces thereof. A conserve is just an expensive jam usually implying more fruit and less sugar or filler. Freezer jams are conserves made with so little sugar that they go moldy quickly unless kept frozen and then used from the refrigerator.

Almost any fruit can be jammed or jellied—and there are many that are only palatable once treated in this way. The fruit is cooked to the point of breaking up the cells so that the juices run. The juice is then turned to a jell with sugar, which acts as preservative as well. Most fruits need to have up to their own weight of sugar added to them to make a setting jell. With jellies the juice is often augmented with the squeezings of the fruit pulp reheated with some water. These juices are thinner and require proportionately more sugar to set.

Jellies are made from the strained juice and set clear and bright. Many people prefer them because of the absence of seeds, skins, etc., though others like the textures of jams simply because of the presence of these things—and don't forget the nutritional value. Picking fruit to make jelly is easier because the odd sprig, hard or underripe fruit or bit of leaf is removed when the liquid is strained. Fruit for jam requires much more careful picking and preparation. My solution for, say, black currants is carefully to pick the very finest berries first, and then more roughly pick the bulk of the fruit to jelly. As the bulk is going to be strained, there is no need to be so careful to keep out the sprigs. The bulk is simmered down to a pulp, strained and then *before* it is set with the sugar, the finest berries are added and quickly cooked. White sugar, not brown, is traditionally used for jamming and jellying unless a strong caramel flavor is required. Honey is not really successful as the flavor is strong and it goes off when heated. Similarly, concentrated juices can add too much flavor. The amount of fruit can be increased and the sugar decreased according to your expertise at jam-making and the speed at which you eat a jar! Organic sugar is now available, but if not pure white it may add a caramel flavor to delicate preserves.

Ideally, simmer down the fruit with a minimal amount of water, strain if it is for jelly, add the sugar, bring to a boil, skim off any scum, and then pot in sterile conditions. Hot jars and clean lids put on *immediately* improve results. Store once cold in a dark, cool place. Some fruits are difficult to set, particularly strawberries in a wet year. Adding chopped apples to the jelly fruits or their purée to the jams will supply the pectin needed to make any fruit set. Extra acidity, for a pleasing tartness which brings out the piquant flavor of some jams, is often achieved using lemon juice. However, white currant juice is a good substitute and redcurrant even better—especially where their color is also an advantage. White or redcurrant juice is also an aid to setting difficult jams. Their flavor is so tart yet mild that their jellies make good carriers for more strongly flavored fruits in shorter supply, especially for raspberries and cherries. *Important tip!* It is far quicker and easier to make four five-pound batches of jam than one twelve-pound one. And the result is always better—large

There is nothing like homemade strawberry jam.

With strawberries, pick only the perfectly ripe fruits for freezing. For jam you can be a little more tolerant.

batches have a low heating and evaporating surface compared to their volume and take much longer to process, so the fruit degrades more. Remember: quickly simmer down to pulp, add the right amount of sugar, bring back to boil, skim, pot, and seal. No standing around watching some great cauldron bubble all day!

Chutneys, sauces, and relishes are just like jam-making with vegetables! But because these are prone to go off, we add vinegar and salt to the sugar, or even to replace it entirely. Many vegetables, such as zucchini, onions, rutabagas, and cucumbers, are combined with fruits, such as apples, raisins, and tomatoes, in chutneys and these are truly a feast of goodness if well made. Tomato sauce is ripe tomato jam with vinegar and spices; many other sauces are based on this with more or less chili/tamarind/ pepper. The vegetables may be salted first, but otherwise are often almost raw in relishes such as piccalilli (wee bits in a mustard sauce). What healthier food could there be?

Drying is a traditional way of preserving. It loses some flavor but concentrates the food in a much smaller volume—so use dried herbs sparingly. Many foods can be dried if they are simply sliced thinly and exposed to warm dry air. Sealed in dark containers, kept cool and dry, they will last for long periods to be eaten dried or reconstituted when required. However, in the humid air of the U.K. and much of maritime Europe and North America, drying is not quick enough, nor is it helped by the low temperatures in the same regions. Making solar-powered dryers—simply wire trays under glass with good ventilation—allows fruit to be dried to a larger extent, but in the regions with the highest humidity the food may still go moldy before it dries. And of course flies etc. must be excluded!

I find that slicing the food thinly and hanging the pieces separated by at least their own thickness on long strings over my cooking range provides the dry warmth and ventilation needed to dry most within a day or two. The easiest kinds, such as apples, will dry overnight. Oven drying with artificial heat is risky because it can cook the food, destroying the value, texture, and keeping properties. It is possible if the temperature is kept down and the door kept partly open. Oven-drying is convenient, though, for finishing off partly dried samples after you have done other baking—the decaying heat desiccates well with little risk of caramelizing or burning.

Herbs for drying are usually best gathered once the dew has dried off them. Hang them in small bunches, upside down, in a dark, very airy place. Bright light bleaches out the color, so some shading may be necessary. Once they are completely dry, they can be crushed to go in jars or sealed in paper bags in a tin.

Freezing captures flavors lost by drying. It is especially good for herbs which can be frozen and need almost no time to defrost—especially parsley and basil. These can even be conveniently frozen as portion-controlled ice cubes in water or oil. Most fruits freeze easily with little preparation, unlike vegetables which need blanching first. Blanching is merely chopping the vegetables up and immersing them in boiling water for a minute or more and then chilling them again before freezing. It is extra work and uses fuel but then you can eat your own produce throughout the year.

Obviously only the very best is worth freezing, few things are improved by the process! Most fruits turn to soggy lumps in a pool of juice when defrosted which is not as appetizing as the well-textured fresh product. However, they are still packed full of sweetness, flavor, and vitamins, so are well worth having for culinary use especially in tarts, pies, sauces, and compotes. A mixture of frozen fruits is marvellous if they are dechilled, but not totally defrosted, so they retain their frozen texture like pieces of sorbet, and served with cream.

For most fruits and blanched vegetables merely putting them in sealed freezer bags or boxes is sufficient. However, they do tend to freeze in a block, making later piecemeal usage difficult. You can avoid this by freezing them loose on open wire drying trays or greased baking trays before packing them. Fruits that are cut or damaged need to be drained first or, if you have a sweet tooth, they can be dredged in sugar which

'Boskoop Glory' produces heavy crops of sweet grapes which can be juiced and frozen for later use.

absorbs the juice before freezing them. Stone fruits are best pitted before freezing, as the pit can give an almond taint. The tough-skinned fruits such as tomatoes or plums should have their skins removed after freezing and before use. The easiest way to do this is carefully to squeeze the frozen fruit after immersion in very hot water when the skin will slip off easily. Foods lose nutritional value slowly in the freezer, although fruits do not deteriorate as badly or as quickly as vegetables, meats, or fatty products.

Simple and preferable ways of cooking efficiently, ecologically and organically

Undoubtedly if you wish to grow crops naturally you will also wish to prepare them for the table in the same manner. Having achieved freshness, flavor, and quality with all your homegrown fruits, herbs, salads, and vegetables, don't spoil your wonderful ingredients by using a rancid oil or a stale or adulterated spice; grind your own from fresh and always buy "organic" if you can. Avoid processed and altered foods especially hydrogenated oils and trans-fats, preservatives, ersatz meats, and genetically modified ingredients. You are what you eat, shouldn't it be the very best? Indeed, you can now find almost everything you wish grown organically, though mail order is more productive than local stores. Even clothes and sheets of organic cotton and wool can be had.

There are many ecological alternatives to everyday household products that are obviously preferable to anyone with a greener outlook. It is possible to have a fly-free and clean kitchen without vaporizing fly-killers giving off chemical poisons, and lethal bactericides being poured over every surface. Gentler, more natural washing-up liquids and cleaners are sold in most supermarkets. Multiple waste buckets make sense, with separate ones for compost, hens, recycling, and the garbage can. This last ought not to get too full too often, as obviously there ought not be many tinned, bottled, or prepackaged products used in a household that grows its own! Indeed, a pantry full of dried, pickled and preserved, as well as fresh produce, means such a household often recycles the containers for storage from neighbors who shop more often!

Naturally the bulk of one's food ought to be whole, and raw, but we still need to cook some foods. A pressure cooker or a steamer is more efficient to cook with than boiling. Good planning is important, too. If you cook or bake several meals together for simple reheating later, you can have a range of homemade ready-meals for those rushed days. Of course, if you have a freezer, this becomes easier. I believe it is advisable to stop using aluminum or nonstick surfaces—and, especially with acid or salty liquids, copper and brass are downright dangerous for most cooking purposes, because they poison the food! Stainless steel or, failing that, cast iron is preferable.

THREE CULINARY TIPS FOR GARDENING GOURMANDS

1 Use only the best ingredients Never cook with, serve or eat less than the very best. Food is far too important to spoil by using even one inferior ingredient. If a meal can't be made with love it is probably better to pass it by and have some fruit to be going on with. If you are only eating something to save "waste," send it to the hens or compost heap.

2 Do not overkill the flavor If you have fresh, organic, homegrown produce you have the real flavor. Cook delicately and sparingly and add herbs and spices in extreme moderation, so as never to overwhelm the true glory of your food.

3 Always whet guests' appetites with delicious smells, serve crudités, then soup, and never ever dish up all the main course at once, but only small portions so they must come back for more!

Flavorful guidelines Bay leaves add aroma to every savory dish, and basil can be almost as widely used especially with tomatoes and any combination with garlic. A parsley or cheese sauce will go with almost any savory dish, or enliven a plate of steamed vegetables. Mint sauce is delicious with most vegetables. A "bunch of herbs" for soups and other dishes contains a sprig each of parsley, thyme, and bay—though I always add rosemary as well. A bouquet garni is just the same thing tied up in a bit of cloth with some peppercorns. "Fines herbes" for French-style egg dishes and sauces are just finely chopped chervil, chives, parsley, and French tarragon. Mixed herbs are anything you like, but usually parsley, thyme, marjoram, and summer savory. Angelica and sweet cicely make rhubarb and fruit dishes sweeter, and bay or lavender can be added to milk dessert dishes. There are countless combinations, so do experiment.

Most vegetables and fruits can be peeled and though some fiber is good, some, such as tomato and potato skin, may be an irritant to some people. The area under the skin contains the most valuable nutrients so it is often best to cook first and slip the skins off afterwards. Water that has been used to steam or boil food is full of goodness and should be used as a stock, fed to the stock or at least added to the compost heap.

A better salad Bored with the blandness of many salads, I experimented with adding fresh herbs to enliven them. I also reasoned that more varied foods, especially using more herbs, would provide healthier nutrition. Once I had started, I soon found the herbs outgrew the "lettuce and cucumber" portion. During really hot summers when lettuce crops failed, I discovered that by blending many herbs I could make delicious salads without any lettuce or most other conventional saladings at all. The more herbs I blended the pleasanter the overall taste, as long as I used the very bitter and strong herbs with the utmost moderation. Although some of my more conservative friends have looked askance at these strange mixes, they have nearly always gone on

A melon such as this deserves careful treatment: keep it at room temperature until the perfume evolves, then chill for several hours. Allow it to rewarm slightly for half an hour before serving.

to enjoy them. The basic principle is to use as many different edible herbs as possible without letting any one flavor dominate. Go to each herb and take small quantities and chop them fine. By varying the proportions the mix can be adjusted to suit most tastes. Of course, for some people the flavor will be too strong, but this can be tempered by adding saladings to dilute the herbs. Much of the year it is possible to continually crop small amounts of very many different herbs, though the choice is not as wide in late winter and early spring. It is then that the hardier herbs and vegetables such as sage, rosemary, thyme, chives, cabbage, and kale can be valuable by providing the most part of salads.

Flowerdew's super salad Add, mix, and adjust to taste as available. All should be finely chopped:

Small amounts of rosemary, thyme, sage, marjoram, sweet cicely, summer savory, shungiku, cilantro, and fennel.

Large amounts of parsley, chervil, dill, French tarragon, and basil.

Lots and lots and lots of chives and arugula.

Varying quantities to taste of mint, nasturtium leaves and flowers, purslane, iceplant, good King Henry, grated horseradish, land cress, citrus leaves, radicchio, and alpine strawberries.

Mix all the above up thoroughly to be diluted with background saladings of: shredded carrot, grated red and green cabbage, shredded kohlrabi, chopped red, green and some of the hot peppers, cucumber and gherkin bits, tender curly kale leaves, corn salad, *Claytonia* and even lettuce, chicory, endive, almost any edible green, and baby peas. Then add pot marigold, day lily (*Hemerocallis*), pelargonium and shungiku petals, borage and rosemary flowers, some violets, pansies, bergamot, and loads of rose petals. When ready to serve top with sliced 'Gardener's Delight' tomatoes and sprinkle over hull-less pumpkin, poppy, celery, and sunflower seeds. I rarely use salad dressings on this, but prefer to serve it with a well-moistened dish such as taramasalata, hummus, egg mayonnaise, etc. (I have also eaten, but cannot and do not recommend including, *very* small amounts of clary sage, salad burnet, lovage, hyssop, winter savory, lemon verbena, lemon balm, and lavender.)

Bob's toast topping A very nutritious meal for those in a hurry. Soft-cook an egg (or eggs), make some toast and chop up fine a handful of any tasty herbs, but especially chives and chervil. Put the chopped herbs in a small bowl and add (to taste) grated cheese, mayonnaise, some tomato ketchup and a dash of hot chili or Worcestershire sauce. As soon as the egg is cooked, shell and chop it into the bowl, mix quickly and spoon onto the buttered toast. This goes well with the salad above and the kohlslaw below to make a mega-healthy meal.

Kohlslaw This is like coleslaw but made from grated kohlrabi instead of cabbage, plus carrot, apple and onion, mixed with mayonnaise (or similar), a little garlic and paprika. I often add grated celeriac, red and green sweet peppers, and small amounts of dill and other herbs. This is a moist dish to complement salad or to go with baked potatoes or toast topping.

Household products, pot pourri, and strewing herbs

Like culinary, the medicinal uses for herbs require a book on their own so I will not venture to deal with them here. It is worth noting a few of their more handy uses around the home, though. Handfuls of fresh or dried herbs wrapped in cloth and tied under the hot tap create a wonderful and relaxing bath to finish off a hard day in the garden. Pot

above
The floor of my fall store for squashes and marrows is strewn with leaves and lavender.

o v e r l e a f
Poultry adds a new dimension to the garden and diet.

pourris are air fresheners made from dried herbs; special recipes are quoted needing exotic ingredients, but any dried herb in a bowl will eliminate unpleasant scents and give off its own aroma. My favorite is based on lemon verbena leaves with some rose petals, eau de cologne mint, and 'Herba Barona' thyme. Try whatever you have available. Dried herbs tied in bags keep pests out of drawers and cupboards, giving them a pleasant smell. Lavender is the best base for this. Strewing herbs are better than pot pourri for scenting a room and ideal for floor coverings in potting sheds, where they give a pleasant—if dusty—atmosphere. They tend to get carted around on feet in the house. I prefer mints and cotton lavender for working areas, hyssop by the boot rack. For the summerhouse and in my car footwells, thick layers of lavender create a tranquil atmosphere. In the fruit store I use southernwood to give a clean scent and drive away pests. The barbecue can scent the air and drive away gnats and flies if small bundles of fresh or soaked dried herbs are added to the coals. They can flavor, and smoke, the food as well.

Sharing our garden with backyard friends

Along with the satisfaction of growing your own food and flowers, the pleasure of real freshness and flavor, the greatest joy of successful organic gardening is spying a rare butterfly, a grass snake or a dragonfly by your pool. All the natural fertility you make in your soil, the many forms of life it supports and the inviting and sustaining habitat you create will attract the wildlife we all love and wish to see. These are disappearing in the wild and our aim is to preserve and bring them to strength again within our bounds. We may lose some crops to them, but in return they give us pleasure, control many pests, and improve our fertility. Surely we can afford to share a little of our and nature's surplus with them? But not only may we have wild friends who live with us, we can have pets and livestock. These latter are a cunning way to convert medium-grade household and garden wastes into high-grade food and also high-grade compost material. By feeding animals leftovers and any other edible items that would otherwise go to waste, we can recycle the food value back as eggs, meat, or milk. This is also a way of converting the surpluses of summer into a more storable form. Don't be put off by the added responsibility of looking after animals—having chickens is much easier than keeping a cat or a dog—and their eggs are far better!

TWO-LEGGED FRIENDS AND THE GARDENER

Chickens It is an exceptionally good idea to run chickens underneath fruit trees as they improve the fertility, control the grass, and reduce pest problems to a minimum. Cynically, it is said, they are even more effective if you do not feed them too much. Bantams give more beaks and eyes for the same amount of food, lay as many but slightly smaller eggs, and are more prone to escapism than the bigger breeds. Marans or Rhode Island Reds are good breeds for most households.

A couple of hens can be kept and run on a small lawn in a mobile ark which is moved each day. It is gratifying how much grass they then neatly eat. For several birds a hut is needed. If permanent, site it next to the compost heap or to plums and peaches as these will benefit from the additional nutrients in the localized droppings. Ideally the hut should be mobile, so the hens get access to different areas. The more they run around on new sites the better the egg quality and production will be. And you don't need a cockerel if you just want eggs. The birds will need nice fat perches in their hut, nest boxes, water, grit, and oyster shell. (They can be given back eggshell, but only if it is baked and crushed first.) Household scraps plus garden wastes and grain will make a couple of hens happy, and they will give you eggs from early spring to late fall for about five years. In winter, you just do without eggs unless you give them extra light and hot mashes. Their parasites can be kept down if you give them a dust bath to roll in.

Chickens, just like the wild birds, love their greens and if you let them among brassicas they choose cauliflower and broccoli leaves first, but they also really like lettuce, beet, and chard leaves. Neighbors are often only too happy to give away their scraps and why not encourage their children to feed your hens for you. In some areas foxes may be a problem. A solid hen house with a shutable pop-hatch simply opened each morning and closed at dusk will have them sleeping safe. Automatic ones are also available. Keeping them in till late morning usually ensures they will lay in there where you can find the eggs!

Ducks are more garden friendly than chickens as they do not scratch about and they eat more slugs and snails. Indeed, they are wonderful to watch dibbling their bills in among the groundcover, but they would rather be in your pond or pool. They destroy almost all pond life, so keep them out or preferably have separate ponds! Ducks need no shelter, but appreciate one, and may use a nest box. They can live on grass plus household scraps and some grain and most lay many more and bigger eggs than chickens. I find duck eggs good in cooking but even more use for feeding my young chicks. Muscovy ducks are the best for pest control and they snap up a lot of flies, White Aylesbury's are the best eating and Khaki Campbell or Indian Runners can, amazingly, lay an egg for almost every day of the year.

Geese make great lawnmowers. They will live on grass alone, but tend to eat the carrots and steal any windfall apples before you can get to them. They debark young trees and low branches and rip off dangling labels, so trees may need protecting with guards. Geese are very good at destroying

buttercups and can be used to clear them from pasture, unfortunately clearing the clover as well. They must have water to wash their eyes but do not need to swim though they love it. They are fastidious cleaners and a small pool is a kindness, a plastic child's sandpit will suffice. Geese are hardy, though a hut and nest box is still a good idea. They lay a large number of very big eggs that make excellent egg custard and cakes. As with the ducks I freeze the surplus eggs to be the fat and protein feed for my young chicks.

FOUR-LEGGED FRIENDS AND THE GARDENER

Cats are much abused for their various antics. However, there is nothing like a few cats about for keeping the birds on their toes and for decimating the rodent population. Rats kill far more birds as eggs and fledglings than adult birds are killed by cats. (Indeed, every year large numbers of young birds fly straight into greenhouses and patio windows!) Neutered males make more slothful pets than females if you want to minimize potential bird losses. Cats can be trained: I have five and most can even sleep with the chicks! (I think they prefer roast chicken and see it as a long stake-out.) Keep cats around by planting catnip, *Nepeta cataria* not *N. mussinnii*, and valerian in warm sheltered corners. Catnip is also useful for driving away their fleas, although most effective is a proper metal flea comb used daily and this saves risking a pesticidal collar. Most cats love catnip, so it can be planted where you want them to lurk; a patch near the strawberries can really keep down bird damage. If you are bothered by cats visiting your garden to leave free fertilizer packages in your seedbeds, try this compromise. Cats are notoriously lazy devils, so provide them with a well-sited tray of soft, deliciously fresh and crumbly material. They will use it rather than dig holes in the firmer beds and borders. The tray's contents can then be emptied regularly and buried under trees or shrubs, putting the fertility where it is safe and useful.

Dogs can be much more damaging in gardens, depending on their temperament. It is up to the owner to train them to treat the garden well. Dogs can be taught to use a mulched and hedged off area for their bathroom and their droppings can be buried under trees and shrubs. Like cats, their parasites can be controlled by careful grooming. The bitches urinating on a lawn will cause bald patches unless the area is washed immediately with a gallon or so of water to dilute the urine. Both dogs and cats are natural carnivores; it is cheaper, more ecological and probably healthier to feed them cheap meat than tinned food which is four fifths added water.

Rabbits and guinea pigs make good pets and with a mobile run can be very efficient grass cutters. Their droppings can be safely added to the compost heap, too. Rabbits are also often kept for the table in rural France and I looked after them as a boy on the farm. They will convert much garden and kitchen waste into meat as efficiently as chickens and with the light breeds the meat is almost like chicken.

Goat and sheep are dangerous creatures to have near a garden, as they will both merrily debark and crop almost any valued plant they can get at. Given they can climb like a monkey and have *all day every day* to apply their wicked ingenuity, then sooner or later they will get out! Goats, of course, give milk, but are not grazers and will not do well with just grass—they are browsers, and *need* to eat your trees and shrubs! Sheep make better lawnmowers as they are by nature grazers—they just *enjoy* eating your trees and shrubs. Sheep can have more health problems and the milk is less desirable than goat's.

Cows are relatively cheap to buy, live on grass and can give a lot of milk every day which you then have to find a use for. The milking is chore enough without the time taken to make cheese, butter, yogurt, etc. So a cow only makes sense where there are many people, say three families or so to divide up the labor and all the dairy produce. Cows will select the plants they need, but can pick up bad food habits just like us. Clear their pasture of ragweed, bracken, larkspur, and other poisonous weeds. Hedge garlic and similar strong-flavored weeds will taint their milk.

. . . AND AT THE OTHER END OF THE SCALE

Honeybees It is ironic how nowadays city beekeepers prosper more than their country cousins. The cities have caused a poverty of country wildlife by incessant taking of land for roads, building, and for more food production. There are now so few areas of uncultivated land and wildflowers that many country beekeepers despair, while city gardens are filling with expensively planted flowers. Urban beekeepers also find that the shelter and warmth from all the buildings extends the honey season by many weeks. Bees are an ideal occupation for someone with a small garden and who is good at slow, gentle movements and taking methodical care. The amount of work is not great, but it must be done at the right date and often at the right time of day so it suits the retired. A modest investment will set you up with honey and beeswax for life. You can also spend a lot of time just watching bees. If you have the space, you can help them by planting the right sort of flowers, and thereby increase the quality and flavor of your honey. Bees do not use their sense of smell much and tend to go for blue or white flowers, though other colors are not excluded.

. . . and fish Well, why not? I have goldfish in my water butts to keep down the gnat larvae and they breed up and produce a surplus.

The best bee plants

The following garden flower families commonly grown in beds and borders have built up a close relationship with bees and will attract them:

Aconite, *Allium, Anchusa, Arabis*, aster, *Borago, Campanula, Centaurea, Chionodoxa, Colchicum, Delphinium, Echinops, Echium, Endymion, Erigeron, Hyssopus, Kniphofia, Lavandulus, Limnanthes, Limonium, Lobelia, Lychnis, Lysimachia, Lythrum, Malva, Matricaria, Melissa, Mentha, Monarda, Muscari, Myositis, Nemophilia, Nepeta, Nigella, Omphalodes, Origanum, Papaver, Phacelia, Platycodon, Polemonium, Pulmonaria, Reseda, Salvia, Scabiosa, Scilla, Thymus,* and *Veronica.*

Trees and shrubs have also come to depend on bees and lindens are well known for filling hives with honey. Most members of the following families are good for bees, but avoid sterile, double-flowered varieties:

Acer, Aesculus, Alnus, Berberis, Betula, Caragana, Catalpa, Ceanothus, Cercis, Chaenomeles, Cistus, Cotoneaster, Crataegus, Daphne, Elaeagnus, Escallonia, Fagus, Fraxinus, Fuchsia, Hedera, Hypericum, Ilex, Laurus, Liquidambar, Liriodendron, Malus, Mespilus, Olearia, Perowskia,

Physiocarpus, Populus, Potentilla, Prunus, Pyracantha, Quercus, Rhamnus, Rhus, Ribes, Robinia, Rosmarinus, Rubus, Salix, Senecio, Skimmia, Sorbus, Spiraea, Symphoricarpus, Syringa, Tamarix, Tillia, Ulex, Viburnum, and *Weigela.*

In the vegetable and fruit garden leave unwanted brassicas, leeks, and onions to go to flower as bees love these. Strawberries, especially the alpine ones, are always popular, but raspberries, blackberries and their hybrids are favorite. Clovers sown in sward and as groundcover or green manure are one of the biggest yielders of honey. On farms, field bean and oilseed rape are the largest sources. Sweet basil, summer savory, lemon balm, and the mints are all much loved. On a cost-effective basis the mints are probably the best for large areas as they spread so well.

Weeds are, of course, by definition unwanted, but the flowers of some are loved by bees: Agrimony, bellflower, betony, corncockle, clovers, cranesbill, flax, forget-me-not, hound's tongue, mallow, meadowsweet, melilot, mullein, ox-eye daisy, pansy, poppy, ragged robin, scabious, soapwort, tansy, teasel, trefoil, valerian, and yarrow.

above right

Limnanthes douglasii—the most useful bee plant, as it is also good for hoverflies and as a weed-suppressing green manure.

Unfortunately goldfish are not tasty and are bony, even the cats refuse them, and most other cold water fish that could be kept are not great meals. Tasty fish like trout need sparkling running water. However, they used to have fish ponds in the Dark Ages and in the East, so it may be worth pursuing. Certainly many cunning schemes have centered around alternating sunken livestock grazing meadows with ponds every couple of years. Fish and livestock have different parasites; the fertility left in the mud grows good grass; and, when flooded, grassland produces rich food for fish.

chapter ten

SUCCESSFUL ORGANIC PEST AND DISEASE CONTROL AND GAINING FREEDOM FROM WEEDS

Simple strategies for avoiding problems; how to deal with them organically and effectively

Any gardener wanting to have a natural organic garden must have a very different approach to the conventional spraying routine of drenching plants and soil with chemical poisons. Primarily, we help the plants to hel p themselves by enabling them to resist attacks in the first place. We also manipulate the natural checks and balances to our favor by encouraging the pests' natural enemies. As organic gardeners, we rely on a series of measures with progressive strengths of action, and use pesticides only as a last resort. We expect to have pests in our gardens, after all some are needed to feed all the predators we are encouraging. What we are after is balanced control not elimination. We use our wit and cunning to make life difficult for the pests and diseases, so that we get our crops despite them. After all, plants endure minor infestations in much the same way as we shrug off spots or a cold. Most commercial pesticide use is to ensure the appearance of the crops not improve the yield. For home consumption, a minor blemish is acceptable, and seconds can be used for processing or preserving.

Sophie has promised to make sure
no mice run off with the carrots—
though she is letting the root fly in
under the netting.

Japanese wineberries fool the birds for a while—they are red when ripe and don't darken as most other blackberries do.

Apart from building up self-regulating systems, direct action is occasionally needed and is more effective the earlier it is taken. Regular observation is essential so that small infestations can be nipped in the bud before they spread. Observation also allows potential problems to be spotted so that preventative measures can be in place for the following year if not in time for this. It is a good idea to get things in proportion and not to be a plant hypochondriac. After all, the greatest losses are caused by inclement weather ruining whole crops. Close behind bad weather comes bad practice, such as overcrowding and poor weed control. Only then do pests come into the ranking, with birds worst of all. They eat seed, seedlings, leaves, fruits, and buds, but also many pests. In some areas two-legged "rats" are the next greatest source of damage and loss, followed by slugs and snails—most other pests and diseases are far less common or troublesome than these!

What must also be considered is the economics—whether or not the increase in yield is really worth the extra time, cash and labor needed to achieve it. For example, flea beetles make shot holes in radish and brassica seedlings; maintaining moist conditions reduces their damage and is worthwhile, but spraying with derris may cost more than a radish crop is worth. Similarly, pheromone traps for codling moths cost say £5; with one tree the extra fruit saved may not be worth it, with four or five trees near each other it may be very worthwhile. On the other hand, in an orchard of twenty trees, where four traps would be required, the extra clean fruit may not be needed anyway.

The ten lines of defense against pests and diseases

There are many different approaches for reducing pests and diseases. Few problems are solved with just one measure but by combinations of several. They are presented here in order of minimum intervention, with the passive methods first and the less natural—or more unecological—last.

1 Good husbandry Good method is 95 percent of successful organic gardening. So organic gardeners choose suitable plants, avoiding those that are inevitably prone to problems. It is pretty daft to try and grow watermelons in the U.K. (I know, I keep trying), rhododendrons if you live on chalk, or cauliflowers in hot, dry, sandy soil. Grow plants adapted to your conditions and they succeed. Keep plants healthy by making sure they are growing steadily and they will overcome minor problems. Never let your plants become checked by being pot bound, crowded, dried out, cooked, frozen, or choked. Any check reduces yield and may lead to disease, so crops grown in season always do better than extra early or late sowings. It is also daft trying to have strawberries in winter—another of my follies.

Of all the checks to growth water imbalance is probably the most common. Obviously desiccated plants will die, but if they even start to wilt they have already been severely checked. Waterlogging can be equally serious, especially in cold, low-light conditions. Plants in containers are as often sickened by overwatering in winter and spring as they are by drought in summer. Dry roots and damp or stagnant air inevitably lead to mildews and botrytis rots, especially for roses and climbers on walls.

Fertility imbalance is rarely a problem for organic gardeners, but conventional growers may over-stimulate their plants into lush growth with excess nitrogen, making them more susceptible to pests and diseases. Air and light are also very important factors when preventing infection, so give each plant sufficient space. Never crowd plants, grow a few well rather than many poorly. Vigorous and woody plants need pruning or tying not only to allow air and light, but also to give predators access.

2 Hygiene Regular inspection of all parts of the garden and prompt action to remove infected material will significantly reduce further pest and disease attacks. For example, the removal of any infested tips controls aphid attacks on broad beans. Similarly, coral spot is a common disease of woody plants—prompt removal prevents its spread. All diseased and infested material should be immediately burned, well composted or deeply buried. Pruning shears, saws, and knives should be sterilized with alcohol between operations to prevent cross-infection. Care needs taking not to introduce any problems with bought-in plants, manures or dirty tools. Never bring in soil-grown brassica plants because of the danger of clubroot (see page 163). A good idea is to keep new plants in isolation for a while before putting them with others. Do not become over fastidious though, a small level of pest infestation is necessary to maintain predator populations.

3 Resistant varieties In many ways the very plants we grow have been selected because they are inherently trouble free, but few cultivars are immune to all pests and diseases. The more important crops are grown most frequently and thus have acquired the most pests and diseases to bother them. For these important crops much research has been done to find varieties resistant to the commonest ailments. Most success has been against diseases—for example, there are blackspot-resistant roses, scab-resistant apples, and canker-resistant parsnips. Pests are harder to discourage, but there are lettuces which are resistant to root aphids and carrots that do not attract their rootfly. However, choosing resistant varieties may entail some loss of flavor or quality compared to other varieties. Red and oddly colored varieties often suffer less pest attacks because they are naturally camouflaged.

4 Cunning cultivation methods Rotation is the most important of these methods. Move the plant each season and pests and diseases over-wintering in the soil emerge to find their target has gone. (The same applies to replant disease—never replace a dead plant with one of the same.) Rotation also changes and modifies the conditions in the soil, ensuring that few pests or disease spores survive until the crop returns.

Timing can be important. Although plants grown in season are the healthiest and survive most diseases, there can be advantage in early or late sowing so that the crop misses the worst pest attacks. For instance, early potatoes are out of the ground before blight becomes a problem most years. Overwintered broad beans usually are too tough too early for the black aphid to bother them, while early peas miss mildew and early carrots miss the rootfly which is most preponderant when the weed cow parsley is flowering.

Raising plants in pots under cover can help to get better early or late starts and thus miss attacks, but can also prevent them entirely by isolating the crop during its more vulnerable stage. Beets sown in the open are razed off by birds, but survive if planted out when bigger.

Accurate sowing and indoor propagation also avoid the need to thin, which can attract pests to the scent as with carrot root fly or onion

205

fly. Most shrubby plants benefit from summer pruning which controls growth, so encouraging flowering and fruiting. This can simultaneously remove a burgeoning pest population, especially aphids, as these cluster on tips.

Raking heavy mulches aside in winter disturbs many hibernating pests, killing them either directly or through exposure to hungry birds. This is useful against gooseberry sawfly and raspberry beetle. A heavy mulch before growth starts in spring seals spores and infectious material underneath, where they cannot be splashed up onto the buds. It is recommended for most plants, particularly blackspot-prone roses.

Seaweed and occasionally herbal sprays, applied to supplement fertility, are also good for reducing pest and disease problems. They do not act directly as pesticides, but aid the plants to make resilient, vigorous growth that throws off attacks— much the same as us taking vitamin supplements. The smell of the sprays may also help by confusing pests.

5 Encouraging predators and parasites

Building up self-regulating ecosystems means good provision for predators. You need plants for nectar, fruits and pollen, shelter on the large and small scale, sites for nests and hibernation quarters, water and sacrificial plants to maintain colonies of pests on which the predators and parasites can feed. Thus for effective predator and parasite encouragement it is essential to provide a continuity of companion plants throughout the seasons, and particularly so early in the year. Not all flowers are equally useful; the deep-throated ones are only accessed by moths and butterflies, and double flowers wrought by man for their beauty may have no nectar or pollen for insects.

6 Hide and seek companion plants

The great variety of plants favored by good gardeners creates diverse

Asparagus berries provide for the birds in winter.

ecosystems which prevents the build-up of pests and diseases. In a mono crop not only is there a vast amount of susceptible material, but it is all in contact so any problems can easily spread. Once plants are mixed and intercropped, it is harder for an initial infection to occur and much harder for it to spread. Growing several varieties of a crop is also useful, because each will mature at a different time and each may be more or less susceptible to pests and diseases. This greatly reduces the risk of total loss and also spreads the workload at harvest.

Not only do we find that mixtures of plants are less attacked than monocultures, but we can also use companions, such as the aromatic herbs, deliberately to camouflage or disguise the scent of the crop. French marigolds are particularly effective at this, their presence prevents whitefly coming into a greenhouse and they also kill soil nematodes. Many gardeners believe some companion plants, such as nettles and alliums, can help prevent fungal and bacterial attacks to other plants. Chives and garlic are often grown under roses and fruit for this purpose.

Some plants act as sacrificials, grown to attract pests away from the main planting. They may be the same plant grown around the perimeter or a more attractive lure. For example, red currants will keep birds off the black currants. In a similar manner surplus leaves or seedlings shredded when transplanting and spread around transplants will fob off the slugs. Trap plants work in a similar way. For example sweet tobaccos, especially *Nicotiana sylvestris*, have sticky stems and leaves and are very attractive to whitefly and thrips. Growing these among other plants concentrates the pests so they can be further stuck on with a spray of sugar solution and removed with the plant.

7 Barriers and traps

There are many simple mechanical methods to exclude pests and thin out their numbers. These cause little harm to the environment as many can be made from recycled materials. Nets are the best way of protecting crops from many pests. A complete cage is best and makes economic sense, but any pieces of net held in place with clothespins can be used to protect a branch or two. The netting bags fruit and nuts come in are good for individual fruits and bunches, nylon stocking legs do as well. Whole stockings or tights can be pulled over long branches of fruit, such as red currants or cherries. Fine mesh bags can exclude wasps as well as birds, but may encourage mold or botrytis. Fine netting, woven fleeces, and punctured plastic sheets can all be used to keep pests off vegetables as well as fruits and are very effective at preventing carrot root fly attacks. (This fly is about the size of a housefly and has to lay its eggs next to the seedling.) A barrier gives 100 percent control. The same materials can also be used to protect cabbages from root flies and butterfly caterpillars and to keep birds off beets and saladings. Cabbage rootflies need to lay their eggs in the soil next to the stem so a barrier made of squares of old carpet, tarred roofing felt or cardboard fitting snugly around the stem will seal the soil underneath.

Carpet can be used to seal larger areas trapping insect pests underneath when they emerge from hibernation or their pupae. This can considerably reduce infestations of gooseberry sawfly, raspberry beetle, and pear midge. Carpet laid on a wet lawn will bring up leather jackets and other soil pests to the surface overnight and can be swept up or left to the birds in the morning. Cloth bands, carpet bands, and corrugated cardboard bands tied round trunks and stems simulate shredding bark and attract many insects. The beneficial ladybugs can be retained on inspection and the pests evicted. Many creatures, especially earwigs, are attracted inside hollow tubes and can be blown out into a bucket. Earwigs are especially attracted to straw filled flowerpots on sticks. Sticky bands stop pests climbing up trunks, while few predators need to. They are especially effective against the female winter moth, which cannot fly, earwigs, and ants. Ants "farm" aphids by moving them to tender shoots and milking them for honeydew. A sticky band reduces the aphid populations as the ants cannot tend and protect them.

Sticky bands can be applied to the bark of old trees, but are better on top of a foil strip on young bark as it may soak in. Tie-on sticky bands on paper are even more expensive than the paint-on mixture which can be made to go further on rough surfaces if applied on top of cheaper pruning compound.

Sticky boards and flypapers are especially good in the greenhouse where they trap many pests, especially whitefly and thrips. More pests are lured to them if they are bright yellow. Sticky traps are even more effective if they are given a pheromone scent. When hung in fruit trees they are a very good way of reducing codling moth and plum fruit moth attacks.

Mouse traps are too well known to need describing. They are needed near peas and beans when sown or stored, and near crocuses, which mice love. Mole traps are similar and there are humane traps for both, so you can release them elsewhere.

Lures can be made for many pests. Cans or yogurt cartons buried in the ground with bits of potato or carrot will attract mostly millipedes and wood lice. Slugs and snails will come to rotting fruit, and wireworms to bran or germinating grain. Dead-fall traps are just the same without the lure. Isolation trenches of about a spade's depth all around vegetable beds present mice, slugs, and other small creatures with a barrier, and so exclude them more than the conventional short drop.

Bird scarers are psychological barriers. They all work for a short time, but garden birds rapidly learn not to fear them. Use several and change them daily. Scarecrows, glitter bangs (coffee packaging bags are good), flashing or humming tape (video or cassette works, but remove it before the coating degrades). Black cotton gives them a fright when they touch it. Use an artificial spider's web to give them arachnaphobia. Hosepipe snakes, paper hawks and fur-hat cats all disturb them for a day, but they will be back.

8 Direct action Hand picking is effective against many pests—gooseberry sawfly or cabbage caterpillars, for example. Many minor infestations can be terminated with finger and thumb before they become a plague. A squidge in time saves nine. . . Slugs and snails come out on warm, wet evenings and tend to return to the same site so can be spotted with a flashlight and picked off—scissors are nastier, but effective. Battery-operated vacuum cleaners are excellent for rounding up flying insects like whitefly or flea beetles which jump when disturbed. Using a water hose to produce a strong jet can knock aphids and other pests off plants especially rosebuds; some may return, but many will not. Combining this with sticky bands works well.

9 Bought-in predators and parasites These have been used commercially and now many are available to gardeners by mail. They are most suitable for greenhouse pests which are difficult to control because of the absence of natural predators, and because they can't escape. Once the predator has been introduced, almost all pesticide use has to stop. They are most effective if introduced early in the season, but not before the pest has appeared or they will starve. If pest populations get large before the predators arrive, thin out the numbers with traps, trap plants, and safe sprays before introducing them. Full instructions come in the packets, which may be just opened or emptied onto the plants. Often a large packet is enough to be shared among friends and much cheaper than buying a small one each.

Aphididoletes aphidmyza is a parasitic midge for controlling aphids. *Cryptolaemus montrouzieri* is a ladybug, its white shaggy larvae rapidly control mealy bugs. Cabbage white and other similar caterpillars can be safely killed with the naturally occurring disease *Bacillus thuriengiensis*: this is sprayed onto the crop and as the caterpillars eat they pick it up and very soon die. *Trichoderma virides* is a predatory fungus used to prevent other fungi attacking pruning wounds. It is applied before or instead of a sealing compound. It can also be used to cure silver leaf disease in plums and Dutch elm disease if these have not progressed too far. Pellets are inserted into holes drilled in the trunk and the predatory fungus permeates the tree. *Trichoderma* apparently prevents posts rotting and has been used in watering systems to prevent wilt in seedlings, but unfortunately is not available to amateurs in the U.K.

10 Organic pesticides Organic gardeners prefer not to use poisonous substances unless they are needed to save a valuable crop. However, they are there as last resort and can be used to kill pests, but you must take great care with them and not disrupt ecosystems that have slowly built up. Take special care not to harm bees and use poisons only after the bees have retired. Follow the instructions on the packaging as to their uses, application rates, and precautions. Keep them in a safe, secure place.

Insecticidal soap is just that. Traditionally used to kill aphids, spider mite, white fly, and other pests, it has been reformulated to be more effective. Extremely safe to use and made from natural products it is the preferable pesticide, but cannot deal with the larger insect pests. Quassia solution is made from a tree bark and kills aphids, but few beneficial insects. I believe it is no longer available in the U.K. on its own. Pyrethrum is also no longer available to U.K. gardeners in pure form, as required by organic purists, though both it and quassia are legal in the U.S.; in the U.K. pyrethrum is commonly supplied with a synthetic synergist. However, if it becomes available again, it is a useful powder or liquid for killing many insect pests including small caterpillars. It also

kills beneficial insects and fish, but is very safe for mammals. It is made from the flower heads of a chrysanthemum and breaks down in half a day once exposed to air and light. Derris (rotenone) liquid or powder is extracted from various tropical plants and kills most insects and caterpillars, friends and foes, indiscriminately. It is particularly effective against mites, but is also lethal to fish, pigs, and tortoises. It breaks down in sunlight and is slower to act than pyrethrum. Ryania, sabadilla, nicotine, and false hellebore are similar plant-based insect killers but are unavailable to U.K. gardeners.

Bordeaux mixture is a fungicidal suspension of copper sulphate and slaked lime. Although a chemical, it is allowed under organic standards because it is not very harmful to us or to soil life. It is effective against potato blight, peach leaf curl, raspberry cane spot, and many other fungal diseases. It is a preventative not a cure and must be applied thoroughly and in good time.

Sulfur is the pure element and is allowed under organic standards as a control for powdery mildews on fruit, flowers, and vegetables, and for preventing rots in overwintering bulbs and tubers. Take care with fruit trees and bushes as a few varieties are allergic to sulfur, so read the label carefully.

Sodium bicarbonate solution was once used as a fungicide and was particularly useful against gooseberry mildew, but is not allowed under U.K. pesticide legislation.

The usual diseases and their treatment

Mildews are broadly of two types: powdery and downy. The powdery forms do less damage in general than the downy, grey matted mildews. They both attack plants under stress, "eating" them from the outside. The

commonest causes are plants being too dry at the roots and stagnant air. Good growing conditions suitable to the plant, careful pruning, and training to allow access of air and light will do much to alleviate mildews. Having many alliums growing nearby may offer some protection, but this needs time to work. Removing diseased material will reduce the spread. *Equisetum* tea, seaweed, garlic and nettle sprays are all claimed to make the plants tougher and more resistant, as may mustard-seed flour.

Rusts in many ways are very similar to mildews, and like mildews they tend to appear on different plants at the same time, because the conditions are suitable. It is not because the rust has spread from one plant to the other, because in general it does not. However, some rusts do have alternate hosts where they spend part of the year on one plant and then move to another for the winter. For example, wild berberis harbors wheat rust over winter. Hygiene and the permissible fungicides cited above are usually effective if used in time.

Botrytis or gray mold is nearly always associated with high humidity. Improving air flow and drier conditions arrest it. Some fungicides may help and, horrifyingly, it has been found that fresh urine sprayed on stops attacks on soft fruit!

Wilts and rots are soil-dwelling organisms of all sorts which attack unhealthy plants which soon succumb. These are most often only a problem with young seedlings. Once plants are growing well they are rarely attacked. Rather than the futile effort of sterilizing the soil, add real live garden compost and the goodies soon eat the baddies! *Trichoderma* also proves useful but, as mentioned above, it is not available to amateurs in the U.K.

Bacterial or virus diseases Good garden hygiene, healthy plants, and the control of vectors spreading the diseases are the most effective controls. For example, removing the mite-swollen buds from black currants helps prevent reversion attacks.

The usual pests and their treatments

Ants Black ants do not sting but may bite; red ants sting. They are all attracted to the honeydew excreted by aphids. The black milk and move aphids to better feeding sites, and they overwinter aphids and eggs in their nests. They also effectively keep almost all predators away from their flocks! Ants may do the same for other pests such as scale insects, whitefly, and mealy bugs. They may, however, prey on some other pests, and they may be pollinating plants unbeknown to us. For example, Chinese citrus growers have used them to control caterpillars.

Ants uproot seedlings and even large plants with their burrowing. The main problem is their arrival in the house or store. Strewing the mint family especially spearmint or pennyroyal will repel them. Growing mints or tansy near their entrance point will similarly help. Non-drying sticky bands are a very effective preventative barrier.

Nasty option: put out some sugar, watch where the ants take it home to, then pour boiling water down their hole.

Aphids are generally considered a plague, but often do little real harm. They do not suck sap, but allow it to be pumped through them, taking what they want and letting the sticky sweet sap residue fall on leaves where it turns moldy. They can do serious damage by spreading virus diseases, but otherwise aphids are usually just taking surplus nutrients without

Himalayan balsam (*Impatiens roylei*) is a good green manure, benefits insects, and grows to head height in shady, moist places.

affecting overall growth. The curling of leaves especially of tip growth has the same result as summer pruning—for many plants, red currants and sweet cherries in particular, withering the tips causes young buds lower down to convert to fruit buds instead of staying vegetative. There are many different aphids, some are specific to a few plants while others are less particular. Chives discourage aphids on many plants, nasturtiums although themselves attacked will keep broccoli clear.

Ladybugs and hoverflies are the best control, so plant attractants like *Limnanthes douglasii*, buckwheat, and *Convolvulus tricolor*. If these fail then soft soap works well. Traditional but now illegal was the use of plant extracts such as elder or rhubarb leaves combined with the soap. Never ever use detergent! Likewise, fumigating aphids with burning tobacco is no longer allowed. In the greenhouse, diseases, parasites, and predators are all available to control aphids.

Flea beetles make many tiny holes in the young leaves of plants especially turnip, radish, and Chinese cabbage. They dislike moist conditions, so frequent watering is most effective and usually only required while the seedlings are small. Interplanting lettuce or spinach deters them and they can be discouraged with mint, wormwood, and elderberry leaves. Pieces of tomato plants are most effective. Sticky flypaper waved close overhead thins them out rapidly, as they jump up when disturbed.

Caterpillars are often not spotted till rather too late, but then it is worth hand picking or shaking them off on to a sheet. Sticky bands can stop them climbing back. For many, such as the cabbage white caterpillars, you may use a bacterial control, *B. thuriengiensis,* which rapidly stops their attacks. Surprisingly, nature will control caterpillars in time to prevent real damage; often the outer leaves of my brassicas are damaged, but the plant soon recovers.

Slugs and snails can be stopped by barriers of salt, lime, wood ashes, soot, pine needles, crushed eggshell, or sawdust. They are reluctant to climb over smooth rings cut from plastic bottles. Slugs can be trapped in "slug pubs"—saucers or yogurt pots half full of fermenting jam and beer, in which slugs obligingly drown themselves. "Friendly" ground beetles also drown unless you give them some twigs to climb out on.

Slugs and snails also unwittingly congregate under tiles, melon or orange shells, and upturned saucers from where they can be collected. Do not destroy the now rare predatory slug *Testacella*. It is yellowish with a small but noticeable vestigial shell on the tail. Many beetle species eat the mollusc's eggs, some such as glowworms attack directly and *Tachinid* and *Sciomyzid* flies parasitize the adults. All of these thrive under moist groundcover. There is a parasitic nematode available you can water onto the soil to kill slugs and snails where they hide.

Scale insects and mealy bugs Scale are most troublesome on plants under cover and on walls. The little flat helmets hide an aphid-like pest which soon proliferates and they cunningly hide out of sight on the backs of leaves and branches. Naturally controlled by beetles, ladybugs, lacewings, and anthocorid bugs. Help build up numbers of the latter by planting willows, which produce an abundance of catkin pollen in early spring. Hand pick minor infestations, spray with soft soap or derris, and buy in predators. Mealy bugs are very similar, but mobile, and can be treated with bought-in predators such as the beetle *Cryptolaemus montrouzier*. The bugs are attracted to potato shoots, so can be trapped there, then sprayed with soft soap and derris.

Whitefly are mostly a problem under cover. They are unrelated to the pest of outdoor brassicas, though the same physical methods and sprays work for both. Thin out flying adults with a vacuum cleaner, use trap plants as suggested above, and spray with soft soap. Indoors, introduce the commercially available biological control. Whitefly parasites *Encarsia formosa* are small wasps that rapidly reduce whitefly populations and have been used since the 1920s. The white scales turn black once attacked by the wasps. As these fly when disturbed, infestations of aphids or other less mobile pests can still be controlled by dipping the tips of plants, where the pests concentrate, in soft soap solution. Remove yellow sticky traps from greenhouses once the wasps are introduced. Other predators are available. Out of doors, grow hops, as they breed up the *Stethoras* ladybug that attacks whitefly.

Spider mites are a serious threat to plants under cover, on walls, and even in the open. They cover shoots with fine webbing that repels sprays

As grapes ripen, more are lost to wasps and birds than to all other pests put together.

and turn leaves yellow and desiccated with thousands of tiny pinpricks. Spraying water and keeping the air humid discourages them. Attract them onto plants of sweet tobacco which are then composted. Spray with soft soap and derris and introduce a biological control. The predators *Phytoseulis persimilis* are tiny, but still bigger than the pests and work very well if introduced early enough. Outdoors, many beneficial insects do the work for us, especially lacewings and ladybugs.

Wasps are very beneficial early in the season because they hunt other insects in great numbers, but when they turn to fruit they need trapping. A bottle half full of water and jam capped with foil with only a small hole allows the wasps to crawl in, but not to fly out. Do not use these near flowers or with honey, as bees may also be lured. Dusting wasps with flour enables you to follow them home. The nest can be destroyed by flooding or by puffing derris dust in

the entrance. When they fly in at dusk, they carry it in with them. Repeat the dusting a week later.

Vine weevils The adult weevil is dark gray, beetle-like with a very long snout and takes rounded bits out of leaves. However, most harm is done by the grubs, which have a gray-pink body and brown head and destroy the roots of many plants. Adults may be trapped in rolls of corrugated cardboard, bundles of sticks or under saucers, in which they hide during daytime. Vine weevils are very difficult to control, as the troublesome larvae live in the soil or compost, but there is a parasitic nematode you simply water on that eradicates them. For vines and plants in pots make an excluding lid that fits snugly around the stem or stand them in double saucers with a water moat between. Outdoors, vine weevils are controlled by trapping, clean cultivation—and very effectively by keeping chickens.

Eelworms or nematodes The larger saprophytic varieties are mostly harmless—the nematodes that are pests are too small to see, though they may cause visible damage. On potatoes they form cysts on the roots. Many fungi attack eelworms, so organic soils rich with compost suffer less. *Tagetes* marigolds give off secretions that kill nematodes and can be planted to clean the ground. *Crotalaria*, castor oil plants, and pot marigolds (*Calendula officinalis*), may discourage them. Some are themselves parasites of other pests.

Rabbits Only netting the area will keep rabbits out. In case they get in, have a plank ramped against the fence so they are not trapped inside and eat even more. If the perimeter cannot be secured, surround or wrap each plant in wire netting. If this is impossible *feed* the rabbits when snow stops them finding their own food and *before* they remove the bark from your plants! Just the smell of a ferret or its droppings will drive them away. Humane traps work!

Moles Countless suggestions have been made to deter moles, but none has ever proved consistently efficacious—find one that always works and you will have fame and fortune. Try euphorbias, *Incarvillea*, and castor oil plants if you must, but only if you like irritant and poisonous plants. Poke sharp, twiggy, thorny things down their holes, flood them, gas them with car exhaust, pour foul, disgusting things down their runs. You will only discourage them for a while or drive them to the neighbors temporarily! Why not accept them and appreciate the pest control, ventilation, and fine soil they leave? Some dogs and cats can be taught to catch moles.

Two-legged rats These can be the worst pests of all and their senseless damage is worse than their thefts. Fences, barriers, and locks are sadly now required especially for succulent fruit. Signs saying "Beware of the wasps nests!" can be singularly more effective than "Keep out." Dogs are considered the best guards, but geese are as good and have other benefits.

The safest and least effort methods for breaking new ground and killing off established weeds

At some time most of us want to make a new bed where none was before. Before embarking on the actual task it is a good idea to check that there are no pipes or wires under the ground. Traditionally, you have to hack off the top growth, dig it all over and pull out the weed roots as you go. There are easier ways. Easiest of all is cutting it out of a lawn, so if possible put the whole area down to closely cut grass for a year or two.

"Weeds" may also be valuable parts of a complex ecosystem keeping the rest of your garden free of a particular pest.

Then just cut out the bed.

Good weed control is easy even though as organic gardeners we also spurn chemical herbicides. These do not just kill the unwanted plants, but microscopic ones and other forms of life as well. Instead we rely on mechanical means combined with wit and cunning. As with pests the aim is control not elimination—weeds have their uses as well as drawbacks, but for optimum yields they must be controlled; further, as crops receive most damage the earlier they are checked, so weed control is most effective the earlier it is done. But too early control reduces the fertility created by the weeds as they grow, so precise timing is needed. The timing and best method of control varies with type of weed, situation, and crop. So much effort can be saved with a little planning and knowing your weeds.

Friendly and unfriendly weeds Weeds are just plants in the wrong place, many are otherwise valuable garden plants, or even crops such as poppies. In some gardens, weeds may be the last remnants of the original flora and so help preserve insect and wildlife populations. A stand of weeds not only fixes and stabilizes the soil, but can act as a miniature hedge and windbreak sheltering emerging seedlings but it needs eradication before it competes too much. Most of all, weeds are a useful free source of fertility, admirably well suited to their conditions by self-selection. They produce a wealth of green manure at times when our crops cannot use the soil and act as valuable groundcover, but are also superb mineral accumulators, making these accessible to crops after incorporation. Some, such as clovers and vetches, fix nitrogen; comfrey is well known for accumulating potassium, as are nettles and thistles; phosphorus is collected by fat hen, sorrel, yarrow, and thorn apple. However, these plants can also be a problem, out-competing and choking our crops, spoiling the appearance, locking up fertility in seeds and roots, and harboring pests and diseases.

Their control probably takes up most gardening time, after grass cutting. What is needed for effective control is recognition that weeds come in two types, annuals and perennials. Once the latter have been totally eliminated, the former are easy to control, with very little time or effort.

Annual and perennial weeds Annual weeds spring from seed as soon as soil is exposed to the light, warmth, and wet. They can be suppressed from so doing by mulching or deep burial. Allowed to germinate, they are relatively easy to kill by any method, but rapidly get progressively tougher. Some can even set seed lying on the ground if they have reached flowering. From the point of view of weed control, it doesn't matter if the seedling weed is a biennial or perennial—it is small and easily killed because it has not long established.

Established perennial weeds are much more difficult, the worst creep, spread, and regrow from pieces of root. It is effectively clearing each and every bit of these that makes for future ease! Clearing them methodically reduces later weed control effort to seedlings, which can be easily hoed or mulched. Planting up beds or borders without first removing or killing all perennial weeds allows them to interpenetrate the crop roots, and then weeding is far more difficult. Once all the perennial weeds have been cleared from an area, there are almost certainly going to be thick flushes of weed seedlings for a year or two. But once the soil has had some seasons of regular weeding, there will be fewer seedlings. Digging or deep raking will bring up more seeds, or some selected weeds or other favored plants can be allowed to seed to give good winter cover on otherwise bare vegetable beds and other areas. Where the weeds are being mulched, dug or hoed in their goodness is retained in situ, but it can be removed to the

Bindweed is beautiful and beneficial, but nearly impossible to eradicate.

compost heap and thus concentrated for more important crops. All weeds can be composted, but those with pernicious roots should be withered on a path for some days first. Diseased weeds may be best burned.

Weeding methods There are many ways to kill weeds, but not all are suitable for every occasion and some are impractical in small gardens. Digging up weeds, root and all, is a useful way to gain control of small areas, while hoeing off the tops of seedling weeds is a better method for maintaining control. Mulching is probably most important as not only does it suppress weed seeds from germinating, it also has benefits for fertility and water conservation. Hygiene is valuable for preventing undesirable new weeds as dirty manures, uncomposted mulches, and especially bought-in plants in pots can smuggle in seeds and even whole live specimens. Protect sensitive areas such as flower beds, gravel paths, and drives by never letting anything set seed nearby or upwind. Rotation is as useful in weed control as it is in pest and disease control. Moving the crop and changing the conditions means

that no weed species is favored and allowed to establish—the conditions under say peas or beans being different to those between brassicas or corn.

Digging is easy for starting a new bed or border where the ground has been under turf or grass for a while. Regular cutting will have reduced weed populations favoring grasses and rosette weeds. From late fall till midspring the turf can be skimmed off and stacked for loam, used elsewhere or dug in. Tap-rooted weeds can be pulled as they are uncovered and wilted for compost. But if there are many creeping weeds then digging them up becomes exceedingly laborious—excluding light with mulches is easier. Dig in green manures and overwintering groundcover weeds during early spring when they have time to decay before the crop is planted. Dig and chop small spits methodically rather than labor with larger pieces. Alternatively, the surface can be lifted and inverted in shallow slices and the weeds prevented from rerooting by later hoeing.

Rotary cultivating is really chopping up the weeds and not like digging. It kills earthworms, damages some soil textures and is noisy, dangerous work. It is not really suitable for breaking badly perennial infested ground as most rotary cultivators have insufficient power. If they succeed, they chop each weed up into many bits which then regrow. Rotary cultivators are better for incorporating lush green manures and overwintered annual weeds which are less likely to regrow. They can also be used for regular weed control, provided the plot is laid out in long, straight, wide-spaced rows. They are most definitely for the larger not the smaller garden because of their awkwardness in confined spaces. To break in a large plot, rotary cultivate two or three times, two weeks or so apart in spring. This will incorporate the turf or light weed cover, and any regrowth as it occurs.

Hand weeding is often resorted to when an earlier hoeing has been missed. Hand weeding is really best saved for getting weeds out from among other plants and, though laborious, converts perennial weeds into fertility if every new leaf appearing is cut or pulled off each week until the root system expires. Some much-feared weeds, such as ground elder or bindweed, can be eliminated in a season if every leaf and shoot is removed weekly. Any lapse, though, and they may recover from just one little piece. Gloves make hand weeding more pleasant, and I prefer the plastic mesh-covered fabric "brickies" gloves sold in hardware shops. Kneeling pads as used by skateboarders protect the knees and a sharp knife helps cut under stubborn roots rather than pulling them up with a large clod.

Never ever pull up weeds growing in among your plants, as you rip out their intertwined root systems, doing more harm than the weeds. Remove the weeds in among and close by the plants first, then the ones between. Small seedling weeds may be killed with the edge of the knife, a hand rake, onion hoe, or scuffler. Use an old washing-up bowl or bucket to collect the weeds and transfer them to barrow or heap when it's full, to save getting up and down too often.

Hoeing is the most widespread method of maintenance weed control. It is using a knife on the end of a stick to cut through the weeds. Severing the top growth just below ground level is most effective. This is difficult with a blunted hoe which will try to uproot them. *Hoes must be sharp.* I always sharpen mine on a wheel and then keen it up every ten minutes or so with a whetstone while working. In heavy, sticky or stony ground it may pay to put a "hoeing mulch" of sharp sand or sieved compost on top of the soil to make the going easier. It is said to be better to work backward so you do not firm in the weeds, but I prefer to go forward and look where I'm going.

There are two basic types of hoe: the swan-necked or draw hoe and the Dutch hoe. The former, used with a chopping action, is good for incorporating seedling weeds and young green manures, but makes hard work. It is also good for pulling earth up to potatoes and can be used for making drills. The Dutch hoe has a blade that is pushed to and fro through the soil just below the surface. This is easier work, but does not incorporate seedlings so well after chopping them off. It deals with bigger weeds more effectively than a draw hoe. Weeds are further damaged by the Dutch hoe's rolling action and this also makes a good dust mulch. It is hard to draw soil up or make a drill with the Dutch hoe.

Hoeing is excellent for maintaining clean soil in beds and borders. If these are only producing annual weeds, they need hoeing every two weeks from early spring till mid-summer, but little thereafter. This does not take much time if done every two weeks in dry weather— leave it longer and the weeds get established and take more effort. Hoeing is effective against perennial weeds but needs doing at least weekly so that the top growth is hoed off before it can replace the resources used to make it and the roots become exhausted and die. This is hard work over a large area unless only a few perennial weeds are present.

Flame-gunning is not as horrendous as it sounds. A gas- or kerosene-powered blowtorch gives an intense blue flame about the size of a wine bottle that will splay out over a foot square or so. This is passed over the leaves at a walking pace and will then ideally cook, but not char, the leaves—leaving them to weaken the root system further as they wither. It only warms the soil but is very effective against young seedlings. However, if they are well established, some may recover from the roots and need a second treatment a week or so later. It is possible to kill perennial weeds with repeated weekly applications, but this wastes potential compost material.

Timing a flame-gunning just before a crop emerges can be very useful as it removes the weed competition without disturbing the crop or soil and bringing up more weed seeds. For example, carrots take at least ten days to germinate, so if these are sown into a weeded seedbed then all new weeds emerging in the next ten days can be removed in perfect safety with a treatment on day nine. The carrots then emerge and establish, deterring further weeds germinating.

Flame-gunning is most useful for weeding large areas such as seedbeds, gravel drives, and so on, but should obviously be kept away from automobiles, buildings, and flammable materials. Because of their thermal mass and the insulation of their bark it is possible to use flame guns under and up to trees and even tough stemmed plants like mature Brussels sprouts. Conifers, evergreens, dead leaves, and hedges, on the other hand, catch fire easily! Herbaceous plants can also be flame-gunned while dormant to kill winter weeds if the crowns are covered with sand— this works particularly well on asparagus beds. Small hobby blowtorches are superb for weeding rockeries and can also be used with care on weeds growing in the cracks and crannies of paths and patios.

A lesser evil Ammonium sulphamate is not allowed under organic standards as a weedkiller, but is the least obnoxious from the organic point of view if you need to kill off a tree stump that cannot be dug out. It is very indiscriminate and kills almost all plants, but breaks down into the relatively harmless ammonium sulphate, a common nonorganic fertilizer.

Mulching is probably the most important method of weed control. Mulching materials can be expensive to buy, but can save much time and effort by suppressing weeds. They all help water conservation and moderate and improve soil temperature, encouraging growth. Organic mulches also add fertility and improve the soil texture. Mulches do have a few drawbacks other than the cost, though. They may encourage some burrowing pests such as voles and moles, loose mulches are scattered onto lawns by birds. There is a danger that a deep mulch in damp conditions will encourage the rotting of crowns or bark, and grafts may root if the union is covered by a mulch. Mulches can also seal the soil warmth in, so that growth above them becomes more prone to frost than it would over bare soil. This is important for strawberries and bush peaches in flower and with mulched potatoes. Mulches are generally an alternative to green manuring, but do not utilize sunlight, so do not increase biomass.

Mulches are the easiest way of breaking new ground initially, as well as a good way of keeping weeds down later. Providing the top growth is not woody and has been at least cut with a rotary mower, an area can be turned into weed-free, clean soil in six months with little effort or preparation.

All weeds are killed by excluding light and preventing any bit of them reaching it with impenetrable mulches. The tougher perennial weeds are stopped only by thick opaque plastic or fabric, such as old carpet. But the majority of weeds can be killed off with a thick mulch of straw, hay or grass clippings on top of cardboard and newspaper. In any case, some hand weeding is needed if any weed appears through a hole. It

Horticultural paper and carpet underfelt keep this squash's roots moist and weed-free.

helps if an isolation trench a foot deep and wide is dug round the perimeter first and the mulch continued over the edge.

Mulching new ground works best if the impenetrable mulch is put down just as the weeds have started into growth, flattening them underneath. This is usually early spring when the soil is also full of water; later than midspring is far less effective. The weeds turn yellow through lack of light and rapidly rot as do their root systems, feeding soil life and increasing fertility. After a month or so any creatures can be exposed for the birds if the sheet of mulch is rolled back early in the morning. Worms and beneficial insects move quickly and escape, most pests do not. If an area is mulched like this in early spring then it can be cropped from early summer—though the weeds may recover if the mulch is simply removed. Instead, plant vegetables through holes in the mulch where they will grow wonderfully in the moist enriched soil underneath. Tomatoes, zucchini, vegetable marrows, ridge cucumbers, melons under cloches, corn will all do well. The brassicas also thrive, but

some occupy the land through the winter so do not fit in if the area is needed for the fall.

In the fall, after any catch crop has been harvested, the mulch can be removed and the area dug over if thought necessary. Almost all the weeds and roots will have rotted and disappeared leaving a rich texture and natural stratification that may be better left undisturbed. It is quite possible to plant through the mulch and leave it in place providing it will not interfere with cultivation.

In exactly the same way, green manures and overwintered weeds can be mulched in early spring with sheets of plastic or fabric, even grass clippings in quantity. You can then plant through these into the enriched soil. Compost too can be added before mulching for the best results with hungry feeders.

Mulches can be applied onto bare soil or areas covered with annual weeds during fall. This hibernates the bed, protects the soil from erosion and encourages soil life, especially earthworms, so that when removed or planted through in spring the soil will be ready with excellent texture and fertility. Fall mulching can benefit herbaceous and less hardy plants by protecting the roots from frost, though plants that are more likely to rot in damp conditions should only be mulched with light airy materials like loose straw or bracken.

All mulches can be applied at any time, but most benefit comes if they are introduced in early spring before the winter rain has evaporated. Similarly, if there is a long dry period, it is a good idea to rake or roll aside mulches when it rains and replace afterwards to prevent the mulch soaking up all the water.

Different mulches, impenetrable and loose Plastic sheets are a great aid to weed control but unsightly, costly in cash, and environmentally undesirable. They vary in manufacture and use. The clear plastic, similar to that used for polytunnels, can be pinned to the ground to warm up the soil in spring and encourage flushes of weeds. Black or opaque plastic sheeting, thick enough to exclude all light, warms the soil and kills weeds—even perennials. It can be laid permanently and covered with a loose mulch to improve the appearance, so becoming suitable for shrub borders, soft fruit, and other permanent plantings. In the same way, it can be underlayered in gravel paths and drives.

If all perennial weeds are dead it is a good idea to puncture plastic sheets in many places to prevent water problems. Unperforated, they may cause flooding or a lack of aeration to the soil. Preperforated sheets can be bought ready made, but then of course cannot, unaided, prevent weeds passing through. Black and white plastic can be reversed, after the black side has warmed the soil and killed weeds, for the white side to reflect light up onto the plants and confuse pests.

Large squares of plastic tucked into slits round the edge make a superb start for young trees, keeping them weed-free and preventing evaporation for a year or two. Long strips a stride or so wide are excellent for starting hedges, cuttings of easy rooters, such as quickthorn, can even be pushed through them. Strips of plastic can also be used for strawberries, vegetables, and particularly lettuce and saladings which then get less dirty, though slugs may become more of a problem.

I do find the sight of plastic mulches unappealing and with high winds there is a danger of them and the crop blowing away in the open. Woven materials are also available and are similar to perforated plastic, but are heavier. Their porosity allows much better aeration of the soil and less water run off than with

Straw mulches, car-tire cloches, and old glass panes may not be very aesthetic, but they ensure an earlier, healthier crop.

impermeable plastic. Woven materials are far more expensive than plastic, but are better for growing valuable crops through like strawberries where their wear resistance will also be useful. Bed-sized pieces on the vegetable plot will kill and incorporate green manures for many years and are tough enough to have flaps cut for planting through.

Carpet is the best woven material, heavy, weed resistant and not unattractive laid upside down and often available free. This is *the* material for breaking new ground— even a bramble can't push through a nice bit of Axminster or Wilton. Purely artificial carpets last forever and make good paths, especially in the fruitcage and polytunnel. The brighter ones can look much better covered in a skim of loose mulch. Organic wool or cotton carpets rot after a year or two of use, so are perfect for establishing trees and shrubs. Mixed fiber carpets partly rot leaving a stringy mass to dispose of.

Paper and cardboard are no good on their own except in the greenhouse or polytunnel where they

are safe from wind and useful for keeping lettuce and saladings clean. Outside they blow away unless covered with another mulch. Used in this way, they kill many weeds almost as well as plastic or fabric materials, but rapidly rot. Using them under a loose mulch stops birds mixing weed-seed infested soil into the mulch material. They improve the effectiveness of thin plastic sheet which lets some light through. Wet them first to get them to lie flat.

Peat, bark, and coir are very much more attractive to look at than any other mulches. Peat is considered undesirable in the U.K., but on a world scale it is abundant and an excellent material. Bark byproducts are better for the U.K. as they are produced there, coir and other wastes are also replacing peat, but all are very similar. They do not add much to soil fertility and are very expensive compared to the others. However, they are generally weed-seed free, of good texture, and beneficial to most plants. Because of their cost, they are best used for important ornamental areas, but would be advantageous almost anywhere. They can be made to go further if used on top of newspaper or cardboard and improve the appearance of plastic mulches. On their own, at least a finger's depth is needed and this will need topping up every year. Do not use thin layers—they just disappear—and hold down fine-grade material with a coarse-grade top layer to prevent it being blown around in the wind. Do not put thin, loose mulches down unaided on top of weeds, as the weeds will just grow through.

Compost, well-rotted muck and manures are applied more for their fertility than just as mulches. Sieving beforehand makes them more attractive, but is laborious and they inevitably are full of weed seeds. This makes them most use on the vegetable bed and around trees and shrubs. In thick layers, they suppress many existing weeds, but not creeping or vigorous ones. These mulches disappear quickly and so need continual topping up.

Straw and hay may be available in quantity and make good mulches under trees and in the fruitcage, especially for strawberries. There tend to be quite a lot of annual grass seeds after these mulches, so be prepared to keep mulching once you start. Best on top of a newspaper layer, a three-inch-thick slab of straw or hay will then last for two years or more and look quite attractive as the color mellows. Put on loose, these materials are good for covering less hardy plants in severe weather, bracken fronds are better. Take care with moldy straw or hay and with bracken as inhaling dust from these can be a health hazard.

Grass clippings are freely available, homegrown and for the asking. Put down in one place they make a wet smelly mess, but put in inch layers and topped up regularly they make one of the very best mulches. They feed the soil and encourage worms, so benefit almost every area of the garden. Multiple layers are good for earthing up potatoes and soft fruit bushes and trees. Grass clippings "glue" down the edge of plastic sheets and can help disguise them as a skim on top. They can be made more effective and longer lasting if

A weed is also a wild flower. Violets like these will rapidly colonize a shady woodland's edge.

put down over newspaper.

Sand and gravel are not usually thought of for mulching; however, they do have many advantages though adding no fertility. They can be very attractive and are cheap and sterile. They keep moisture in the soil, but do not get wet themselves which makes them good for winter protection of less hardy plants. One of the best mulches for ornamental areas and for fruit where they reflect up ripening heat and light. Sand is excellent for asparagus, but should be darkened with soot or it will not warm up quickly enough. Be warned—anything seeding into gravel germinates, so practice good preventative hygiene nearby. It is a good idea to put gravel over perforated plastic confining the worms and soil underneath.

Weed control in nonsoil areas Paths, drives, and patios are often a problem as windblown seeds lodge in every niche. Prevention is better than cure, so either point up holes and cracks with cement or mastic after cleaning them all out by hand with a knife and a pressure hose, or grow plants you want there. A mixture of potting compost and thyme and chamomile seeds worked in will soon establish and prevent other plants getting in. Flame guns are best where they can safely be used, a knife will remove weeds from cracks between slabs, and I use a nylon line trimmer to flay them—though the occasional stone has done for a window or two. A carpet or plastic sheet laid on top for a few weeks will kill many off, it can be permanent if graded and covered with fresh gravel.

Groundcover Under shrubs and over large areas mulching becomes expensive in materials and time as there will always be some weeds that arrive on the wind. It then becomes more effective to go over to groundcover plants which then add fertility from captured sunlight—especially grass, which is so simply maintained. In shady areas, ivy will be better and is easily weeded by trimming anything that grows up out of it. Planting bulbs, primroses, violets, and other naturalizing plants can further improve the appearance and the wildlife habitat without upsetting weed control. The most vigorous and beneficial groundcover wherever height allows are the mints, these suppress most other weeds and are loved by insects when they flower. They can be kept in bounds by a mown grass path.

Worst weeds and garden "weeds" There are weeds and there are wild flowers. The least desirable weeds are annuals that should not be allowed to increase and perennial weeds that are very difficult to deal with: annual meadow grass (*Poa* species); Canadian fleabane (*Onyza canadensis*); hairy bitter cress (*Cardamine hirsuta*); shepherd's purse (*Capsella bursa pastoris*); bindweed (*Convolvulus*); couch grass (*Agropyron repens*); ground elder (*Aegopodium podagraria*); horseradish (*Cochlearia armoracia*); horsetails (*Equisetum*); Japanese knotweed (*Polygonum*); lesser celandine (*Ranunculus ficaria*); winter heliotrope (*Petasites fragrans*).

These garden plants are among the worst seeders and spreaders: *Allium*, *Ajuga*, bluebells, feverfew, forget-me-nots, foxgloves, golden rod, Himalayan balsam, honesty, *Hypericum*, *Lamium*, loosestrife, mints, periwinkles, poppies, Russian vine, *Rhododendron ponticum*, Shasta daisies, *Sisyrinchium*.

A good experiment is to put your garden soil in a pot, water it and leave it on a windowsill where you see it every day, and watch what comes up. You can remove many of the duplicates and anything else as soon as you recognize it: these are your common annual weeds. Once you know them, it is easier to spot the rare finds such as tree and shrub seedlings.

What weeds are telling you is the conditions they are growing in. Any piece of ground gets covered with weeds very rapidly if left untended, these compete with each other and different species dominate temporarily. As weeds slowly build up the fertility of the soil, it becomes suitable for nettles, brambles, and tree seedlings. If these—especially nettles—occur in profusion it can indicate a potentially rich site. Deep-rooted weeds such as dock and thistle are good as they bring up nutrients from deep down, making them available for future crops. The types of weed will always be those most suited to the conditions, so if the population consists of acid lovers the topsoil is probably acid. Lime-rich soils are similarly indicated by the plants that grow readily on them, while damp conditions encourage rushes—and more obviously wet feet. Lots of docks mean horses or their manure have been on the land as the seeds pass through unchecked. Similarly, lots of tomato seedlings could mean sewage sludge has been used. Beware of any land that grows few weeds!

The most common "weeds"

"Weeds" or native plants that occur most frequently on acid soil:
betony, birch, black bindweed, broom, cinquefoil, corn chamomile, cornflower, corn marigold, corn spurrey, daisy, foxglove, fumitory, gorse, harebell, heather, horse or marestail, lesser periwinkle, mercuries, pansy, rhododendron, rowan, scabious, shepherd's cress, small nettle, Scots pine, sorrels, spurrey, and tormentil.

"Weeds" or native plants that occur most frequently on lime-rich soil:
agrimony, bellflower, black medick, candytuft, cat's ear, clematis, cornelian cherry, cowslip, dogwood, goat's beard, greater hawkbit, hawthorn, hazel, horseshoe vetch, knapweed, lamb's lettuce, mignonette, ox eye daisy, penny cress, privet, rose briar, salad burnet, spindle, stonecrop, tansy, valerian, wallflower, white mustard, wild carrot, and yarrow.

"Weeds" or native plants that occur most frequently in a heavy clay:
annual meadow grass, creeping buttercup, cowslip, goosegrass, hoary and ribwort plantain, meadow cranesbill, nipplewort, and selfheal.

"Weeds" or native plants that occur most frequently on light dry soil:
annual nettle, bramble, broad dock, bulbous buttercup, charlock, dandelion, groundsel, knotgrass, mouse-eared chickweed, stinging nettle, petty spurge, poppies, red dead nettle, rose bay willow herb, shepherd's purse, and speedwell.

"Weeds" or native plants that occur most frequently in wetter places:
alder, bugle, bulrush, buttercups, comfrey, cuckoo flower, docks, great willow herb, hemp agrimony, Himalayan balsam, loosestrife, marsh marigold, meadowsweet, mint, plantain, primrose, ragged robin, sedge, stinging nettle, thistle, water avens, willow.

On prospective land you want to see masses of stinging nettles! Other favorable weeds are chickweed, dock, forget-me-not, goosegrass, groundsel, thistle, and yarrow. What you most definitely do not want—and it may be best to move home—are white-flowered bindweed, *Equisetum*, horseradish, Japanese knotweed, lesser celandine, Leyland cypress hedges or poplars on or close to the sunny side of the garden, *Oxalis*, or winter heliotrope.

However, some generally feared weeds are common, very tough and require several attacks a week apart to die, but do succumb to persistent attacks. These include: bramble, coltsfoot, couch grass, creeping buttercup, dock, ground elder, knotweed, nettle, thistle, and tree saplings.

Don't forget that the more growth the weeds make, the more material you have for the compost heap. A bed of nettles will get you up and running in fertility for the next couple of years, which is the times it takes to kill them off by regular raids for their succulent growths.

The best of luck and keep on composting!

A YEARLY CALENDAR

The following are reminders of the most essential tasks for the majority of gardeners. Obviously the exact timing varies with locality, site, and soil, and of course you may not grow exactly the same things as I do, but even unusual plants have similar requirements at much the same times.

Late winter

Check stores, remove and use anything starting to deteriorate before it goes over and infects others.

Make a health and hygiene check: examine every plant for pests, diseases, and dieback. Check straps and stakes after gales. Apply sticky bands and inspect the sacking bands on apple trees, and other trees if they suffered from many pests. Pick off big buds on black currants.

Empty insect traps and nests, collect and destroy snails. Make and hang bird boxes, slug pubs, insect traps, and bottle cloches. Put out food, hang up fat, and provide water for birds.

Put out cloches and low tunnels to warm soil. Put down carpet and sheet mulches on new ground or green manures.

Spread a good layer of compost or well-rotted manure under and around everything possible, preferably not just before a period of heavy rain.

Spread a good layer of mulch under and around everything possible, preferably just after a period of heavy rain.

Spray everything growing with diluted seaweed solution at least once, and anything showing deficiency symptoms more often. Spray peaches and almonds with Bordeaux mixture against peach leaf curl if buds are beginning to swell.

If conditions are mild, cut the grass with blades set high and return the clippings. Plan and make changes to shapes of grass paths, lawns, and their beds and borders.

Once ground becomes workable, plant out hardy trees and shrubs that missed the fall planting. Firm in roots of fall plantings after hard frosts. Do major pruning work to trees and bushes missed earlier, but not to stone fruits or evergreens unless damaged by storms. Prune fall-fruiting raspberries to the ground.

Make sure no weeds are getting away—they come up easily at this time. Hoe whenever it's dry enough and add extra mulches on top of thin, weedy ones.

Repair and clean tools and equipment, tidy sheds and greenhouse. Sieve and mix homemade potting composts, top up indoor beds. Order seeds and plants for coming season and plan their positions.

Chit potato "seed" on trays in light, frost-free place. Plant potatoes in pots, and garlic, onion sets, and shallots in pots or in situ. Sow the following under cover in warmth: indoor tomatoes and cucumbers, early peas, broad beans, cabbages, cauliflowers, lettuce, spinach, turnips, carrots, radishes, onions, scallions, leeks, sweet peas.

Early spring

Check stores and make a health and hygiene check as above.

Put out food, hang up fat, and provide water for birds.

Spread more mulch under and around everything possible, preferably immediately after a period of heavy rain. Once ground becomes workable, plant out evergreen and less robust hardy plants, roses, soft fruit, artichokes, asparagus, rhubarb, and grapevines. Protect these from frost and wind their first season.

Cut back evergreen and conifer hedges. Prune herbs, tender plants, evergreens, and hollow-stemmed shrubs such as buddlejas. Protect their new growth against frost afterwards.

Ensure good weed control, by hoeing fortnightly; add extra mulches on top of thin, weedy ones. Compost, dig in or invert green manures and any weed flushes.

Cut the grass at least once fortnightly, preferably weekly, returning the clippings or raking them into rings around trees and bushes. Feed turfed areas with sieved compost, seaweed or diluted personal liquid waste. Move, lay and repair turf in nonfrosty weather.

Spray everything growing with diluted seaweed solution at least once, and anything with deficiency symptoms more often.

Spray peaches and almonds a second time with Bordeaux mixture against peach leaf curl as buds swell.

Spread wood ashes under and around plants, giving priority to gooseberries and culinary apples. Feed spring greens with comfrey liquid or seaweed solution.

Pollinate early-flowering plants and those under cover by hand.

On still, cold nights, protect blossom and young fruitlets from frost damage, using net curtains, plastic sheeting or newspaper.

Plant garlic, onion sets, shallots, potatoes. Sow any plants grown under cover or for later planting out. Under cover in warm: tomatoes, cucumbers, eggplants, sweet peppers, celery, celeriac, hardy and half-hardy annual flowering plants. Outside in warm soil or under cover: peas, broad beans, onions, leeks, beets, kohlrabi, cabbages, cauliflowers, lettuce, spinach, turnips, carrots, chards, salsify, scorzonera, parsnips, herbs, radishes, scallions, sweet peas, hardy annuals.

Midspring

Check stores, remove and use anything starting to deteriorate before it goes over and infects others. Use up stored fruits and vegetables, clean out stores once empty.

Make a health and hygiene check: examine every plant for early signs of pests and disease. Check straps and stakes after gales. Firm in roots of earlier plantings after hard frosts. Retouch sticky bands. Pick off more big buds on black currants.

Ensure good weed control by hoeing weekly and adding extra mulches on top of thin, weedy ones.

Cut the grass at least weekly, returning the clippings or raking them into rings around trees and bushes.

Spray everything growing with diluted seaweed solution at least once, and anything with deficiency symptoms more often.

Water all plants established within the previous twelve months if there has been little or no rain for a week.

Deflower or defruit new plants to give them time to establish. Pollinate plants under cover by hand.

On still, cold nights protect blossom and young fruitlets from frost damage, using net curtains, plastic sheeting, or newspaper.

Feed and top-dress all permanent container plants with compost. Tie in new growths of vines and climbing plants under cover.

Make layers of plants that are difficult to propagate. Take cuttings of herbs and less hardy plants, repot house plants.

Prune and cut back most early-flowering shrubs once flowers die. Remove seed heads from bulbs as they die back.

Plant out the less robust hardy plants under cover or with protection; also plant out potatoes, onion seedlings, perennial herbs. Sow plants grown under cover or for later planting out. Under cover in warm: tomatoes, ridge cucumbers, gherkins, melons, zucchini, squashes, corn, half-hardy flowers. Outside and under cover: peas, broad beans, French beans, runner beans, most brassicas, lettuces and saladings, herbs, spinach, turnips, carrots, rutabagas, salsify, scorzonera, radishes, kohlrabi, fennel, leeks, parsnips, sweet peas, hardy annuals.

Cut the grass at least weekly, use clippings for mulching.

Put out slug pubs and pheromone traps, and make nocturnal inspections of the garden, especially the sowing and propagation area. Harvest and use, or store and preserve, anything that is ready.

Weed and hoe everywhere every chance you get.

Late spring

Make a health and hygiene check thrice weekly and examine each and every plant in your care for escalating pests and diseases, especially aphids, cabbage caterpillars, and spider mite indoors and out. Note what will soon need harvesting and any specimens or seedlings that need repotting. Top up and check slug pubs and other traps. Retouch sticky bands and note any specimens or seedlings that need repotting.

Ensure good weed control by hoeing fortnightly or weekly, add extra mulch on top of weeds in mulches.

Cut the grass at least fortnightly, preferably weekly, returning the clippings or raking them into rings around trees and bushes.

Water all new plants established within the previous twelve months, especially if there has been little rain. Establish a watering round for all pot-grown plants at least daily. Feed indoor pot plants with comfrey liquid or seaweed solution weekly. Pollinate plants under cover by hand.

Deflower or defruit new perennial plants.

Spray everything growing with diluted seaweed solution at least once, and anything with deficiency symptoms more often.

On still, cold nights protect blossom and young fruitlets from frost damage, using net curtains, plastic sheeting, or newspaper.

Prune out crowded and ill-placed shoots on apricots and peaches. Rub off any buds and small shoots that are pointing in the wrong direction, prune indoor grapes, and redirect new growth. Cut back most flowering shrubs once flowers die. Tie in and support growing climbers and tallest herbaceous plants.

Keep planting potatoes. Harden off and plant out tomatoes, peppers, eggplants, melons, corn, ridge cucumbers, zucchini and squashes under cover—or even in open if last

frost is well past. Incorporate compost with soil for all transplants.

Once frosts are over, sow in situ under cloches outside: tomatoes, ridge cucumbers, gherkins, zucchini, squashes, corn, half-hardy flowers. Outside without cover sow: peas, broad beans, French beans, runner beans, most brassicas, lettuces and saladings, herbs, spinach, turnips, carrots, rutabagas, salsify, scorzonera, kohlrabi, fennel, leeks, parsnips, hardy annual and biennial flowers.

Harvest and use, or store and preserve, your crops as they come into their prime.

Pause at least once to enjoy the result of your labors.

Early summer

Make a health and hygiene check thrice weekly. Top up and check slug pubs and other traps. Retouch sticky bands, note what will soon need harvesting and any specimens or seedlings that need repotting.

Water all new plants established within the previous twelve months, especially if there has been little rain. Increase frequency of watering for pot-grown plants to at least thrice daily! Feed indoor pot plants with comfrey liquid or seaweed solution weekly.

Ensure good weed control by hoeing fortnightly or weekly, add extra mulch on top of weeds in mulches.

Plant out tender plants or move them out for summer.

Cut the grass at least fortnightly, preferably weekly, returning the clippings, using them for mulches or raking them into rings around trees and bushes. Raise cutting height of mower.

Spray everything growing with diluted seaweed solution at least once, and anything with deficiency symptoms more often.

Dead-head roses and cut back most flowering shrubs once flowers die. *Summer pruning, part one of three:* from one third of each plant remove approximately half to three quarters of each new shoot, except for leaders. This applies to all red and white currants, gooseberries, and all trained apples and pears. Thin raspberry canes. Prune grapevines back to three or five leaves after a flower truss; if no flower truss by sixth leaf stop anyway and mark for later removal. Tie in new growths of vine and climbing plants.

Fruit thinning, part one of three: remove every diseased, decayed, damaged, misshapen, distorted, or congested fruitlet. This applies to all apples, pears, peaches, apricots, quality plums, dessert grapes, gooseberries, and figs, and especially to trained forms. Compost or burn rejected fruitlets immediately (of course usable ones such as the larger gooseberries may be cooked). Protect chosen fruit from birds.

Take soft cuttings if you have a propagator. Make layers of difficult subjects.

Transplant last brassica and leek plants. Incorporate compost with all transplants this month.

Feed tomatoes and pot plants with comfrey liquid or seaweed solution.

Spread mulches under and around potatoes.

Sow outdoors: lettuce, saladings, beets, kohlrabi, rutabagas, turnips, spinach, chicory, endive, biennial and perennial flowers.

Harvest and use, or store and preserve, ripe fruits, crisp salads, and prime vegetables.

Pause at least once to enjoy the result of your labors.

Midsummer

Make a health and hygiene check thrice weekly and note what will soon need harvesting.

Water all new plants established within the previous twelve months, especially if there has been little rain. Continue watering all pot-grown plants at least thrice daily. Feed indoor pot plants with comfrey liquid or seaweed solution weekly.

Ensure good weed control by hoeing weekly or at least fortnightly, add extra mulch on top of weeds in mulches.

Cut the grass at least fortnightly, preferably weekly, returning the clippings or raking them into rings around trees and bushes. In orchards let grass grow to help ripen fruit. Raise cutting height of mower even more.

Spray everything growing with diluted seaweed solution at least once, and anything with deficiency symptoms more often. Spray maincrop potatoes with Bordeaux mixture if warm and humid.

Summer pruning, part two of three: from the second third of each plant remove approximately half to three quarters of each new shoot, except for leaders. This applies to all red and white currants, gooseberries, and all trained apples and pears. Prune grapevines back to three or five leaves after a flower truss; if no flower truss by sixth leaf stop anyway and mark for later removal. Black currants may have a third to half their old wood removed after fruiting. Raspberries may have old fruited wood removed. Stone fruits are traditionally pruned now to avoid silver leaf disease. Tie in new growths of vine and climbing plants.

Keep on dead-heading. Cut back evergreens and conifer hedges. Take soft cuttings if you have a propagator, root strawberry runners, and layer tips of black and hybrid berries.

Fruit thinning, part two of three: remove every diseased, decayed, damaged, misshapen, distorted, or congested fruitlet. This applies to all apples, pears, peaches, apricots, quality plums, dessert grapes, gooseberries, figs, and especially to trained forms. Compost or burn rejected fruitlets immediately. Harvest and use or preserve ripe fruits. Protect ripening fruit from the birds. Provide water for birds instead.

Sow lettuce, saladings, carrots, rutabagas, turnips, Chinese cabbage, winter spinach, kohlrabi, finocchio, chards.

Harvest and use, or store and preserve, ripe fruits and vegetables. Dry peas and beans for use as seed and in kitchen. Dry and freeze herbs. Dry onions and garlic in sun. Use or store early potatoes to free ground for sowing.

Pause at least once to enjoy the result of your labors.

Late summer

Make a health and hygiene check twice weekly.

Water all new plants established within the previous twelve months, especially if there has been little rain. Decrease frequency of watering for all pot-grown plants to twice daily as growth slows. Feed indoor pot plants with comfrey liquid or seaweed solution weekly.

Ensure good weed control by hoeing fortnightly or adding extra mulch on top.

Plant new strawberry plants, if you can get them.

Cut the grass at least fortnightly, preferably weekly, returning the clippings or raking them into rings around trees and bushes; in orchards let grass grow to help ripen fruit. Raise or lower cutting height of mower if weather is particularly dry or wet.

Spray everything that is growing with diluted seaweed solution at least once, and anything that has deficiency symptoms more often.

Summer pruning, part three of three: from last third of each plant remove approximately half to three quarters of each new shoot, except for leaders. This applies to all red and white currants, gooseberries, and all trained apples and pears. Cut out old fruited wood of brambles and hybrids, root the tips of these. Prune grapevines back to expose fruit to sun.

Fruit thinning, part three of three: remove every diseased, decayed, damaged, misshapen, distorted, or congested fruit. Compost, burn or use rejected fruit immediately. Protect ripening fruit from birds and wasps.

Sow under cover: winter lettuces and saladings, early carrots. Outdoors: winter lettuces, saladings, Japanese onions and scallions, winter spinach, turnips, Chinese greens; plant potatoes in pots.

Make and turn compost heaps and sieve for use or cover and store. Sow green manures and winter groundcover on bare soil that is not mulched.

Harvest and use, store or preserve ripening fruits, potatoes, and onions. Save seeds.

Order hardy trees and shrubs for fall planting.

Clean, paint and repair timber, gutters, and brickwork.

Pause at least once to enjoy the result of your labors.

Early fall

Make a health and hygiene check once weekly. Note what will soon need harvesting or taking under cover.

Water all new plants established within the previous twelve months, especially if there has been little rain. Decrease frequency of watering for all pot-grown plants to once daily as growth slows. Feed only most vigorous indoor pot plants with comfrey liquid or seaweed solution fortnightly.

Ensure good weed control by hoeing fortnightly or adding extra mulch on top.

Transplant pot-grown biennial flowering plants and those that can be dug with a decent rootball or moved with little disturbance.

Plant garlic, daffodils, and most other bulbs. Sow hardy annuals to overwinter; green manures and winter groundcover on bare soil that is not mulched. Sow bare turf and grass down orchards.

Cut the grass at least fortnightly, preferably weekly, returning the clippings and any fallen leaves or raking them into rings around trees and bushes. Raise the height of cut.

Spray everything that is growing under cover with diluted seaweed solution at least once, and anything that has deficiency symptoms more often.

Cut back herbaceous plants to six inches as their stems wither. Make and turn compost heaps and sieve for use, or cover and store.

Remove old canes and tie in new for all the berries.

Apply sticky bands and sacking bands to apple trees, and to others if they suffer from many pests. Go on a pest hunt to thin them out for winter. Rake around old mulches.

On still, cold nights, protect flowers, fruits, and tender plants from frost damage, using net curtains, plastic sheeting or newspaper. Protect first the tops, then the stems and roots of more delicate plants before frosts come. Bring indoors tender plants in pots.

Take cuttings of plants as they start to drop their leaves.

Harvest and use, store or preserve vegetables, fruits, and nuts aplenty. Make fruit juices, cider and wine with surplus/scavenged fruit.

Collect and dry seeds, lift gladioli and bulbs as they wither.

Pause at least once to enjoy the result of your labors.

Mid fall

Make a health and hygiene check once weekly. Note what needs harvesting, pruning or taking under cover.

Decrease frequency of watering round for all pot-grown plants to "as needed" as growth slows.

Ensure good weed control by hoeing fortnightly or adding extra mulch.

Transplant pot-grown biennial flowering plants and those that can be dug with a decent rootball or moved with little disturbance. Plant out deciduous shrubs, trees, and soft fruit, preferably bare rooted, if soil is in good condition and they are dormant.

Plant garlic and many bulbs.

Cut the grass at least fortnightly, preferably weekly, collecting the clippings with the fallen leaves or raking them into rings around trees and bushes. Lime the grass, aerate and spike if needed, adding sharp sand and grass seed.

Top up sticky bands and inspect sacking bands on apple trees, and on others if they suffered from many pests.

Check straps and stakes before and after gales.

On still, cold nights, protect ripening fruits from frost damage, using net curtains, plastic sheeting or newspaper.

Take cuttings of hardy plants as they start to drop their leaves.

Prune most plants as they start to drop their leaves. Cut back herbaceous plants to six inches as the stems wither. Rework and winter prune apples, pears, grapes, and nonstone fruits.

Check stores, remove and use anything starting to deteriorate before it goes over and infects others.

Sow under cover: winter lettuces and saladings, brassicas, broad beans, sweet peas, and hardy annuals and grass seed in warm seasons. Sow green manures in greenhouse and polytunnel.

Protect all less hardy plants against frost; move pots indoors. Cloche saladings and fall strawberries.

Collect up all wastes for composting or shred for mulching. Make and turn compost heaps and sieve for use or cover and store.

Make new beds and borders, move turf or stack it and rot down. Spread mulches under and around everything possible.

Order seed catalogs, potatoes, evergreen and herbaceous plants for spring.

Harvest and store last fruits and root vegetables in hard areas. Collect and dry seeds and berries for seed and to feed birds.

Pause at least once to enjoy the result of your labors.

Late fall

Make a health and hygiene check once weekly. Note what needs harvesting, pruning or taking under cover.

Decrease frequency of watering for all pot-grown plants to "as needed" as growth slows.

Ensure good weed control by hoeing fortnightly or adding extra mulch on top.

Cut the grass at least fortnightly, collecting the clippings with the fallen leaves or raking them into rings around trees and bushes. Lime the grass, aerate and spike if needed, adding sharp sand.

Lime the vegetable beds.

Plant out bare-rooted deciduous shrubs, trees, and soft fruit if soil is in good condition and they are dormant. Incorporate compost with all plantings this month.

Top up sticky bands and inspect sacking bands on apple trees, and on others if they suffered from many pests.

Rework and winter prune apples, pears, and nonstone fruits. Check straps and stakes before gales.

Spread a good layer of mulch, compost or well-rotted manure under and around perennials, preferably not immediately before a period of heavy rain. Mulch and mark crowns of herbaceous plants.

On still, cold nights, protect ripening fruits from frost damage, using net curtains, plastic sheeting or newspaper.

Take cuttings of hardy plants as they start to drop their leaves.

Check stores, remove and use anything starting to deteriorate before it goes over and infects others.

Harvest and store some root vegetables in harder areas.

Order seed catalogs, potatoes, evergreen and herbaceous plants for spring.

Pause at least once to enjoy the result of your labors.

Early winter

Make a health and hygiene check once fortnightly.

Decrease watering for all pot-grown plants to minimum as growth slows.

Plant out hardy trees and bushes if soil is in good condition and they are dormant. Check straps and stakes before and after gales.

Cut the grass if weather is mild. Collect the fallen leaves and use for leaf mold or rake them in rings around trees and bushes.

Lime most grass swards one year in four, more often on acid soil, but not among ericaceous plants or lime haters, and never at the same time as manure or compost.

Clean out gutters and drains once last leaves have settled.

Top up sticky bands and inspect sacking bands on apple trees, and on

others if they suffered from many pests.

Clean greenhouse, coldframe and cloche glass and plastic.

Prune hardy trees and bushes, roses and do major work to trees and bushes (but not to stone fruits or evergreens.)

Make a bonfire of diseased and thorny material saved up and burn it the same day so no small creatures can be inside.

Check stores, remove and use anything starting to deteriorate before it goes over and infects others.

Make your seed orders up and get them in early so you get the best choice in time for the new season.

Order seeds, potatoes, evergreen and herbaceous plants for spring.

Pause at least once to enjoy the result of your labors.

Midwinter

Make a health and hygiene check. Check straps and stakes after any gales.

Check stores, remove and use anything starting to deteriorate before it goes over and infects others.

Empty insect traps and nests, collect up and destroy hibernating snails. Make and hang bird boxes, slug pubs, insect traps, and plastic bottle cloches.

Make sure your seed orders are in.

Take it easy and look back over the successes and mishaps of the previous year, enjoy the fruits of your labors and plan for even more fun and endeavor in the coming seasons.

The best of luck, and happy and successful gardening

Some interesting addresses

American Horticultural Society, 7931 East Boulevard Drive, Alexandria, UA. www.ahs.org

Gurney's Seed and Nursery Company, PO Box 4178, Greendale, IN 47025-4178. www.gurneys.com

The Cook's Garden, PO Box 1889, Southampton, PA 18966-0895. www.cooksgarden.com

Ronnigers Potato Farm, Star Rate "B", Moyie Springs, ID 83845. www.ronnigers.com

Johnny's Selected Seeds, 955 Benton Avenue, Winslow, Maine 04901. www.johnnyseeds.com

W.Atlee Burpee & Co., 300 Park Avenue, Warminster, PA 18974.www.burpee.com

Thompson & Morgan Seed Catalogue, PO Box 1308, Jackson, NJ 08527-0308. www.thompson-morgan.com

Shepherd's Garden Seeds, 30 Irene Street, Torrington, CT06 790. www.shepherdseed.com

Totally Tomatoes, PO Box 1626, Augusta, GA 30903. www.totallytomato.com

Seed Savers Exchange, 3076 North Winn Road, Decorah, IA 52101. www.seedsavers.org

Recommended reading list

These are a few of the many books worth looking for that contain useful and relevant advice. Some are out of print and need unearthing from libraries and secondhand bookstores:

George E. Brown *The Pruning of Trees, Shrubs & Conifers* Faber & Faber, 1972

J. Cherfas (ed.) *The Veg Finder* HDRA, 1994

William Cobbett *Treatise on Gardening* 1821

The Diagnosis of Mineral Deficiencies in Plants HMSO, 1943

Fruit, Berry & Nut Inventorry Seed Saver, 1993

Roy Gender's *Scented Flora of the World* Granada, 1977

Hillier's Manual of Trees and Shrubs David & Charles

L.D.Hills *The Good Fruit Guide* HDRA

Richard Mabey *Food for Free* Fontana/Collins, 1972/75

The Oxford Book of Food Plants Peerage Books, 1969

The Plant Finder Hardy Plant Society

Plant Physiological Disorders ADAS, HMSO, 1985

Robbins, *Crafts & Raynor Weed Control* McGraw Hill, 1942

Sir John Russell *Soil Conditions and Plant Growth* Longmans

Tropical Planting and Gardening Macmillan, 1949

Vilmorin-Andrieux *The Vegetable Garden* John Murray, 1885

INDEX

Access to garden, 60-1
Addison, Joseph, 11
Air, 55
Almonds, 129-30
Ammonium sulphamate, use of, 213
Angelica, 149
Animal manures, 83-4
Anise, 154
Annuals, 37-9
  bedding plants, 60
  hardy, 40
  list of, 40-1
Ants, 209
Aphids, 209
Apples, 124-5
  rootstocks, 110
  varieties, 105
Apricots, 129
Arches, 51
Arugula, 150
Asparagus, 155-6
Aubergines, 179

Bananas, 183
Basil, 151
Bats, 28
Bay, 147
Bedding plants, 59-60
Beds, digging, 212
Bees, 22, 24, 200
Beetles, 22, 25
Beets, 162-3
Bergamot, 149
Biennials, 38
  bedding plants, 60
Bilberries, 122
Biodynamics, 14
Birds
  beneficial nature of, 26
  nest building, 26
  plants attracting, 26-7
Blackberries, 121-2
Blackcurrants, 117-18
  cuttings, 111
Blueberries, 122
Bog garden, 72
Bok choy, 152
Bonfires, 78
Borage, 154
Bordeaux mixture, 15
Borders
  designing, 59
  herbaceous, 59
Botrytis, 208
Bought-in manures, 83
Bought-in plants,
  planting out, 94
Boysenberries, 122
Broad beans, 157-8
Broccoli, 138, 164
Brussels sprouts, 165
Bulbs, 41-2
Bullaces, 131
Bush, planting out, 94
Butterflies, 22, 24
Buying in plants, 94

Cabbages, 138, 163-4
Calcium, 82
Cape gooseberries, 182

Caraway, 155
Carbon dioxide,
  importance of, 15
Cardoons, 156
Carrots, 161
Catalogs, buying from, 94
Cats, 199
Cauliflower, 138, 164
Celery, 152
Chard, 162-3
Cherries, 128
Cherry plums, 131
Chervil, 150
Chickens, 198
Chicory, 152
Chili peppers, 179
Chinese cabbage, 153
Chinese greens, 152
Chives, 147
Citrus trees, 182
Claytonia, 151
Climbers, 47
Cloches, 57, 169-70
Cobs, 132-3
Coldframes, 57, 170
Companion plants, 18,
  35-6, 112, 206
  herbs, 144
  vegetables, 143-5
Compost
  choosing, 92
  homemade mix, 92
Compost heap
  location, 73
  starting, 79
  turning, 80
Composting, 17, 79-80
Concrete paths, 62
Conservatories, 171-2
Containers
  fruit grown in, 109
  growing in, 98-9
Coppice, 72
Coriander, 155
Corms, 41-2
Corn, 138, 166
Corn salad, 151
Cottage gardens, 32-3
Cowberries, 122
Cows, 200
Cranberries, 122
Cumin, 155
Currants, 104
Cuttings, 95

Daily round, 76
Damsons, 131
Dandelion, 149
Day length, plants
  sensitive to, 54
Deciduous plants, 39
Digging, 77
Dill, 150
Diseases
  bacterial, 208
  defenses against, 205-8
  gardening under
    cover, 175-6
  natural control of, 7, 16
  treatment of, 208-9
  virus, 208
Dogs, 199
Drainage, 87

Drives, 62
Drought-tolerant
  shrubs, 46
Ducks, 198

Ecological damage,
  minimizing, 17
Eel worms, 210
Eggplants, 179
Endives, 151-2
Evergreen plants, 39
  foliage, 51
  shrubs, 45

Feeding plants, 79
Fences, 57
Fennel
  herb, 147
  vegetable, 153
Fertilizers
  soluble, stopping use
    of, 18
  use of, 12
Fertility, maintaining, 79
Figs, 132
Filberts, 132-3
Fish, 201
Flea beetles, 209
Florence fennel, 153
Flowers
  beauty, growing for, 52
  cutting, for, 60
  families, 200-1
  sowing, 29
  winter, 177
Foliage, 51-2
Forest glades, 34
Frame cucumbers, 179-80
Framework, 50-1
French beans, 158
Frogs
  breeding places,
    decline in, 21
  habitat, 25
Front garden, 72
Fruit. See also
  individual fruits
  birds, attracting, 26-7
  cages, 70, 106
  choice of, 104-5
  companion plants, 112
  container growing, 109
  cooking, 193-6
  culture, 101
  drying, 192
  early ripening, 187
  freezing, 192-3
  growing organically, 102
  growing under cover, 180-3
  harvesting, 106, 185-7
  homegrown, taste of, 102
  initial cost of
    growing, 102
  jamming, 190-1
  jellying, 190-1
  juicing, 189
  microclimate, 108
  multiple plants, 111

nutrients, 102-3
orchard, 72, 106
planting, 112
pollination, 108
processing, 189-93
productivity, 102
propagation, 111
replacement plants, 111
soil and site for, 107-8
spacing and stalking, 109-10
storing, 106, 187-8
trained, 70
training, 112
varieties, choosing, 105-6
wildlife, garden for, 104
work involved with
  growing, 103
Fruit trees, 44-5
  annual maintenance, 115
  attraction of, 103
  citrus, 182
  cordons, 112
  ecology of, 104
  espaliers, 112-13
  fans, 113
  flexibility, 103
  planting, 112
  regular fruiting,
    inducing, 115
  rootstocks, 109
  spacing and stalking, 109-10
  summer pruning, 114
  training, 112
  watering, 116
  winter pruning, 114
Fungicides, ceasing use
  of, 18

Garden
  access, 60-1
  features, 52-4
  framework, 50-1
  furniture, 58
  planning, 49-50
  themes, 52-4
Gardening under cover
  bonus crops, 178-80
  cloches, 169-70
  coldframes, 170
  conservatories, 171-2
  greenhouse, 171
  heating, 172
  hotbeds, 173
  light, 175
  microclimate,
    controlling, 169
  old deep freeze,
    propagation in, 173
  pest and disease
    control, 175-6
  plastic-covered
    tunnels, 171
  soil care, 176
  soil-warming cables, 172
  tender and early
    fruits, 180-2
  tender plants,
    hardening off, 176
  tropical fruit, 183

ventilation, 173
water control, 174-5
Gardens
  bog, 72
  bolt-on areas, 70-2
  cottage, 32-2
  forest glades, 34
  front, 72
  large country, 69
  large suburban, 68-9
  natural, 34
  potagers, 33-4
  rock, 72
  small and large,
    advantages of, 67
  small country, 69
  small town, 68
  taste in, 31-2
  vegetable, 33-4
  wild, 34
Garlic, 147
Gateways, 51
Geese, 199
Gherkins, 166
Ginger, 183
Globe artichokes, 156
Goats, 200
Good King Henry, 150
Gooseberries, 118-19
Grapevines, 123-4, 181
Grass cutting, 77
Grass paths, 62
Grassed areas,
  establishing, 62
Gray mold, 208
Gray water, 87
Green manures, 81-2
Greengages, 131
Greenhouse, 71, 93, 171
Ground rock dusts, 84-5
Groundcover, 216
  natural, 64
Growth, unhindered, 16
Guavas, 183
Guinea pigs, 200

Half-hardy plants, 39
Hamburg parsley, 161-2
Hardy plants, 39-40
Haricot beans, 158
Harvesting, 76, 185-7
Hazelnuts, 132-3
Heating, 172
Hedges, 55, 57
  planning, 66
  plants for, 66
  trimming, 78
  types of, 66
Herb bed, 70
Herbicides, ceasing use
  of, 18
Herbs, 135. See also
  individual herbs
  annual, 136, 150-2, 154
  companion planting, 144
  cooking with, 194
  culinary, 146
  drying, 192
  flowers, used as, 154
  growing conditions, 136

harvesting, 187
household uses, 197
medicinal uses, 197
perennial, 146-50
salads, in, 194-6
seeds, grown for, 154-5
toast topping, 196
Horseradish, 147
Hotbeds, 173
Hoverflies, 22, 24
Hygiene, 205
Hyssop, 150

Iceplant, 151
Indoor cucumbers, 179-80
Infestations, treating, 204
Insecticides, stopping
  use of, 18
Irrigation, 86

Japanese cucumbers, 166
Jerusalem artichokes, 157
Jostaberries, 119

Kale, 164
Kiwi fruit, 182
Kohlrabi, 153
  kohlslaw, 196

Lacewings, 25
Ladybugs, 25
Lamb's lettuce, 151
Land cress, 151
Large country gardens, 69
Large gardens, 67-8
Large suburban
  gardens, 68-9
Lavender, 148
Lawns, 62-5
Layering, 95
Leaf mustards, 152
leaves, collecting, 77
Leeks, 159-60
Lemon balm, 150
Lemon grass, 183
Lemon verbena, 148
Lettuces, 151-2
Light, 54, 175
Lincolnshire asparagus, 150
Liquid feeds, 85
Livestock, 72
Loganberries, 122
Lovage, 148

Maintenance,
  importance of, 73
Manure
  animal, 83-4
  bought-in, 83
  composting, 79-80
  green, 81-2
Marginal plants, 47
Marjoram, 148
Marrow, 165
Meadow, 72
Mealy bugs, 209-10
Measures, 9
Medlars, 127
Melons, 180

Microclimate
  fitting plant to, 169
  matching needs of
    plants to, 8
Mildews, 208
Mineral accumulators,
  82
Miners' lettuce, 151
Mint, 148
Moisture, 56
Moles, 211
Moths, traps for, 204
Mowing, 64
Mulberries, 131
Mulching, 56, 87, 214-
  16
Multipurpose plants, 36
Mushrooms, 157
Mustard and cress, 152

Nasturtiums, 154
Nature
  pests and diseases,
    control over, 7
  processes, using to
    advantage, 8-9
Nectarines, 129-30
Nematodes, 210
New Zealand
  flatworms, 209
Newts
  breeding place,
    decline in, 21
  habitat, 25
Nitrogen, 82
No-dig methods, 77
Nut patch, 107
Nylon line trimmers,
  65

Okra, 179
Onions, 160
Orchard, 72, 106
Organic garden
  tending, 11
  wildflowers and
    wildlife,
    encouraging, 12
Organic gardening
  approach of, 13
  benefits of, 12
  life in soil, guarding
    and increasing, 14
  principles of, 14-16
  soil, feeding, 15
  techniques of, 9
Organic products,
  standards for, 14
Organic Standards, 13

Paddock, 72
Parasites
  bought-in, 207
  encouraging, 206
Parsley, 152
Parsnips, 161-2
Passionfruit, 183
Paths, 51, 62
Patio area, 70
Peaches, 129-30
Peanuts, 182
Pears, 126-7
Peas, 158-9
Peat, use of, 18
Peppers, 179
Perennials
  annuals, grown as, 37-8

herbaceous, 42-4
  list of, 41
  low- to medium-
    growing, 43
  medium- to tall-
    growing, 43
  semipermanent nature
    of, 38
  shrubby, 39
  soft, 39
  taller-growing, 43-4
  true, 38
  very low-growing,
    42
  well-scented, 44
Pergolas, 51
Permaculture
  gardening, 14
Pesticides
  industry, 11
  organic, 208
  plants, harm to, 7
  withdrawal of, 12
Pests
  barriers and traps,
    206-7
  control, need for, 21
  defences against, 205-
    8
  direct action against,
    206-7
  elimination, no need
    for, 21
  gardening under
    cover, 175-6
  natural control of, 16
  nature, control by, 7
  subsystems, 21
  treatment of, 209-11
Phosphorus, 82
Pineapples, 183
Pit composting, 80
Planning, 49-50, 73, 75
Plant names, 37
Planting out
  bought-in plants, 94
  larger plants, 94
  seedlings, 93
Plastic-covered tunnels,
  171
Plastic products,
  avoiding, 18
Play area, 72
Plums, 131
Pollination, 40, 108
Pollinator subsystems,
  22
Pond plants, 47
Poppies, 155
Pot marigold, 154
Potagers, 33-4
Potassium, 82
Potatoes, 166-7
  new, 178
Potting up, 91
Predators
  bought-in, 207
  encouraging, 206
  subsystems, 21-2
Pruning, 77-8
  fruit trees, 114
Purslane, 151

Quinces, 127
Rabbits, 200, 210
Radishes, 151
Raspberries, 121

Recycler subsystems,
  22-3
Redcurrants, 118
Replanting, 96
Resources, making best
  use of, 17
Rhubarb, 156
Ridge cucumbers, 166
Rock garden, 72
Root division, 95
Rose petals, 148
Roses, pruning, 78
Rotary cultivating, 212
Rotation, 96, 205
Rots, 208
Runner beans, 158
Rusts, 208
Rutabagas, 162

Sage, 148
Salad bed, 70, 136-7
Salad crops, winter, 177
Salad herbs, 194-6
Salad plants, 151-
  2Salsify, 161-2
Scale insects, 209-10
Scarifying, 64
Scented plants, 54
Scorzonera, 161-2
Seakale, 156
Seasonal activities, 75
Seed beds, 91-2
Seeding lawns, 62-4
Seedlings
  light, temperature and
    water control, 92-3
  overcrowding, 93
  planting out, 93
  watering, 93
Seeds
  covering, 91
  growing from,
    drawbacks of, 95
  life of, 90
  plants grown from, 95
  protected varieties, 96
  sale of, 96
  saving, 90
  storing, 89
  tender plants grown
    from, 93
  watering, 93
Shallots, 159
Sheep, 200
Shelter, 56-7
Shrubs, 44
  birds, attracting, 26
  drought-tolerant, 46
  evergreen, 45
  tough and reliable, 46-
    7
  well-scented, 45-6
Shungiku, 152
Silica, 82
Slugs, 209
Small country gardens,
  69
Small gardens, 67
Small town gardens, 68
Snails, 209
Soil
  air, importance of, 98
  analysis, 98
  feeding, 15
  fertility, increasing, 17
  fruit growing, for, 107
  heavy clay, 96

lime-rich, 97
  loamy, 96
  matching needs of
    plants to, 8
  natural substances,
    use of, 15
  organic improvement
    of, 96-8
  organic, increasing
    life in, 15
  peaty, 97
  plant cover,
    increasing, 17
  sandy, 96
  silty, 97
  stony, 97
  subsoil, 98
  thin, chalky, 97
  type, recognizing, 96-
    8
  wet, 97
Soil Association, 13
Soil-warming cables,
  172
Sorrel, 150
Sowing
  astrological timings,
    29
  compost, 92
  light, temperature and
    water control, 92-3
  methods, 89
  pots and multicell
    packs, in, 91
  rows, in, 91
  situ, in, 95
  time of, 28-9
Spanish chestnuts, 133
Spider mites, 210
Spiders, 25
Spinach, 153
Spraying, 203
Steiner, Rudolph, 14, 79
Strawberries, 119-21,
  181
  runners, 111
Sulfur, 82
Summer savory, 152
Sunflowers, 154
Surplus plants, selling,
  96
Sweet cecily, 148
Sweet chestnuts, 133

Tarragon, 148
Tayberries, 122
Tender plants, 39
Theft, 211
Thyme, 149
Toads
  breeding place,
    decline in, 21
  habitat, 25
Tomatoes, 138, 178-9
Tool shed, location, 73
Topsoil, maintenance
  of, 14
Trees
  birds, attracting, 26
  buying in, 95
  fruit, 44-5
  height, adding, 44-5
  planting out, 94
  plants being, 44
  specimen features, 44-
    5
Turfing, 64

Turnips, 162

Vegetable garden, 33-
  4, 72
  blocks, 142
  catch cropping, 143-4
  companion planting,
    143-5
  fixed beds, 142
  intercropping, 143-4
  laying out, 140-1
  planning, 137, 140-1
  raised beds, 142-3
  rotation, 141
  rows, 142
  season, extending, 143
  shape, 141
  space, allocation of,
    140-1
Vegetables. See also
  individual vegetables
  alliums, 159-60
  brassicas, 163-5
  birds, attracting, 26-7
  bolting, 138
  choosing crops, 138-
    40
  chutneys, 191
  cooking, 193-6
  cucurbits, 165-6
  drying, 192
  freezing, 192-3
  gourmet crops,
    cultural requirements
    for, 136-8
  growing under cover,
    178-80
  harvesting, 185-7
  homegrown produce,
    value of, 135
  legumes, 157-9
  nutrition from, 140
  overbred, 137
  perennial, 155-7
  processing, 189-93
  relishes, 191
  roots, 160-3
  salad beds, for, 152-3
  salad, 196
  sauces, 191
  storing, 187-8
  value of, 140
  varieties, 155
  yields, 139
Vine weevils, 210
Vines, 123-4, 181
Vineyard, 72

Walls, 57
Walnuts, 133
Warmth, 55
Wasps, 22, 25, 210
Waste, recycling, 17
Water
  accessibility of, 21
  drainage, 87
  gray, 87
  water control, 86
  water features, 70
  water plants, 47
  water storage, 87
  water stress, freedom
    from, 16
Watercress, 150
Watering
  cans, 86
  containers, 99

daily, 76
  drought, during, 86
  fruit trees, 116
  gardening under
    cover, 174-5
  importance of, 86
  seeds in pots or cells,
    of, 93
  transplanted plants, 94
Watermelons, 180
Weeding, 77
Weedkillers, 11
Weeds
  annual and perennial,
    212
  conditions for, 217
  control of, 211
  established, killing
    off, 211
  favorable, 217
  flame-gunning, 213
  friendly and
    unfriendly, 211
  groundcover, in, 216
  hand weeding, 213
  hoeing, 213
  mulching, 214-16
  nonsoil areas, control
    in, 216
  types of soil for, 217
  weeding methods, 212
  wild flowers, 216
  worst, 216
Weekly routine, 76
White currants, 118
Whitefly, 210
Wild gardens, 34
Wildflower lawn, 72
Wildflowers,
  encouraging, 12
Wildlife
  categorization of, 19-20
  control of, 20-1
  encouragement of, 12,
    18-20
  fruit garden, in, 104
  pollinator subsystems,
    22
  predator subsystems,
    21-2
  recycler subsystems,
    22-3
  sharing garden with,
    197-201
  water, accessibility of,
    21
Wilts, 208
Windbreaks, 55
Winter purslane, 151
Winter salads, 177
Winter savory, 148
Worcesterberries, 119
Worm compost, 80
Worms, 28

Yearly cycle, 76, 28-9
Yields, increase in, 12
  pesticides, without, 7

Zucchini, 165